RAYMOND A. ANSELMENT is a member of the Department of English at The University of Connecticut.

Marprelate, Milton, Marvell, and Swift are among the best prose satirists in a remarkably rich literary era. Focusing on these key figures, *'Betwixt Jest and Earnest'* examines the theory and practice of religious prose in the sixteenth and seventeenth centuries. Recognizing the difficulties inherent in attempting to transform unimaginative animadversion into effective satire, it analyses the ways in which Marprelate's tracts, Milton's anti-prelatical satires, Marvell's *The Rehearsal Transpros'd*, and Swift's *A Tale of a Tub* variously resolve the decorum of religious satire.

Although the study is not specifically an intellectual history or a rigid definition of religious attitudes towards jest, it does bring together basic arguments central to the decorum of religious ridicule and identify symptoms of altering sensibilities in the period. Marprelate, Milton, Marvell, and Swift represent diverse religious dispositions, but they share a similar satiric vision. Each recognizes the central importance of manner, and all develop dramatic satire heavily dependent on character, an emphasis which often displaces the immediate issues contested, but never obscures the larger concerns the satirists pursue. Their preoccupation with the nature of tradition, their emphasis on the self, and their sensitivity to language reflect similar involvements in questions of certainty and absolutism. The virtues and abuses they find in such central questions are not unique to them or their time, but their emphases are, for they wrote in an age in which sensitive men could confront revolution and reaction with an assurance not easily attainable once that era had passed.

RAYMOND A. ANSELMENT

'Betwixt Jest and Earnest'

MARPRELATE, MILTON, MARVELL, SWIFT & THE DECORUM OF RELIGIOUS RIDICULE

UNIVERSITY OF TORONTO PRESS
Toronto Buffalo London

© University of Toronto Press 1979
Toronto Buffalo London
Printed in Canada

Library of Congress Cataloging in Publication Data

Anselment, Raymond A.
'Betwixt jest and earnest' : Marprelate,
Milton, Marvell, Swift and the decorum of religious
ridicule.

Includes bibliographical references and index.
1. Satire, English–History and criticism.
2. English literature–Early modern, 1500-1700–
History and criticism. 3. Church polity in
literature. 4. Religious thought–Great Britain–
Controversial literature–History. 5. Great
Britain–Church history–Modern period, 1485-
I. Title.
PR931.A55   827'.009   79-12498
ISBN 0-8020-5444-7

FOR CAROL

Contents

Acknowledgments

GRANTS FROM The University of Connecticut Research Foundation helped make possible a sabbatical year of research at the Bodleian Library as well as additional study at the Beinecke Library of Yale University and the Houghton Library of Harvard University, and also supported part of the expenses involved in the preparation of this book. The book has been published with the aid of an additional grant from The University of Connecticut Research Foundation as well as a grant to University of Toronto Press from the Andrew W. Mellon Foundation. Some of the ideas in chapters three and five were published in different form in 'Rhetoric and the Dramatic Satire of Martin Marprelate,' *Studies in English Literature*, 10 (1970), 103–19; 'Satiric Strategy in Marvell's *The Rehearsal Transpros'd*,' *Modern Philology*, 68 (1970), 137–50; and '"Betwixt Jest and Earnest": Ironic Reversal in Marvell's *The Rehearsal Transpros'd*,' *Modern Language Review*, 66 (1971), 282–93; they appear in this study with the kind permission of the journals' editors.

The final form of this book benefited from the criticisms of the anonymous readers for University of Toronto Press and the suggestions of its editors Prudence Tracy and Joan Bulger. Two other close and sympathetic readers also offered invaluable commentary: I am grateful to David Sonstroem who generously took the time from his own scholarly work to criticize the manuscript, and I am indebted to my wife Carol who again provided sensitive guidance.

'BETWIXT JEST AND EARNEST'

1

Introduction

IN AN EIGHTEENTH-CENTURY ESSAY concerned with the post-Shaftesburian question of laughter as the test of truth Anthony Collins contends: 'Let any Man read the Writings of our most eminent Divines against the *Papists, Puritans, Dissenters,* and *Hereticks,* and against one another, ... and he will find them to abound with *Banter, Ridicule,* and *Irony.*'[1] To prove his assertion, and thereby refute a specific argument proscribing laughter in serious issues, Collins cites numerous clergymen both for and against the established church who countenance and even employ various forms of ridicule. Although the writers and the works cited in Collins's extensive survey of the seventeenth and early eighteenth centuries are sometimes distorted to support his admitted bias, the sheer number of examples from both Conformist and Nonconformist writings suggests that the propriety of religious laughter was an issue of some concern even prior to the controversy over the *Characteristics.* The earlier preoccupation with the limits of ridicule, however, is generally less philosophically detached and abstractly conceived than the protracted eighteenth-century dispute. In the relatively stable Georgian society men who ventured into extended examination of the relation between laughter and truth did so with the knowledge that their religions were not contested. Their predecessors in the late sixteenth and seventeenth centuries, caught up in the forces that produced the turmoil and change of two revolutions, confronted an emotional issue in which the decorum of ridicule was a practical concern.

Among the myriad works of these prose controversialists the pseudonymous Martin Marprelate's tracts, John Milton's antiprelatical writings, Andrew Marvell's *The Rehearsal Transpros'd,* and Jonathan Swift's *A Tale of a Tub* are especially significant. All are at least initially inspired by a central problem of their time, church polity: Marprelate's first illegal publications in 1588 revive the Admonition Controversy; while fifty years later at the onset of civil war John Milton's alliance with the Smectymnuans supports Puritanism; the first part of Marvell's satire originally appeared in 1672 in response to a reactionary Erastianism; and Swift's perplexing work is, among other things, a late seventeenth-century defence of Anglicanism. Together the four writers accent important moments in a crucial span of time. Individually the authors also share significant literary concerns, foremost of which is an interest in religious ridicule. Their willingness to blend serious religious considerations with acceptable jest – which they define across a spectrum ranging from simple buffoonery to ironic wit – reflects the pressure of writers responding to involved and immediate issues, but the satiric prose that results is more than expedient attack.

Used imaginatively, laughter's element of distortion and its natural emotional appeal help sustain fictions that shape memorable satires from polemical contexts,[2] a transformation that raises serious issues of decorum and form. Although the practice of religious ridicule had long been established among earlier church writers,[3] contemporary reactions to the four satirists studied here and their own defences of their methods suggest that its propriety remained unresolved. In the following chapters it will also become apparent that Marprelate, Milton, Marvell, and Swift challenge an antiquated tradition of prose controversy. Their deliberate departures from the established notions of polemical animadversion are strikingly individualistic, but in common they reveal an intensified awareness of the restrictions confronting the religious satirist.

The issue, expressed quite crudely by Orpheus Junior in *The Golden Fleece*, involves a basic pragmatism. 'Doe not wee see,' the author asks, 'Pamphlets, Ballads, and Play-bookes sooner sold, then elegant *Sermons* and the *Books of Piety*? ... Therefore vnlesse a *Booke* containe light matters as well as serious, it cannot flourish nor liue *Iouially*.'[4] In the hands of more sophisticated apologists of the revolutionary era laughter's rhetorical power becomes a strong inducement to overcoming misgivings about its use in important matters. Several seventeenth-century commonplaces also reinforce the temptation to overlook its prohibition. Besides citing Aristotle's observation that man's uniqueness depends upon a capacity for both reason and laughter, writers also note that Socrates was an originator of ridicule as well as the father of philosophy.[5] Laughter is thus respectable and, as Thomas Jackson proves syllogistically in *A Treatise of the Holy Catholike Faith and Chvrch*, inevitable: 'If the power of laughing proceede from the nature of man, and the nature of man consist in reason: it will bee very hard for any man to refraine laughing, that hath but so much reason as to consider the vanitie of this assertion.'[6]

The laughter is at times neither noteworthy nor effective; yet attempts to expand through ridicule the potential of polemic literature often met with a resistance symptomatic of the need for change. An embattled polemicist such as the fiery pamphleteer William Prynne could ignore both personal safety and recognized conventions to pursue an unrestrained assault on corrupt prelacy. But when later himself the object of attack, he is quick to complain that his anonymous opponent has not followed 'an orderly or Scholasticall manner' and to argue that 'the fairest natural or artificiall Bodies, may soon be metamorphozed into the most *misshapen Monsters*, if torne into confused *fragments*, and then patched up together into a disorderly Chaos.'[7] Another vociferous contemporary, Thomas Edwards, reveals even more clearly the incongruities of an emerging double standard. Throughout the tedious pages of *Gangraena* and its supplements Edwards has no scruples about his role as an ecclesiastical scandalmonger; in fact he presents arguments to justify his often harsh and personal attacks. Despite these apologies he can find nothing but righteous indignation for the poetic justice with which John Goodwin answers him in turn.[8] This contradictory attitude reflects an ambivalence about ridicule that prompts writers throughout the late sixteenth and seventeenth centuries to invoke vague standards of disputation which they themselves choose to ignore.

In this study the general attitudes of the period towards religious ridicule establish a perspective from which to view four innovative satirists. Isaac Barrow's sermon on Ephesians 5:4 provides in the first chapter the prevailing understanding of the Pauline prohibition, 'nor foolish talking, nor jesting, which are not convenient.' From classical and patristic authorities the sermon draws together the traditional pronouncements on laughter and shapes them according to the reassessment of jest current among some prominent members of the Royal Society and the Anglican clergy. Using the sermon as both a focus and a point of departure, the first chapter develops from a diverse range of sixteenth- and seventeenth-century commentaries a sense of the contemporary views of religious jest. In addition, close analysis of the sermon itself shows that a thoughtful interpretation of Paul's pronouncement is presented in a manner that embodies the conditional nature of its resolution. The structure, as well as the content of the sermon, makes clear that the tolerable limits of religious jest are not easily established and are even then only justified by manner. Through his sensitive, balanced analysis Barrow confirms what the four satirists illustrate: any use of religious jest must be its own defence.

The chapters that follow therefore assume that, despite each of the satirists' formal apologies, the satires themselves offer their own most significant justifications. Thus one of the most radical of prose satirists, the anonymous Martin Marprelate, presents conventional arguments for his unique interpretation of the proverbial wisdom, 'Answer a fool according to his folly'; but the method by which he attacks with poetic justice remains far more interesting and important than the arguments themselves. His efforts in the last tract to justify an approach too extreme for his contemporaries are later successfully realized in Milton's arguments for a 'grim laughter' which is characteristic of Milton's own concept of zeal and suited to his image as an English Elijah. Zealous laughter is countered in *The Rehearsal Transpros'd* with a Horatian ease and Aristotelian *eutrapelia* that typify Marvell's sophisticated, playful earnest. Finally in *A Tale of a Tub* the extremes of zeal and urbanity come together in an exuberantly serious development of religious ridicule that like the satire itself resists simplification or labelling.

This study is not specifically an intellectual history of the period or a rigid definition of religious attitudes towards jest, although it does bring together basic arguments central to the decorum of religious satire and also recognizes symptoms of altering sensibilities. The authors whose works are analysed here represent diverse religious dispositions, but they share a similar satiric vision. Contemporaries who reacted to their methods and even grouped the satirists together denounce in them what they term 'personation.' Each of the satirists recognizes the central importance of manner, and all develop dramatic satire heavily dependent upon character. Their departures from conventional polemic may thus be seen as explorations of the satiric potential inherent in animadversion's adversarial nature. The importance the satirists give to character often displaces the immediate issues contested, but the larger concerns they pursue are never obscured. Their preoccupation with the nature of tradition, their emphasis on the self, and their sensitivity to language reflect a similar involvement with questions of certainty and absolutism. The virtues and abuses they find in the central questions of traditionalism and individualism are not unique to the authors or their period, but the emphases are. Marprelate, Milton, Marvell, and Swift represent a historical period in which sensitive men confront revolution and reaction with an assurance no longer easily attainable once that era passes.

This discussion of their particular visions and achievements assumes that their accomplishments are best appreciated through close textual studies. A formal and descriptive analysis reveals the integral relationships of character and provides insights into complex strategies; it makes more accessible works that are by their nature very challenging. Read either separately or in relation to each other, the analyses establish bases for exploring the satirists' remarkable ability to resolve immediate and often personal confrontations through enduring artistry. Marprelate, Milton, Marvell, and Swift are among the best prose satirists in a remarkably rich literary era; the discussion of their theories and practice which follows adds not only to an appreciation of their significance but also to the knowledge of an area of prose important in the understanding of English satire.

2

'Nor foolish talking, nor jesting, which are not convenient'

THROUGHOUT THE PERIOD bounded by Marprelate and Swift writers schooled in rhetoric, who were acquainted with patristic authors and sensitive to the Bible, return continually to the same sources to form or to justify their own attitudes towards religious ridicule. With characteristic eclecticism and with considerable repetition they cite familiar passages from Horace, Chrysostom, and Genesis to form at least in theory a decorum of laughter.[1] Among these many discussions Isaac Barrow's sermon on Ephesians 5:4 is particularly important. His elucidation of a biblical passage in which, as Richard Greenham had earlier observed, 'The true rule of mirth is set downe'[2] draws together ideas traditional in the late sixteenth and seventeenth centuries and shapes them in a manner which reflects current and future preoccupations. Its comprehensiveness and lucidity warrant the praise given to it by Corbyn Morris in his eighteenth-century essay on wit,[3] for the sermon, published in 1678, remains a significant introduction to the period's use of jest and a valuable perspective on the religious satires of Marprelate, Milton, Marvell, and Swift.

From his vantage point in the Restoration Barrow recognizes the traditional pronouncements on religious jest available to Marprelate and Milton as well as the contemporary reappraisal central to Marvell and Swift. Indeed his moderate, possibly latitudinarian disposition and his close association with both his fellow members of the Royal Society and the eminent theologians of his day enhance the value of his observations.[4] The sermon on Ephesians 5:4 establishes him as a thoughtful, sensitive writer who shares his peers' concern with the manner proper to a post-revolutionary era. Even though his position seems removed from Marprelate's and Milton's earlier, more radical points of view, it too reflects the central role that revolution plays in shaping the allowable limits of religious ridicule, and it thereby offers a convenient basis for assessing the change in sensibilities. By its very nature the sermon provides an ideal against which the actual practices of the four satirists may be considered. An analysis of it reveals that even in theory the decorum of religious jest is not easily formulated.

Paul's strictures for behaviour 'as becometh saints' pose the essential difficulty in the prohibition, 'nor foolish talking, nor jesting, which are not convenient.' Construed in a conservative sense, as in Erasmus's paraphrase of the New Testament, Paul seems to condemn any lapse from serious demeanour: 'For christians in theyr most spedy iourney to heauen, haue continuall battayle with vyces, and so daungerous battayle, that they can haue no leasure to applye suche tryfles and sportes, but rather thei haue to wepe.'[5] The basis of this interpretation is Chrysostom's belief that 'pleasant iesting' is unsuited to the Christian caught up in 'a time, of battell, & fight, & watching, & warding, and arming & of standing in battell raie.'[6] Other patristic and classical writers agree: '*Quid nobis cum fabulis, cum risu? non solum profusos, sed etiam omnes jocos arbitror declinandos*, saith *Bernard* [*de ordin.* vit.]. What have we to do with tales and jests? *Tertulian* saith, he was *Nulli rei natus nisi pœnitentiæ*, born for nothing else, but for repentance. *Crede mihi, res severa est gaudium verum*, saith *Seneca*, True mirth is a severe businesse.'[7] Not all, however, apply this stern interpretation, and even those who agree occasionally have reservations. John Mayer, whose 1631 commentary claims to represent the 'Divers Expositions thereof, out of the Workes of the most Learned, both ancient Fathers and moderne Writers,' prohibits a 'sharpnesse of wit' designed to create mirth or laughter 'because this can hardly be without some biting, and there must needs be some affectation herein not consonant unto pietie.' Yet in an apparent afterthought he notes: 'it is a marvaile, that even amongst learned men, and amongst some Divines, that should condemne it in others, this kinde of jesting should be so much affected, and studied after.'[8]

For many commentators this contradiction disappears when jesting is interpreted in its Vulgate sense, *scurrilitas*. Within the larger context of the epistle's admonition 'but fornication, and all uncleanliness, or covetousness, let it not be once named among you, as becometh saints; neither filthiness, nor foolish talking, nor jesting,' the passage may be understood merely as a denunciation of obscene jesting. Well before Henry Hammond's learned annotations support this interpretation with philological arguments drawn from the Greek and Hebrew versions, commentators anticipate his interpretation: 'And so all unclean gestures, and obscene talking, or unsavory jests to cause laughter, which are all unbeseeming a Christian.'[9]

Others, among them Isaac Barrow, find in the original Greek text a connotation quite different from the Vulgate rendition. By 1650 English biblical commentators observe that Paul originally wrote *eutrapelia*, which a seventeenth-century writer translates as 'the handsome turning, or changing of a word'; moreover, they also recognize that Aristotle uses the same word in *Ethica nicomachea* to denote a moral virtue.[10] Confronted with this linguistic complication and an apparent choice between Paul or Aristotle, James Fergusson confesses an understandable confusion. 'It is a task of no small difficulty,' he declares in 1659, 'to keep within the bounds of lawfull and allowed mirth and recreation, especially in recreating our spirits by pleasant and delightfull discourse, so that we exceed not either in matter or manner; considering that what is inoffensive at one time and place, and to some persons, may be irritating and offensive at, and to others: for, therefore it seemeth the Apostle designeth this vice in speech by that name, which (as I shew) agreeth also to that which is lawfull and allowed, implying, that in this particular there is an easie passage from what is allowed to that which is forbidden.'[11] Fergusson's ingenious explanation for the use of *eutrapelia* in a passage that he believes can see jest only in 'an evil sense for scurrility' and his tacit endorsement of some uncertainly defined but acceptable jest reveal an obvious reluctance to dismiss either Aristotle or wit. In the sermon which he delivered almost twenty years later Barrow effects the reconciliation of Aristotle and Paul through a more precise definition of jest and a more comprehensive confrontation of the shibboleths of time, place, and persons.

Choosing to read Paul's statement as a 'sober caution' rather than a rigid prohibition, Barrow derives his interpretation largely from the phrase 'which are not convenient.' The Greek 'convenient' becomes in his translation 'pertinent,' but its denotations of profitable or of 'good purpose' are not unlike the word 'edifying' found in other annotations.[12] Any jest 'innocent and reasonable, conformable to good manners, (regulated by common sense, and consistent with the tenour of Christian Duty, that is, not transgressing the bounds of Piety, Charity, and Sobriety,)' should not be prohibited.[13] Lawfulness, in short, is his main concern; and after a preliminary definition of jest the bulk of the sermon determines its allowable limits.

Guided partly by the term *eutrapelia*, Barrow's conception of jest is both representative and particular, general and precise. Earlier annotators recall Aristotle's use of this word to describe 'urbanity, facility and facetiousnesse of speech, in a harmlesse way';[14] Barrow freely interchanges 'facetious speech' with 'facetiousness,' and he also uses 'wit,' 'jocularity,' and 'raillery' synonymously. Of these descriptions, raillery would not, of course, be current before the middle of the century; the definition of jest also puts a distinctly Restoration premium on 'a manner of speaking out of the simple and plain way, (such as Reason teacheth and proveth things by,) which by a pretty surprizing uncouthness in conceit or expression doth affect and amuse the fancy, stirring in it some wonder, and breeding some delight thereto' (p 45). While part of this distinction recalls Quintilian,[15] the fundamental opposition between reason and fancy embodies a contemporary view. So also does the importance given to 'a nimble sagacity of apprehension, a special felicity of invention, a vivacity of spirit, and reach of wit more then vulgar: it seeming to argue a rare quickness of parts, that one can fetch in remote conceits applicable; a notable skill, that he can dexterously accommodate them to the purpose before him; together with a lively briskness of humour, not apt to damp those sportful flashes of imagination' (pp 45–6). These qualities, integral to the desirable 'gayety and airiness of spirit,' represent Barrow's interpretation of the Greek words for 'dexterous' and 'easily turn' found in Aristotle. As such he provides another version of Walter Charleton's 'Festivity of Wit ... which the Greeks name εὐτραπελία the French, Raillerie, and we Jesting'; for the sermon elaborates more definitely the intangible quality that for Charleton denotes 'the Alacrity of his Disposition, and Tranquility of his Spirit (both signs of Virtue) and often also the Dexterity of his Wit, in that he is able to give a delightful and new colour to the absurdity at which he moves his company to smile.'[16]

Barrow's succinct catalogue of the forms in which this admired facetiousness manifests itself draws together points made earlier in Cicero's De oratore, in Quintilian's Institutio oratoria, and in their numerous sixteenth- and seventeenth-century imitators. Because of his ultimate interest in fancy and dexterity, Barrow values verbal facility, and he lists clever allusion, play on words or phrases, unique similitude, and quick retort among the kinds of jests which typify a fanciful agility. Like his predecessors he recognizes the potential in language used ironically, hyperbolically, or metaphorically. And he does not dismiss 'acute Nonsense' or what may be considered a dramatic mode of jest: 'sometimes a scenical representation of persons or things, a counterfeit speech, a mimical look or gesture passeth for it: sometimes an affected simplicity, sometimes a presumptuous bluntness giveth it being; sometimes it riseth only from a lucky hitting upon what is strange, sometimes from a crafty wresting obvious matter to the purpose: often it consisteth in one knows not what, and springeth up one can hardly tell how' (pp 44–5). Protean by its nature, jest seems to defy more precise definition; yet Corbyn Morris believes that, 'if the *Point* was, to exhibit all the various Forms and Appearances, not of Wit only, but of *Raillery, Satire, Sarcasms*, and of every Kind of *Poignancy* and *Pleasantry* of Sentiment, and Expression, he seems to have perfectly succeeded.'[17] But in acknowledging the methods of jest traditional to both his own and the previous century Barrow relinquishes to his audience's 'imagination and experience' the freedom 'to supply the defect of such explication'; he is more interested in describing jest's acceptable and unacceptable limits.

Barrow first dismisses the notion that 'jocular discourse' is not convenient or profitable to Christianity. Opposite the Horatian marginalia '---*ridentem dicere verum Quid vetat?*' he briefly proposes that jocularity possesses an ability to instruct and to enlighten; however, he is mainly concerned that life without recreation would become stultifying. 'It would surely be hard,' he argues, 'that we should be tied ever to knit the brow, and squeeze the brain, (to be always sadly dumpish, or seriously pensive,) that all divertisement of mirth and pleasantness should be shut out of conversation' (p 48). Although another marginal reference cites Seneca's *De tranquillitate animi* as a source, the seventeenth-century audience would more commonly encounter Barrow's notion that jest revitalizes or re-creates the mind for serious business in Cicero's *De officiis*.[18] Barrow's contemporaries would also largely assent to his assertion that 'Christianity is not so tetrical, so harsh, so envious, as to bar us continually from innocent, much less from wholsome and usefull pleasure.'

Barrow's several references to 'this pleasant and jocular Age' imply that a Restoration audience would appreciate the compatibility between Christianity and jocularity, although laughter is commonly accepted throughout the late sixteenth and seventeenth centuries as well. All Christians well knew that man 'is in a vale of tears, he is ful of wofull sicknesses, he is in the midst of fearfull enemies'; ideally they might also conclude: 'were it not unseemly for a souldier to lay downe his weapon in the field and fall to jesting and laughing?'[19] Though they might cry out, 'These are hard and strange sayings, who can hear them?' they are nevertheless reminded by William Chillingworth that the Bible does not allow Christians to jest.[20] Strict interpretations of passages like Luke 6:25 ('Woe unto you that laugh now! for ye shall mourn and weep') or Ecclesiastes 2:2 ('I said of laughter, *It is* mad: and of mirth, What doeth it?') and the authority of patristic writers give further evidence of the condemnation of laughter. A few might even concur with Thomas Granger in his 1621 commentary on Ecclesiastes that, 'if *Adam* had neuer fallen, there should neuer haue beene laughter, nor weeping, but an heart possest with heauenly ioy, euen ioyful sobriety.'[21] In fact, however, the Christian in this period rarely condemns laughter outright; rather, he believes that God intended its use.

As the eminent Puritan theologian William Perkins emphasizes in *A Direction for the Government of the Tongve according to Gods word* (1593), man has an obligation to use his God-given faculty of laughter. Perkins's frequently republished directions for both speech and writing popularize the medieval notion that man must realize that he is *'animal rationale, mortale, risus capax'*;[22] he also follows tradition in his further qualification, 'but the vse of it must bee both moderate and seldome, as sorrow for our sinnes is to be plentifull and often. This we may learne in Christs example, of whome we reade that he wept three times, at the destruction of Ierusalem, at the raising of *Lazarus*, and in his agonie: but we neuer read that he laughed.'[23] The observation that Christ never laughed, usually attributed to Chrysostom,[24] does not imply that man should not laugh. While Perkins may be cautious in his support, he has no hesitation in resolving the biblical injunctions against laughter. In a passage which reproduces all of the major prohibitions he explains,

The Preacher Saith, *There is a time to laugh, and a time to weepe. When the Lord brought againe the captiuity of Sion, wee were like them that dreame. Then was our mouth filled with laughter, and our tongue with joy.*

Now this mirth must be ioyned with the feare of God, otherwise *Salomon* saith well, *I haue said to laughter, thou art madde: and of ioy, what is that thou doest?* And Christ saith, *Woe to you that now laugh, for ye shall weepe*, Secondly, with compassion and sorrow for Gods people in affliction and miserie ... Thirdly, it must be sparing and moderate. *Paul* condemneth such as are *louers of pleasures, more then of GOD*. Fourthly, it must be void of the practise of sinne. *Moses* is commended that *hee refused the pleasures of sin.*[25]

Moderation and proportion are Perkins's foremost considerations; each is central to a Christian sense of priorities that can countenance laughter as long as it does not interfere with the essential love of God and neighbour.

One further distinction provided by Jeremy Taylor dispels the sternest objections of the church fathers and their proponents. In his sermon *The Good and Evil Tongue* Taylor argues that the most uncompromising patristic criticisms of laughter never intended to condemn all laughter. Aquinas had advanced a similar qualification which Taylor now finds equally appropriate in his own answer to the later writers in the Pauline tradition who denounce jesting. He interprets the word *eutrapelia* in the negative sense of 'stultiloquy, or talking like a fool.'[26] The Greek conjunctive, he suggests, implies that jesting is to be equated with foolish talking, and, read in this sense, the epistle actually reproves only the sort of jesting associated with professional fools and stage players notorious for their licentious amorality. The many patristic denunciations reproduced in the sermon are directed against only jesters and actors who play the fool for a living; not all jesting is forbidden. A list of eight conditions for allowable jest amounts to another variation of the rubric of time, persons, and place; moderation again is of paramount importance; and Taylor's general tenor resembles Perkins's: 'But when a jest hath teeth and nails, biting or scratching our brother, when it is loose and wanton, when it is unseasonable, and much, or many, when it serves ill purposes or spends better time, then it is the drunkenness of the soul.'[27] Most contemporaries, for whom the adjectives 'moderate,' 'sober,' and 'innocent' are useful qualifiers and even catchwords, would accept jesting thus defined.

But like many of these same contemporaries Taylor is not content to argue that jest is merely allowable; he also condones its beneficial properties. Indeed the careful answer to the patristics and the warning for seasonable moderation seem only preliminary to the sermon's praise of Christian delight. With mounting emotion and increasingly poetic diction Taylor envisions the cheerful, festive spirit of the harmonious soul and proposes that 'if a facete discourse, and an amicable friendly mirth, can refresh the spirit, and take it off from the vile temptations of peevish, despairing, uncomplying melancholy, it must needs be innocent and commendable.'[28] Other writers who lack Taylor's command of language invoke only the phrase 'honest mirth,' although they have in mind the same ideal.[29] Even those commonly characterized as dour, morose Puritans seldom denounce all mirth in their attacks on drama, poetry, or the pleasures of dicing and dancing. Writers such as John Northbrooke, Henry Crosse, and Robert Barclay vary in their toleration, but all assent at least in principle to Edward Reyner's conclusion that mirthful speech is useful in 'sober and honest delight, for recreation of the minde, and refocillation of the spirits, to make them quick and nimble, when they are dull and heavie, and us fitter and fresher for the duties of our callings ... Wee should make it the end of our mirth, to move such a delight as hath profit or advantage joyned with it to our selves and others, and make us more serious and quick in what we have to say or do.'[30] When used for the further profit of instruction, jesting is even more readily accepted.

Though its bounds are not clearly circumscribed in either century, a firmly established tradition recognizes that jest is a powerful rhetorical weapon. At the beginning of the sixteenth century Erasmus's *De copia* acknowledges Aristotle, Cicero, and Quintilian as important sources; and their authority remains unquestioned throughout the seventeenth century.[31] Although Aristotle's analysis of jest in the *Poetics* no longer existed, he declares in the *Rhetoric*: 'As to jests. These are supposed to be of some service in controversy. Gorgias said that you should kill your opponents' earnestness with jesting and their jesting with earnestness; in which he was right.'[32] A good deal of uncertainty about the exact translation of this passage arises in the eighteenth century; but a seventeenth-century reader with only Hobbes's abridged translation would sense Aristotle's approval.[33] In place of the detailed account now lost, Cicero's long discussion of wit in book II of *De oratore* and Quintilian's similar observations in *Institutio oratoria* remain the most sustained and important pronouncements on the rhetoric of ridicule. Both Castiglione in *The Courtier* and Thomas Wilson in *The Arte of Rhetorique* are indebted to the Roman rhetoricians. Wilson, however, more strongly emphasizes ridicule's pragmatic value, and his rhetoric ranks with George Puttenham's *The Arte of English Poesie* and Henry Peacham's *The Garden of Eloquence* as the most important statements about laughter developed in the English works of rhetoric of the sixteenth century. Other comments scattered throughout the many later rhetorics and the treatises devoted to the art of preaching almost uniformly recognize the same rhetorical value of laughter. Barrow's sermon extensively shows this understanding of ridicule's effectiveness.

Following the first section on delight are seven sanctioning the rhetorical use of jest. Although almost obligatory references are made to Socrates and other great men whose examples lend authority to jest's acceptability, Barrow seems particularly anxious to promote a greater inclusiveness. Since his understanding of *eutrapelia* is often intimately associated with tropes or figures, the sermon argues that 'the limits which sever Rhetorick and Raillery' should not be rigidly maintained. This bid for a more liberal acceptance of jest follows naturally from an earlier inability to determine its exact nature and seems a concomitant of the sermon's recognition that jest is a powerful rhetorical weapon. Barrow supports his contention with specific instances in which jest is both appropriate and valuable.

Facetiousness, he begins, often exposes the vile or contemptible more effectively than reason can. When apparently wrong or evil people resist serious admonition and 'down-right reason,' 'then representing them in a shape strangely-ugly to the fancy, and thereby raising derision at them, may effectually discountenance them' (p 49). Walter Charleton had already noted that the appeal to fancy is central to invective; and the general intent recalls Cicero's suggestion that laughter 'shatters or obstructs or makes light of an opponent, or alarms or repulses him; ... and, best of all, it relieves dullness and tones down austerity, and, by a jest or a laugh often dispels distasteful suggestions not easily weakened by reasonings.'[34] But Barrow offers no rhetorical precedent either here or in the remainder of the discussion; instead he quotes from 1 Kings 18: '*Elias* (saith the Text) *mocked them, and said, Cry aloud; for he is a God, either he is talking, or he is pursuing, or he is in a journey, or peradventure he sleeps, and must be awaked*' (p 50). For the sixteenth and seventeenth centuries the prophet Elijah's retort to the priests who venerated Baal epitomizes a divinely approved use of jest; and this episode from the book of Kings is cited even more often than the divine irony in Genesis 3: 'And the Lord God said, Behold, the man is become as one of us, to know good and evil.'[35]

The sermon, however, considers the divine authorization conditional. While Barrow admits that 'pleasantly-abusive' arguments and 'sarcastical twitches' are sometimes the only effective recourse, he advocates only their 'cautious use.' In keeping with his position as a Restoration divine, his reservation might be expected to reflect a Christian vision of moderation; it is in fact somewhat more qualified. Much of his intent, as well as some of his diction, reiterates the warning in *The History of the Royal-Society* that 'The true *Raillery* should be a defence for *Good* and *Virtuous Works*, and should only intend the derision of extravagant, and the disgrace of vile and dishonourable things.'[36] And while he might not agree with his contemporary John Fell's mistaken notion that Aristotle and Quintilian advocate laughter only as a last resort,[37] he does observe: 'when plain declarations will not enlighten people, to discern the truth and weight of things, and blunt arguments will not penetrate, to convince or persuade them to their duty; then doth Reason freely resign its place to Wit, allowing it to undertake its work of instruction and reproof' (p 50). This basic opposition, one in a series of carefully developed contrasts, accentuates raillery's curative power; but the cure is neither painful nor violent – the wounds will be 'pleasantly rubb'd.' In place of a 'grave' or 'severe' treatment, which would be more in keeping with the barber-surgeon at practice in much earlier satire,[38] a 'free and merry' method may accomplish more lasting results. Replacing chiding with gibing and the contemptuous with the sportful produces, in Barrow's words, both sly laughter and a kind of 'play.' Used against those who resist serious reproof, this appeal to fancy tempers the impression of criticism and disarms the sense of hostility. Reprehension in this manner, 'while it forceth a smile without, doth work remorse within; while it seemeth to tickle the ear, doth sting the heart' (p 53).

The advice would seem common rhetorical knowledge in either the sixteenth or seventeenth centuries; it has, none the less, a distinctly Restoration flavor. Sixteenth- and earlier seventeenth-century writers would not have been acquainted with Barrow's term raillery; nor are its connotations of play or sport central to earlier understandings of jest. Manners, moreover, remain less narrowly described; before the middle of the seventeenth century discussions of manners might include the use of jest; later the emphasis is often reversed and a rhetorical precept becomes a recognized mode of behaviour.[39] In its extreme the growing tendency to consider manners an integral part of jest produces a self-consciousness evident in Tom Brown's late seventeenth-century discussion of Erasmian indirection. Brown praises Erasmus's ability to mix ridicule and seriousness with the 'Air and Gayety of a Gentleman' and the 'Justice of a Philosopher,' and he defends the more notorious sallies of Erasmus's colloquies, declaring: 'Such innocent Freedoms as these, which might fall from a Man of Wit without any Malice, I doubt not but Incensed those of the Reformation, who like the rest of the World were apt to put the worst Construction upon every thing that seem'd to Reflect upon them.'[40] Brown's somewhat smug dismissal of the earlier and ruder era imparts the assurance of a sophisticated individual who knows how to use and to accept laughter. His ideal is the kind of studied ease and naturalness described in Dryden's discussion of satire.[41]

Like Dryden, Barrow observes: 'Many who will not stand a direct reproof, and cannot abide to be plainly admonished of their fault, will yet endure to be pleasantly rubb'd, and will patiently bear a jocund wipe; though they abominate all language purely bitter or sour, yet they can relish discourse having in it a pleasant tartnesse' (p 51). They will accept reproof not necessarily because they know a sophisticated gentleman is expected to tolerate witty admonition but because they will respond to the manner of criticism. Common sense and tact, two of the sermon's notable strengths, suggest man does not readily accept correction, much less that which is condescending and harsh. Jest, on the other hand, is familiar and easy. It allays the natural reluctance to admit error, and it makes reproof more palatable. The ideal is the playful wit Richard Flecknoe earlier describes in his definition of raillery: 'There's nothing in it of abusive, and only as much in it of handsome invective and reproach as may well be owned without a blush.'[42]

This mode of jest, which Flecknoe characterizes as 'a sport onely for your nobler sort,'[43] depends in Barrow's sermon upon a pervasive pragmatism. Regardless of its sophisticated overtones, raillery makes good sense in dealing with certain types of people; besides, any other method would prove futile. It is, likewise, the only way to cope with the false and slanderous. When a person obstinately refuses to heed sound argument, ''tis vain to be in earnest.' The appropriate decorum is to dismiss persistent foolishness with the lightness it deserves. At the same time, the sermon emphasizes, 'perverse obstinancy is more easily quelled, petulant impudence is sooner dashed, Sophistical captiousnesse is more safely eluded, Sceptical wantonnesse is more surely confounded in this, then in the simple way of discourse' (p 54). To refuse to take such behaviour seriously is to deprive it of dignity, and this recourse becomes particularly important in dealing with slanderous charges to which earnest response would give an undue significance.

A composed, facetious manner also often remains the only expedient against those who themselves use laughter. Consistent with its pragmatic vision, the sermon asserts, in heavily patterned cadence, that means must ultimately be judged in terms of ends. Laughter may be used against laughter when all can see 'It is Wit that wageth the war against Reason, against Vertue, against Religion; Wit alone it is that perverteth so many, and so greatly corrupteth the world: It may therefore be needfull, in our warfare for those dearest concerns, to sort the manner of fighting with that of our adversaries, and with the same kind of arms to protect Goodnesse, whereby they do assail it. If Wit may happily serve under the banner of Truth and Vertue, we may imprest it for that service; and good it were to rescue so worthy a faculty from so vile abuse' (pp 55–6). But once again Barrow cautions that jesting is warranted only when more traditional means prove ineffective.

Despite its conditional character the last argument reveals Barrow's increasingly obvious attraction to jest. In an aside to his proposal that facetiousness should be licensed against its misusers, he adds that the world would then see all serious men are not 'lumpish or sour people.' While this corrective would be helpful in an era preoccupied with wit,[44] there remains some uncertainty whether the point is made more for the sake of the sermon or for the author. Throughout the sections analyzing the acceptable limits of jest the careful discriminations and detail are those of an author who has studied with interest the rhetoric of ridicule. The forcefulness with which jest's effectiveness is admitted also indicates someone who appreciates its power. Like many others in a long tradition, Barrow understands laughter's affective appeal, and he may even harbour a desire to be a true wit who 'can speak pleasantly and wittily as well as gravely and judiciously.' He never forgets, however, that laughter must be accepted on condition and then further circumscribed in its use. In spite of the limits he proposes, or perhaps because of them, his final attitude towards jest reveals an important tension characteristic of both the author and his age.

The nature of this complex, ambivalent view of laughter gradually emerges more fully in the second half of the sermon. Until this point Barrow has dealt mainly with the desirability of jest; now he confronts the more difficult task of establishing its acceptability. Jest, he generalizes, may be beneficial as long as it does not undermine traditional values or transgress the obligations of piety, charity, justice, and sobriety. 'When not used upon improper matter, in an unfit manner, with excessive measure, at undue season, to evil purpose, it may be allowed' (p 61). Such abstractions as well as a number of vague adjectives and adverbs show that, quite simply, decorum remains the final arbiter. In the remainder of the sermon Barrow describes the allowable limits of person, place, and time.

Appropriately he begins with the most important subject, religion. Emphatically declaring that 'best earnest' and 'most sober sadness' must always characterize the proper discourse, the sermon condemns all sport, mockery, and loose or wanton jests concerning God and religion. The proscription seems hardly necessary; numerous writers in both the sixteenth and seventeenth centuries agree that 'it committeth a great offence against pietie, when the occasion of mirth & laughter is taken frome ye abuse of reuerend matters, as the holy scriptures, the iudgements of God, magistrates, parents & such like.'[45] Barrow, however, seems particularly appalled by an irreligious wit which a number of his contemporaries claim has become endemic. In a sermon published two years earlier Joseph Glanvill declares: 'And certainly there was never any *other* Age, in which sacred and serious things have been so rudely and impudently assaulted by the prophane abuses of Jesters, and Buffoons, who have been the *contempt* of all *wise* Times, but are the *darlings* and *wits* of *these*.'[46] Glanvill probably had specific writers like Andrew Marvell in mind; others sweepingly proclaim that ''tis *fashonable* to *scoff* and *jear* at all *Religions*.'[47]

Against this form of irresponsible wit the sermon advocates an earnest sobriety that embodies values explained earlier. In a twofold argument Barrow attacks the dangerous immoderation of this religious jest. Wits who lightly trifle with the sacred display a 'prodigious rashness' and an uncouth presumption which any sober man must shun. For the sake of a joke they contemptuously ridicule religion.[48] This rashness confirms, in Barrow's opinion, Koheleth's derisive assertion: 'I said of laughter, It is mad; and of mirth, What doeth it?' The arrogant wit who laughs at sacred beliefs does not only endanger his soul; he also demeans the dignity of religion. The only proper targets for sportful mirth 'are mean and petty matters'; all dignified subjects, 'especially Sacred things do grievously suffer thence, being with extreme indecency and indignity depressed beneath themselves, when they become the subjects of flashy wit, or the entertainments of frothy merriment: to sacrifice their honour to our vain pleasure' (p 63). In view of Barrow's earlier appreciation of the great power of laughter the sermon's emphasis on 'wholesome' speech designed for 'good instruction' or 'good affections' seems natural. Yet some ambiguity remains. Barrow here appears primarily concerned with blasphemy and atheism; his strictures on jest do not exempt from ridicule everything related to religion. Earlier statements that jesting may be a form of piety in 'our warfare for those dearest concerns' indicate that laughter and religion have a relationship only tentatively clarified in the sermon's subsequent sections.

From the abuse of the sacred the sermon moves to a secular parallel, the denigration of reputation. Because it too may cause incalculable harm, Barrow forbids 'All injurious, abusive, scurrilous Jesting, which causelessly or needlesly tendeth to the disgrace, dammage, vexation, or prejudice in any kind of our Neighbour' (pp 65–6). Again not all jesting is forbidden; the sermon prohibits that which is 'without just ground, or reasonable occasion.' But these limits are defined only negatively and by implication; stressed are the evils of scornful or scoffing laughter. Backbiters and mockers who attack their neighbours and disparage the virtuous or pious receive particular attention as Barrow exposes their lack of genuine wit with objections whose corollaries raise issues central to the entire period.

Ridiculers who laugh at men's reputations have traditionally been known as pestilent scorners;[49] in Barrow's depiction of them they warrant even greater opprobrium. Those who create mirth at the expense of others are characterized as uncivil, malignant wits devoid of urbanity. A marginal quotation from Aristotle's *Ethica nicomachea* anticipates the extensive development of this charge later in the sermon. For the present

Barrow closes his initial criticism with the accusation that these wits are also insensitive: they fail to understand that the weaknesses in all men 'do in equity challenge compassion to be had of them; not complacency to be taken in them, or mirth drawn from them: they, in respect to common humanity, should rather be studiously connived at and concealed, or mildly excused, then wilfully laid open, and wantonly descanted upon; they rather are to be deplored secretly, then openly derided' (pp 66–7). Although Barrow has in mind malicious wit, one that is presumably needless and unseasonable, both here and implicitly in the remainder of this section he seems to advocate the tolerant 'amiable humor' of the eighteenth century. His reluctance to malign reputation is of significant relevance to a widely disputed question.

The sensitive issue of name encompasses, obviously, the problem of libel long familiar to writers. Despite the rhetorical precedent supporting the *argumentum ad hominem*, authors in the sixteenth and seventeenth centuries knew the dangers of its injudicious use. The absence of specific names in the vitriolic satires of the 1590s owes at least something to this awareness, and the pressure motivates Ben Jonson to lament in a passage later used by William Congreve: '*Whilst* I name no persons, but deride follies; why should any man confesse, or betray himself? why doth not that of S. *Hierome* come into their minde; *Vbi generalis est de vitiis disputatio, ibi nullius esse personæ injuriam?* Is it such an inexpiable crime in *Poets*, to taxe vices generally; and, no offence in them who, by their exception, confesse they have committed them particularly?'[50] Changing political and social forces during the seventeenth century lessen the reluctance to publish personal attacks, though some of the most liberated writers remain opposed to their own practice. Thus Dryden maintains that satire should expose the error, not the man; and Swift contends: 'Yet, Malice never was his Aim; / He lash'd the Vice but spar'd the Name.'[51] For writers involved in religious controversy the contradiction between theory and practice has special importance.

Barrow summarizes the major conflicts facing a religious controversialist when he admonishes his listeners to remember that slanderous accusations violate Christian charity. Quintilian had noted in his rhetoric that laughter implies derision, and long before Hobbes popularized his theory of superiority, Thomas Wilson mentions in *A Complete Christian Dictionary* (1612) 'that laughing signifieth both rejoycing and mocking, or scorning.'[52] A seventeenth-century audience knew that even without laughter personal attacks and scandalmongering contradict Christ's exhortation to love. Besides fostering selfishness and animus, assaults on reputation threaten Christianity itself. As Richard Greenham preaches in a sermon devoted to this subject, good name enhances the Christian ethos; when calumny deprives the accused of his ability to influence his fellow man, the cause of Christianity is not promoted.[53] The Restoration divine Richard Baxter states this another way: a Christian's character can be more easily ridiculed than his faith, and an otherwise unimpeachable religion will suffer through association.[54]

This danger becomes even more acute when the object of scorn is a dignitary. Barrow firmly believes that people who occupy important or venerable positions deserve esteem; 'their defects are not to be seen, or not to be touched by malicious or wanton wits, by spitefull or scornfull tongues' (p 71). The common fear that detraction will lead to 'publick mischief' is crucial to writers concerned about the propriety of religious ridicule. At times, as in the Augustan dispute surrounding Jeremy Collier's antitheatrical tracts, the inviolability of the clergy threatens to obscure other issues. But the folly of criticizing divine ministers nevertheless entails great harm. 'In publishing the failings and miscarriages of persons engaged in the profession of Religion, what hath he else done but sowne the world with the seed both of blasphemy against God, contempt of his wayes, and obduration of the hearts of wicked and prophane men?'[55]

Against this potential evil is balanced the rhetorical attractiveness of personal ridicule. At the beginning of the seventeenth century, in the aftermath of the Elizabethan extremists, William Vaughan denounces 'detracting and deluding' malice and hopes all will 'spare to speake spitefully against these sicke Brethren of ours, whome we nick-name Puritanes.'[56] Although the civil war challenged his belief that 'It is part of a Brother to endeauour his Brothers conuersion into the vnitie of peace by gentle meanes,' some writers in the 1640s also advocated reasonable discourse and disavowed ironical jeering.[57] But many others embroiled in the bitter debate that divided the nation found that the nature of the conflict demanded harsher methods. Precedents in the writings of the church fathers[58] and the demands of militancy were sufficient for reconciling Christian love and polemical practice.

Polemicists commonly seek to achieve this union without compromising either faith or charity. But as the Dean of Canterbury, John Boys, notes, the two virtues almost inevitably conflict, for 'albeit charity suffereth all things, beleeueth all things, hopeth all things, endureth all things, yet faith can suffer nothing.'[59] Faced with this dilemma at a time when the dangers of civil conflict were yet remote, Boys has little difficulty in siding with the church fathers who uphold faith's adamantine nature. While the evils of slandering a neighbour are considerable, 'It is lawfull also to iest at the vanities of irreligious men, enemies to God and his Gospell.'[60] When the events of later years force neighbours into greater divisiveness over questions of religion, the demands of faith face a more complicated problem. In *A Triall of Ovr Chvrch-forsakers* published on the eve of revolution Robert Abbot expresses a growing awareness of this problem: 'I say as a father of old, *I dare not write against a Bishop of my communion*; the love of brotherly peace is glorious in the Church, even among men that otherwise differ in opinion. But if they put on the armes of an enemy, (because they will be so) with whom I fight for truth, I cannot helpe it, if they meete with a blow, though I glory not in it, yea am sorry that there should be such cause.'[61] As literal arms replace the figurative, zeal more noticeably dispels reluctant passivity. Writers freely cite the example of Christ's reaction to the pharisees or his disciples' against their detractors and urge that love for God supersede personal offence. Thomas Edwards, for example, excuses his voluminous libels with the reassurance that they were undertaken 'out of zeal to the truth of God, and compassion to the souls of men destroyed by these errours, proceeding also from sad and serious consideration of the discharge of my duty.'[62] Although some contemporaries questioned Edwards's motives and sincerity while others supplied him with further items of scandal, the apology does suggest one resolution of the different demands of faith and charity. In exposing deluded men both to themselves and to others Edwards fulfils his obligation to faith and his conception of good. Some seventeenth-century writers found it possible to agree that this loyalty to God and this concern for fellow men constitute true charity.

Among the opponents of zeal, particularly in the reactionary atmosphere of the Restoration, charity is less subordinate to faith and personal ridicule is less tolerated. The temptation to indulge an abusive vein nevertheless occurs frequently into the eighteenth century, and proponents of it like John Edwards continue to object: 'We pretend to make the Scriptures our Rule, and why not in this, as well as in other Matters, that is, in speaking our Minds with Plainness and Freedom, and giving Persons and Things the Names which belong to them?'[63] But his premise that the demands of truth override the concern for names and persons enjoys less support than the similar position of his father Thomas Edwards. The changing sensibility, expressed with considerable detail in a 1684 treatise *Concerning Reproaching & Censure*, reveals the premium placed on sobriety and charity. In this publication William Falkner defines 'true zeal' that prohibits impassioned and uncharitable detraction: 'Christianity doth not only allow, but require a rational and just dislike, and *sober censure* of those, who entertain or countenance *evil practices*, to debauch or corrupt the lives of men, and who spread, promote or receive, false and *unsound principles*, whereby deluded and misguided minds forsake and depart from the truth.'[64] Just censure based on reason dissociates whenever possible the person from the belief and the individual from the party; furthermore it proceeds from 'evident truth' in a sober manner. Although he admits that evil and flagrant absurdities warrant appropriate stricture, his ideal remains a moderate, charitable criticism. 'But in an undue manner to vent expressions of *wrath* or reproach; or of scornfulness or scurrility; and to treat others with an angry and *waspish temper*, and instead of calmness to raise a storm of rage and fury; these things are evil in themselves, being contrary to the meekness and gentleness of Christianity, and savouring of the fruits of the *flesh*, and the root of *bitterness*; and they are also very unsuitable to all sorts of men.'[65] To those zealots who respond that Christ's reproofs were neither meek nor gentle Falkner denies the parallel. According to this not uncommon apology Christ was divinely ordained to reform a badly defaced religion. The magnitude of his mission and the recalcitrant belligerency of the Jews justified sharp reproach, yet Christ never succumbed to reviling. His language transcended personal slander with 'metaphorical and *representative expressions*,' and its '*expressive significancy*' controlled its use. Contemporary Christians face no situation of comparable urgency; therefore when they are moved to 'just indignation,' charity should always temper their reactions. Again intent determines the acceptable censure of personal shortcomings. When the cause is just and a greater good is its end, reproof which derives no secret satisfaction, eschews distorting language, and avoids personal prejudice or harm is charitable.

Most sixteenth- and seventeenth-century Christians agree that reason, sobriety, and certainty are desirable; Falkner's arguments for charitable reproof also disclose a basic preoccupation with order. 'True Zeal,' Edward Stillingfleet explains, 'is accompanied with Meekness, Patience, Gentleness, Long-suffering, Kindness towards others; so false and mistaken Zeal soures and imbitters the Spirits of Men, makes them fretful and impatient of the least Contradiction, morose and inflexible, never yielding to the Conviction of others, but maintaining every thing with an invincible Stiffness; which is a Temper as repugnant to Ingenuity and a peaceable Disposition, as Light to Darkness.'[66] The title of Stillingfleet's sermon, *Peace and Holiness*, aptly describes Falkner's intention. Both react against a zealous enthusiasm which threatens disruption; and each proposes 'to endeavour after Peace, and in lesser matters to yield as far as is consistent with our necessary Duty to God and our Neighbor.'[67]

Charity and holiness find a secular counterpart in the Restoration idea of civility, as reflected in René Rapin's *Reflections upon the Eloquence of These Times*. Rapin, whose mistrust of false eloquence resembles Falkner's fear of zeal, forbids personal detraction. 'We may with civility glance at, but cannot, without rudeness and ill manners, stare upon the faults or imperfections of any man: And I think every man ought to be offended with himself, who violates that religious respect which they owe to the Church and Churchmen.'[68] Emphasis in the main body of his work on reason, judgment, and 'words proportionate to things' anticipates Falkner's call for control. Indeed detraction's potential volatility alone, aside from its association with immoderation, ill-breeding, and contentiousness, may have shaped Rapin's reaction to this form of incivility. At any rate all are important considerations which Barrow recognizes in his own remarks on impropriety.

Malicious jest violates Barrow's conception of Christian charity and breaches his understanding of urbanity. The ideal of Christian civility which the sermon equates with 'genuine facetiousnesse' and opposes to 'uncivil rudenesse' has both classical and contemporary overtones. Marginal allusions to Aristotle and Horace underline its essential balance and perspicuity, while the language and focus echo the values of Rapin and Falkner. The urbane facetiousness envisioned in the sermon maintains a mean which Barrow describes as thoroughly innocent. He agrees with Aristotle and his Restoration imitators that jest in excess suggests the image of a buffoon; more important, it may greatly harm others. 'It is,' in sum, 'an unworthy perverting of wit, to employ it in biting and scratching; in working prejudice to any man's reputation, or interest; in needlesly incensing any man's anger, or sorrow; in raising animosities, dissensions, and feuds among any' (p 72). This apprehension of abusive wit and the sermon's stress on the importance of judgment reflect contemporary reactions to the threat of disorder; Barrow's depiction of 'true wit' also reveals the changing understanding of jest.

In deploring 'biting and scratching' and 'Satyrical taunts,' the sermon reintroduces the notion that 'True Festivity' possesses healing properties. Again the medical analogy points out that innocent jest should only cleanse and never irritate. The older view of the physician-wit used to justify the intemperate outbursts of Elizabethan verse satirists and Caroline pamphleteers followed a standard defence similar to Jonson's rhetorical question: 'If men may by no meanes write freely, or speake truth, but when it offends not; why doe *Physicians* cure with sharpe medicines, or corrosives? Is not the same equally lawfull in the cure of the minde, that is in the cure of the body?'[69] Barrow's negative response may be seen as part of the growing Restoration preference for Horatian *ridiculum* rather than Juvenalian *acre*.[70] Dryden's own hesitation to choose between Juvenal and Horace indicates that not all writers disown sharp reproof; and the vituperative style has its defenders in the late seventeenth century as well. But Barrow finds the appeal of urbane facetiousness considerable.

Although its attractiveness resists simplification, urbanity seems in the sermon inextricably linked to perspicuity. Barrow's specific plea for Christian compassion and his particular denunciation of self-serving libel presuppose the insight of charity. His reference to Horace and his insistence on the need for 'a right knowledge of good manners' also stress this sensitivity. Those who jestingly impugn reputations and thoughtlessly foment discord betray their inability to discern the larger implications of their actions. In fact, these irascible, abusive jesters may deliberately seek this blindness. Empty vanity is concealed in an illusion of wit created by excessive choler. Often 'they who seem to excell this way, are miserably flat in other discourse, and most dully serious: they have a particular unaptnesse to describe any good thing, or commend any worthy person; being destitute of right *Ideas*, and proper terms answerable to such purposes: their representations of that kind are absurd and unhandsome; their Elogies (to use their own way of speaking) are in effect Satyrs' (p 74). Like Rapin's desire to unite words with things and Falkner's advocacy of proper zeal, Barrow's idea of facetious urbanity rests upon true eloquence.

A sceptical fear of distortion and a complementary reaction against rashness greatly influence the delicate balance developed in the remainder of the sermon. The next important section, unseasonable jest, quickly dismisses 'obscene and smutty' humour. It deserves no attention because obscene jesting is the most incontrovertible evidence that a mind is 'utterly debauched from Piety and Vertue' (p 75). This dogmatic attitude is not unusual since Quintilian also declares in his *Institutio oratoria* that 'As for obscenity, it should not merely be banished from his language, but should not even be suggested.'[71] Although in practice this advice is not always followed, rhetorical theory seems agreed about the undesirability of this kind of jest; and Barrow quickly turns to the circumstances and times which dictate the exclusion of all jest.

Of the three unseasonable kinds of jest considered, only one of them contains leeway for disagreement. As the marginal quotation from Quintilian indicates, Barrow has considerable tradition supporting his exclusion of all jests designed to laugh at miserable or unfortunate people. This 'uncivil' and 'inhumane' behaviour runs counter to Christian compassion; it also makes light of God's providence. Christian civility further prohibits the rude use of jests among people who want to be serious. When forcefully introduced, an intemperate manner subverts the value of jocularity, which 'is to sweeten and ease society: when to the contrary it breedeth offence or encumbrance, it is worse then vain and unprofitable' (p 77). Some uncertainty, however, exists in the discussion of the dignified circumstances which allow no jesting; here the ambiguity lies in the question of degree.

Barrow seems to disallow all jests where superiors, sacred duties, or matters of great significance are involved. The first two subjects receive only one sentence, perhaps because the sermon has already touched on the inviolable nature of the sacred and because the wisdom of observing the dignity of superiors was commonplace. In proposing a suitably plain style for resolving important issues Barrow argues at greater length, denying jest in deliberations of church and state: 'The Shop and Exchange will scarce endure Jesting in their lower transactions: the Senate, the Court of justice, the Church do much more exclude it from their more weighty consultations' (p 76). Although the exact meaning hinges upon an interpretation of 'much more,' the sense of the argument seems to deny any jest in deliberations involving matters of church and state. The next sentence, however, modifies this absoluteness with the qualification that 'Whenever it justleth out, or hindereth the dispatch of other serious business, taking up the room, or swallowing the time due it, or indisposing the minds of the audience to attend it, then it is unseasonable and pestilent' (p 76). In view of the sermon's prior acceptance of laughter's beneficial nature, it is by no means certain that Barrow would also exclude jest when it might aid the resolution of the most serious concerns.

This ambiguity stems partly from Barrow's effort to achieve an acceptable mean. The plain, serious style must not be ignored, he continues, because it is both foolish and dangerous 'to be earnest in jest.' Excessive facetiousness reduces man to the level of the buffoon. The adulation of fancy, moreover, is given at the expense of reason, an exchange which for the Christian has momentous consequences. Fancy is little more than a 'brutish, shallow, and giddy power' of doubtful worth, while reason is the essence of man. Earlier in the sermon Barrow admits that fancy may succeed where reason fails; now its power is swept aside in an exaltation of reason. 'It is simple Reason (as dull and dry as it seemeth) which expediteth all the grand affairs, which accomplisheth all the mighty works that we see done in the world. In truth therefore, as one Diamond is worth numberlesse bits of Glasse; so one solid Reason is worth innumerable Fancies: one grain of true Science and sound Wisedom in real worth and use doth outweigh loads (if any loads can be) of freakish Wit' (p 81). While part of the hyperbole may be simply rhetoric, the unreserved acceptance of reason and the contradiction it implies are part of an ancient dilemma.

At least as early as the writings of Plato laughter has been regarded with considerable ambivalence.[72] Quintilian summarizes the major reservations near the beginning of his long discussion of laughter's usefulness when he admits that 'sayings designed to raise a laugh are generally untrue (and falsehood always involves a certain meanness), and are often deliberately distorted, and, further, never complimentary.'[73] Laughter's great rhetorical good involves a basic duplicity which challenges the integrity of reason. The fear of displacing reason is also a major concern of the patristics, who agree with Clement of Alexandria that, 'As rational animals, we must ever maintain proper balance.'[74] Into the sixteenth and seventeenth centuries authors still strive to maintain a tenuous balance, and writers like Henry Peacham continue to warn that laughter may 'outface the truth' if it is allowed in serious controversies.[75] Properly qualified jest is generally accepted; about the middle of the seventeenth century, however, a new awareness of laughter's disruptiveness emerges.

The change is apparent in Richard Baxter's *A Christian Directory*. Baxter adds biblical evidence from Ecclesiastes and Proverbs that prohibits mirth which 'shuts out Reason, and silenceth Conscience, and laughts at God, and jesteth at Damnation, and doth but intoxicate the brain, and make men mad in the matters where they should most shew their wisdom.'[76] Although this position is not unlike that of Perkins and other seventeenth-century churchmen, the stress and the language noticeably emphasize laughter's harmful power. The quotation from Ecclesiastes might, of course, account for the belief that laughter is madness, but the reference to this passage and the emphasis on the brain's intoxication indicate a stronger mistrust of laughter. At its basis are the forces once described as 'The Restoration Revolt against Enthusiasm,'[77] but the renewed interest in the faculties of the mind and the accompanying insights about laughter also influence this reaction.

Thomas Hobbes's *Preface to Gondibert* and Henry More's *Enthusiasmus Triumphatus* are seminal works; their implications in Joseph Glanvill's arguments reveal the changing attitudes towards laughter. In *The Vanity of Dogmatizing*, published a year after the restoration of the monarchy, Glanvill accepts More's interpretation of enthusiasm and attacks confident opinion derived from an imagination influenced by the melancholy humour. Seven years later a letter on drollery and atheism written to More again opposes reason against imagination; this time, however, Glanvill uses Hobbes's language. In criticizing the new breed of drolls that seems to abound, the letter deplores their superficial, flashy wit. 'The *Drolling Humorists*,' who pride themselves on their ability to ridicule the sacred and serious, 'are for the most part, *remarkably defective*, in *close ratiocinations*, and the *worst* in the world at *inference*; which is no wonder, since fancy is a *desultory*, and *roving faculty*; and when 'tis not under the *conduct* of a *severe judgment*, not able to keep it self to a *steady*, and *resolved attention*; much less, to make *coherent chains* of *rational Deduction*.'[78] The droll deliberately resorts to scoffing in order to compensate for his inability to reason. Ignoring judgment and reason, he indulges a fanciful imagination that knows no decorum and accepts no limits. The result is a serious threat to knowledge. '*Philosophy* can shame, and disable all the *reasons* that can be urged against it; but *jests*, and *loud laughter* are not to be *confuted*: and yet *these* are of more force to degrade a thing in the esteem of some sort of Spirits, than the most *potent demonstrations*.'[79]

The reasons why philosophy seems impotent against laughter are readily apparent. Fancy possesses a power which, left unchecked by judgment, can tyrannize the mind. Unlike that of the discursive faculty, its influence is also more easily established. Reason may be incomparably more substantial, but, as Richard Allestree recognizes in *The Government of the Tongue*, 'a dull contumely quickly vanishes, no body thinking it worth remembering; but when 'tis steel'd with Wit, it pierces deep, leaves such impressions in the fancy of the hearers, that thereby it gets rooting in the memory, and will scarce be eradicated.'[80] The image adds to Cicero's description of wit's penetrating ability a greater fear of fancy also apparent in the many allusions to Aristophanes' notorious ridicule of Socrates. From the 1660s onwards[81] this infamous illustration of laughter's harm reflects a corresponding realization that reason is vulnerable to various forms of attack. At the end of his proposal for a new philosophy Thomas Sprat, for example, singles out laughter in particular and expresses the fear that some, by ridiculing his program 'becaus it is *new*, and becaus they themselves are unwilling to take pains about it, may do it more injury than all the Arguments of our severe and frowning and dogmatical *Adversaries*.'[82] Like Glanvill and those associated with the Royal Society, Sprat is not committed to Pyrrhonism; his form of scepticism, on the contrary, values the great benefits of rationality. He is doubtful, however, of man's ability or willingness always to use his reason.[83]

Properly governed by their intended function, however, both faculties may be employed. Glanvill devotes considerable attention to their mutual use in the belief that 'God hath bestowed upon us *Reason*, and understanding to *judge* and *discourse* about things that are *serious*; and the Faculty of *laughter* and *derision* to be exercised upon those things that are vain.'[84] The realm of the serious therefore should always exclude laughter, and conversely common sense dictates that reason should not debase itself with the ridiculous. Among the vanities suitable for laughter Glanvill variously mentions vice, sin, and conceited folly. In addition to its use in exposing evil Sprat further allows it as 'a defence for *Good* and *Virtuous Works*, and should only intend the derision of extravagant, and the disgrace of vile and dishonourable things.'[85] Within these limits laughter is acceptable, and even its most adamant opponents may find it beneficial. Richard Blackmore, for example, forcefully condemns the threat laughter poses to reason and 'useful Science'; yet in his essay on wit he quotes with approval from Archbishop Tillotson's *The Folly of Scoffing at Religion*: 'The proper use of it is to season Conversation, to represent what is Praise-worthy to the greatest Advantage, and to expose the Vices and Follies of men, such things as are in themselves truly ridiculous: But if it be apply'd to the Abuse of the gravest and most serious Matters, it then loses its Commendation.'[86]

In practice the unanimity breaks down since not all writers agree on what defines good or evil or separates the grave from the ludicrous. In the same essay in which he vigorously limits ridicule Blackmore applauds the raillery John Eachard uses to dismiss Thomas Hobbes's philosophy. He is able to maintain that this raillery is acceptable without being inconsistent because in his opinion Hobbes is a 'conceited Philosopher.' A similar qualification also occurs among writers conscious of the propriety that religion demands. Edward Filmer suddenly becomes more narrow-minded than his opponent when he ignores his own advice about the discreet and proper use of ridicule and accuses Collier of demanding respect for all clergy.[87] His objection that Nonconformist ministers do not warrant honour is in fact kinder than the common accusation that all dissenters are fanatical hypocrites. An essay written in the 1650s contends that the 'schismatick' can only be treated with either silence or laughter,[88] and in the 1670s the respected controversialist Edward Stillingfleet lends his authority to a similar 'sport and recreation.' 'Now if any one who pretends to *Inspiration* and *Enthusiasm* cannot be charged with *Fanaticism* without *blasphemy*, we must be exposed to all follies and contradictions imaginable; and to what purpose are we bid to *try the Spirits whether they be of God or no*, i.e. whether their pretence to divine revelation be true or false?'[89] The danger that the dominant religion will always proceed as if it has truth on its side is also apparent to some Restoration thinkers like Thomas Sprat. Archbishop Tillotson would forbid any 'sport' with another's religion 'not with any design to convince their reason but only to provoke their rage.'[90] And the only way to avoid the ambiguities surrounding intention is, as Glanvill decides, to forbid all but the most serious treatment of anything related to religion whether it seems true or false.

Barrow's own delicately poised position observes a measured moderation. Manner as well as intent determines the allowable limits of laughter, and in the last part of the sermon Barrow even implies that it takes precedence. The jest that becomes an end in itself or springs from an inflated conceit contains a disagreeable egotism; ideal jocularity should have the casual, unstudied air which characterizes graceful sophistication. It should also never forget the Christian need for modest and sober seriousness. 'We ought always in our behavior to maintain, not onely τὸ πρέπον, a fitting *decency*, but also τὸ σεμνὸν, a stately *gravity*' (p 84). Violating this standard through excessive levity can only lead to harm, for 'Gravity and Modesty are the fences of Piety, which being once slighted, sin will easily attempt and encroach upon us' (p 85). The extremes balanced in the patterned syntax of the conclusion imply the middle course that Paul might have accepted: 'as we need not be demure, so must we not be impudent; as we should not be sour, so ought we not to be fond; as we may be free, so we should not be vain; as we may well stoop to friendly complaisance, so we should take heed of falling into contemptible levity' (p 85). By opposing the acceptable and unacceptable uses of laughter the larger dialectical movement of the sermon also confirms this conclusion. It is ultimately one of jest and earnest.

The resolution is rhetorically impressive. Structurally the antithetical halves of the sermon convey a sense of moderate, careful deliberation that recognizes alternatives. The movement of the prose confirms with a satisfying inevitability a position that suitably fulfils Barrow's ethos as a Christian minister and decorously meets the demands of a sermon. While the concluding emphasis on grave sobriety may dampen some of the earlier endorsements of laughter, the delicate balance is not upset. By showing that seriousness and jest are not incompatible, the sermon recommends a manner which Cicero long ago admired in Socrates and which Barrow's contemporaries increasingly were to find appropriate to the temper of the late seventeenth century. More precise delineation is unwise and unnecessary. The decorum of laughter, Quintilian reminds the readers of *Institutio oratoria*,[91] can never be satisfactorily established.

Nevertheless the complex era embracing both Marprelate and Swift believed some form of religious ridicule was acceptable. The adverbs in Barrow's conclusion, 'we can use our wits in jesting innocently, and conveniently,' are neither intentionally vague nor evasive. Classical, patristic, and contemporary pronouncements on jest indicate that its allowable circumstances are indeed tentative. When theoretical distinctions are put into practice, the circumstances must be individually judged. The right to blend religious jest and earnest will then depend largely on character. As Barrow illustrates both in his precept and in his presentation, manner determines acceptable decorum and influences individual judgments.

In its sensitive and comprehensive analysis of the period's attitudes towards jesting, the sermon elucidates the central preoccupation of Marprelate, Milton, Marvell, and Swift. Like Barrow, these major satirists recognize that current notions of decorum offer at best general guidelines; the licence to mix jest and earnest must in each instance be individually warranted. The expediency of the moment and the need to answer in kind are certainly considerations, but obligations to truth, charity, and civility remain paramount. Aware that religious ridicule may be easily abused, they too strive to show by their behaviour the 'fitting *decency*' and the 'stately *gravity*' befitting the Christian satirist. Thus apologies for their satiric modes, however necessary, are secondary to a common concern with character development. From the self-dramatizing postures and innovative concept of *decorum personæ* developed by the anonymous Martin Marprelate to the complex, elusive masks of Jonathan Swift the fundamental achievement lies in the satirists' ability to give new dimension to the importance of manner.

3

The Marprelate Tracts

IN THE FOURTH OF THE SEVEN TRACTS issued secretly from the
Marprelate press between October 1588 and September 1589 the
anonymous author admits that his natural inclination is not 'to jest in this
serious matter.' Only the obligation to expose the errors in the polity of
the established church and to promote true Christian government
prompted his expedient course. Most people, the apology explains, had
little immediate interest in the need for reform and would not ordinarily
become engaged in the disputed issues. 'Perceiving the humours of men
in these times (especially of those that are in any place) to be given to
mirth,' Marprelate continues, 'I took that course. I might lawfully do it.
Aye, for jesting is lawful by circumstances, even in the greatest matters.
The circumstances of time, place, and persons urged me thereunto. I
never profaned the Word in any jest. Other mirth I used as a covert
wherein I would bring the truth into light. The Lord being the author both
of mirth and gravity, is it not lawful in itself, for the truth to use either of
these ways, when the circumstances do make it lawful?'[1] This brief defence raises many of the same issues encountered in Barrow's sermon;
traditional apology, however, cannot justify the radical decision to mix jest
and earnest in religious matters. Throughout the satires Marprelate develops his own justification for a manner that gives new significance to
the repeated emphasis on circumstances and the appeal to truth.

The first satires appeared near the end of 1588 in response to John
Bridges's *A Defence of the Government Established in the Chvrch of Englande for
Ecclesiasticale Matters.* This lengthy and significant work of the dean of
Sarum grew from a sermon he preached at Paul's Cross into an official
answer to the challenge posed by a 1584 publication, *A Briefe and plaine
declaration ... for the Discipline and reformation of the Church of Englande.*

Commonly known as *The Learned Discourse*, the tract was probably written by William Fulke[2] and served to reassert the Puritan desire for a church ordered by pastors, doctors, elders, and deacons. The lucid exposition of the reformers' ideals and the demand for open confrontation could not be ignored, for, as Bridges explains, 'when a matter groweth to importance, and is vrged too importunately, admitting it be a wrong and daungerous errour, and yet on all sides it winneth fauour; to let it so passe without all controlement; what were silence then, but grosse negligence, the very yeelding to the errour and danger, yea the wilfull betraying of the truth, and consenting to the ouerture of our state?'[3] The seriousness of the threat prompted Bridges to write a 1400-page defence which, aside from a section on Beza, minutely scrutinizes the proposed reforms. Within the year Dudley Fenner's *A Defence Of The godlie Ministers* countered Bridges's massive work. Promising that 'we shal be forced for the length of his flourishes, to diuide it into seuerall Treatises, and publishe them seuerally as we may,'[4] Fenner limits his refutation to the preface of Bridges's *Defence*. The first of its sixteen books is considered the next year in Walter Travers's *A Defence Of the Ecclesiastical Discipline*. At the end of this tract Travers describes his effort as 'the first part of this my labour,' and there seems to be no end in sight. Fenner had required 150 pages and Travers 228 to answer Bridges; at this point they had defended only 10 pages of the 154 in *The Learned Discourse*, and over 1200 pages of Bridges's tome remained unanswered.

Marprelate's own answers, *The Epistle* and *The Epitome*, seem little more than stopgap measures designed to discredit Bridges while more serious replies were being prepared. Although he agrees with the contention in *A Defence of the Government Established in the Chvrch of Englande* that 'discipline, and of the Churches gouernment' are the main concerns, his initial satires consider Bridges's arguments only superficially and sporadically. Even when Anglican officials protract the controversy with Thomas Copper's *An Admonition to the People of England*, the subsequent Martinist publications do not add to the substantive issues. The list of four petitions in the next to the last satire summarizes demands also found in *The Learned Discourse* for the abolition of ignorant ministers, 'unlawful' or 'sinful callings,' and all offices without biblical sanction; proofs offered in the other pamphlets to substantiate the correct polity are also standard. Throughout their brief course the satires remain primarily vehicles to popularize reform rather than means to dispute their opponents' essential beliefs. As highly effective propaganda they are attuned to the circumstances which favour jest's rhetorical value.

In a milieu sensitive to the relationship between profit and delight these limits at times seem tolerant. The need to hold the audience's attention is recognized by Thomas Wilson who declares in *The Arte of Rhetorique* that 'euen these aunciente Preachers, muste now and then plaie the fooles in the pulpite, to serue the fickle eares of their fletyng audience.'[5] Later he cautions that jest must observe a moderate mean, but this warning does not diminish his appreciation of laughter's lawful and effective uses. Following closely the precepts of Cicero and Quintilian, Wilson adds his colourful and forthright endorsement. 'Now when we would abashe a man, for some wordes that he hath spouken, and can take none aduauntage of his persone, or makyng of his bodie, we either doult him at the first, and make hym beleue, that he is no wiser then a Goose: or els we cōfute wholy his saiynges, with some pleasaunt ieste, or els we extenuate and diminishe his doinges, by some pretie meanes, or els we cast the like in his dishe, and with some other deuise, dash him out of countenance: or last of al, we laugh him to scorne out right, and sometimes speake almoste neuer a worde, but onely in countenance, shewe our selues pleasaunt.'[6] While these techniques might not suit all audiences, a contemporary translation of *The Practice of Preaching* suggests greater tolerance was possible. Distinguishing between a 'scholastical' and a 'popular' audience, Andreas Hyperius describes in detail rhetorical freedom given to the preacher who turns away from the confines of the schools to address the 'large and spacious temples.' His statements on popular appeal, although technically limited to the pulpit, recognize the importance of confutation and allow considerable affective licence.[7] They suggest a new consciousness of the need to reach and to sway a wider audience.

Establishing acceptable boundaries when, as Dudley Fenner contends, 'there is not found any expresse lawe which determineth the ecclesiasticall way of defining controuersies'[8] proves more difficult. Sixteenth-century precedents for the use of religious jest among both continental humanists and English polemicists offer only limited guidance. When he was being examined concerning his role in the Marprelate publications John Penry allegedly cited Philip von Marnix's *The Beehive*, Curione's *Pasquine in a Traunce*, and Beza's pseudonymous mask of Passavontius to excuse the satires' jest as a 'lawfull Course ... that godly men had taken heretofore.'[9] Later critics of Marprelate also mention Beza's influence, and one contemporary objects that Thomas Cartwright 'by his scoffes and flowers of railing traced out a way for *Martin*.'[10] The charge of improper jesting made in the Admonition Controversy by both John Whitgift and Cartwright can also be found in the important confrontation between

John Jewel and Thomas Harding. Jewel justifies his conduct with the contention that 'well may we jest at your unhandsome and open legerdemain that so vainly seek to blind us with a painted shadow of the Spirit of God,'[11] and the earlier controversialist John Frith partly rationalizes his own laughter with the claim that 'euery mā perceiueth that *M. More* his bookes are so full of rayling, gestyng and baudye tales, that if the furious *Momus* & *Venus* had take out theyr partes there should be very little left for *Vulcanus*.'[12] More himself in *The Apologye of Syr Thomas More Knyght* offers only the Horatian quotation that Erasmus used earlier in his own defence and that the 1584 edition of *Pasquine in a Traunce* translates: 'Ridentē dicere verum, quid vetat? Why shuld not a iester or a merie fellow tel truth';[13] more specific apology is not developed. With the possible exception of Erasmus's letters to Thomas More and Martin Dorp defending the laughter in his *Praise of Folly*, in the sixteenth century the defence of religious ridicule remains only a little more certain than the charges of its abuse.[14] Thus when Marprelate answers the adverse reaction to his method, his insistence upon the urgency of the circumstances appears little more than a traditional argument from rhetoric for the lawfulness of jest.

In practice, however, the satiric blend of jest and earnest departs significantly from conventional notions of decorum. At the onset of his attack on Bridges's work Marprelate requests permission 'to play the dunce for the nonce, as well as he; otherwise dealing with Master Doctor's book, I cannot keep *decorum personæ*' (p 17). The introduction of this particular term may allude to the principle in Horace's *Ars poetica* that action should be consistent with character.[15] Marprelate's variation in *The Epistle* implies that Bridges is a fool who deserves nothing but the answers of a fool; or, as he apologizes, 'if I be too absurd in any place ... [it is] Because, I could not deal with his book commendably, according to order, unless I should be sometimes tediously duncical and absurd' (p 17). This rationale recalls a similar appeal to propriety in the *Praise of Folly* and also echoes the counsel imparted in Proverbs 26:5 to 'Answer a fool according to his folly, lest he be wise in his own conceit.'[16] Used several years earlier by Beza to defend his treatment of Genebrard, the proverb is often cited in the next century to argue, in a similar way: 'What ... if I have answered one that deserved no better, *Quasi per ludim, &c.* in a sporting manner, as the times would then bear? *Solomon* sure doth not simply forbid us to answer a Fool; and what hinders but that a man may laugh and speak the truth?'[17] Marprelate's satires, in contrast, invest the words 'according to his folly' with a decorum unique to the tracts.

Biblical commentators in the sixteenth and seventeenth centuries generally agree that strictly observed decorum should exclude the imitation of folly. Relying often on the interpretation developed in Cyprian's letter to Demetrian, they are painfully aware that the previous proverb advises 'Answer not a fool according to his folly, lest thou also be like unto him.' Cyprian resolves the apparent contradiction by suggesting that silence remains the best course unless the circumstances are such that unchecked folly will cause harm.[18] Any correction should be undertaken '*with wisedome as his follie requireth to be answered*.'[19] While some readings of these two proverbs further allow sharp reproof or *ad hominem* arguments, they recognize that the wisdom in answering a fool 'according to his folly' excludes adopting a like foolishness.[20] When polemicists speak of answering a fool they too, as the opening passage in *The Epistle* might imply, intend to ridicule rather than to imitate folly.[21] Marprelate, however, exposes folly with his own form of deliberate mimesis. The title page of the second satire declares: 'lest Mr. Doctor should think that no man can write without sense but his self, the senseless titles of the several pages, and the handling of the matter throughout the Epitome show plainly, that beetleheaded ignorance must not live and die with him alone' (p 115). This mimetic manner adds an important dimension to Marprelate's claim that 'the circumstances do make it lawful.'

Its genesis begins innocuously in the prefatory comments of *The Learned Discourse*. There the hope is offered that a 'peaceable and reasonable way' can be found to unite English Protestants against their common enemy Catholicism. The matter of perfecting the present church structure can be resolved through a mutually accepted 'manner.' The 'best learned, most Godly & moderate men' from each side should be chosen to defend their positions, and the differences should then be carefully established and sufficiently examined 'till eyther by the euidence of truth one part yeeld vnto the other; or the folly and madness of those which gaynesay it, do in equall iudgement become manifest, in regarde of the contradictions and absurdities whereto they shall bee dryuen by the force of Gods worde.'[22] The preface assumes that the reformers would emerge triumphant from open confrontation, and requests for such an exchange were not unusual. However the author of *The Learned Discourse* realizes that truth can easily be distorted, and he proposes a manner of conduct that eschews any rhetorical flourishes. His ideal of fruitful disputation devoid of rancour may be achieved only 'where no authoritie, pregnancie of wit, plausible perswasion of mans wisedome, shall turn the truth aside, but al shal stand in the euident demonstration of Gods spirite.'[23]

Bridges doubts that this desired manner can ever be achieved. Unable to resist suggesting that the reformers fear wit because they themselves are not witty, he more earnestly concedes that rhetorical eloquence is not necessary. 'Our dram of discretion' together with the virtues of obedience, humility, and temperate zeal are 'more woorth in *reasoning* of these cōtrouersies, then al the pregnancie or *readiness of wit*.'[24] Those who want to destroy the existing order have in Bridges's opinion already closed their minds to the truth, and their desire for open disputation is not only self-serving but futile. Developing a position that Hooker would later adopt,[25] Bridges further objects that the logistics of establishing a debate and clarifying all ambiguities would prove formidable obstacles; deciding a victor and satisfactorily implementing the program suggested would be impossible. 'For my part,' he concludes, 'I see little hope of *reconciliation of the matter, by this manner* which they heere set down.'[26]

When Fenner and Travers answer with their rebuttals, 'manner' assumes still greater meaning. In the preface to *A Defence Of the godlie Ministers* Fenner bitterly asserts that Bridges has mistreated their proposal for reform. 'No wordes, no sentences, neuer so clearelie and manifestlie set downe of vs, can escape at his handes most violent and forced interpretations, most ridiculous and slaunderous gloses.'[27] Actually Bridges's long book does not stray far from its promise to remain moderate, and even its occasionally heavy-handed irony might be ordinarily overlooked. But the heavily italicized pages of the work underscore his tendency to intersperse his opponent's words in lengthy animadversions. Fenner, who saw a seven-page request for a plain style proliferate twentyfold in Bridges's scrutiny, reacted critically to his manner. And there is special poignancy in a renewed desire for open disputation that ends: 'Wherefore desiring him in the bowells of Christ *Iesvs*, to leaue slaundring, caueling, peruerting of playne sentences, and to reason pithelie and Syllogisticallie out of Gods worde.'[28] In Travers's continuation, *A Defence Of The Ecclesiastical Discipline*, the criticism of Bridges's tediousness openly reveals the reformers' resentment of implied scorn. 'To see him thus discourse vpon euerie seconde or thirde worde,' Travers complains, 'and to playe and sport him selfe, as if he were at great leysure, and had as little to doe as one that should playe with a feather: may shew howe easilie men of his coate, beare the burden of the Church.'[29] Particularly upset by the disregard for gravity he sees in Bridges's introduction of fables and his occasional attempts to jest, Travers accuses him of using a style suited only for the stage. Referring to Paul's admonition to the Ephesians, he dismisses this manner with the rebuke: 'I leaue his iestes and scoffes to him selfe to consider of, with remembrance that the Apostle sayeth, *These are thinges not seemelie*, and reckoneth this pleasaunt humour amongst a number of other things, whereof all professours of the Gospell, and much more the Preachers of it, shoulde bee ashamed.'[30]

Marprelate makes this preoccupation with manner central to his basic fiction of *decorum personæ*. When he first introduces Bridges in *The Epistle* the dean is referred to as 'a very patch and a dunce' who has written a 'most senseless book.' Later charges that the divine continually plays the fool in the pulpit further reconfirm the initial impression that he is hopelessly 'duncical and absurd.' But throughout the relentless pursuit of the fiction that Bridges's writing appears to reflect 'the brains of a woodcock, as having neither wit nor learning,' a single but explicit reference to the 'worshipful jester' seems to give still another meaning to his lack of wit and his absurdity. Marprelate shares Travers's displeasure with Bridges's levity and assumes that at least part of this witlessness is the intentional behaviour of a divine in motley. As he explains: 'I jested because I dealt against a worshipful jester, Dr. Bridges, whose writings and sermons tend to no other end than to make men laugh' (p 118). His own flauntingly advertised pretence of foolishness accordingly encompasses both interpretations of 'worshipful jester' with an undeniable decorum that ensures its impunity. As the self-proclaimed fool Marprelate has the freedom which liberates the 'common iester or buffoon' from ordinary rules of decency.[31] At the same time he can also claim a literal-minded propriety, since his licence to jest follows Bridges's example and his 'duncical' manner matches the apologist's stupidity. In demonstrating that others may also utilize wit, the satires give new meaning to Aristotle's dictum: 'character may almost be called the most effective means of persuasion.'[32] They also cleverly develop an unexpected answer to Bridges's question: 'why may not a fained fable applyed to truth, aunswere a feyned *perswasion*, grounded on falsehoode?'[33]

The pretence of *decorum personæ* is not, however, evenly sustained throughout the Marprelate tracts. When the unknown satirist entered the growing controversy, he had only Bridges's imposing work in mind. Thomas Cooper's official reply demanded its own answer; and during the period needed to prepare the critique the Marprelate press expediently issued a list of ironic schoolpoints in the broadside *The Mineralls*. The awaited *Hay any Worke for Cooper* returns in part to the tack developed in the first satires with the promise that a companion volume would further expose the bishops' untenable position. All copies of this satire, *More Worke for the Cooper*, were seized by the authorities before they could be distributed. The next publication, *Theses Martinianæ*, describes its 110 theses as 'an after-birth of the noble Gentleman Himself' published in an incomplete form by Martin Junior. Additional theses, along with a parody of Whitgift supplied by Martin Senior, follow in *The Just Censure and Reproofe*, and by the time Marprelate offers his last challenge in *The Protestatyon* much of the earlier imaginative satire is gone. Yet in spite of their extemporaneous nature and the possibility of multiple authorship, all seven satires retain a basic continuity in the tension between the extremes of manner. In transforming the conventions of animadversion into an imaginative attack unlike either traditional polemic or contemporary verse satire Marprelate uniquely justifies the premium Barrow's sermon places on character.

The initial attack in the complementary halves of *The Epistle* and *The Epitome* originates this criticism of manner through a complex ironic mimesis. Marprelate's first satire, largely an *ad hominem* assault on the Elizabethan bishops, draws upon a number of muckraking, scandalous, and often ridiculous exposés gathered some time earlier by John Field.[34] Although it primarily serves to occupy attention until the specific answer to Bridges's work undertaken in *The Epitome* is completed, *The Epistle* is an integral prelude to the Martinist strategy. Its opening charge disregards the political tactfulness of *The Learned Discourse* and asserts that all bishops are 'petty popes and petty antichrists.' Perhaps responding specifically to Bridges's rejoinder that the members of Convocation are not ignorant and that the bishops are above venality, Marprelate's epistle to 'my clergy masters of the Confocation-house' ignores the sanctions prohibiting personal ridicule with specific charges against individual members of the clergy. Its author assumes this prerogative at least partly because he shares the more radical Puritan belief in the sanctity of the individual rather than the office. Religion is for him valid on immediate, personal terms, and he will not limit himself to a general, abstract attack. By stripping away the veneer of respectability he denies to the offices of the established church inherent dignity and implies a widespread perversion of the ideal Christian manner. As an unexpected kind of epistle dedicatory or address to the Christian reader *The Epistle* also ironically suits the satirical appreciation of Bridges's defence. It suggests that the dean's defence of such a corrupt institution could appeal only to those devoid of Christian sensitivity, while his manner, which both parts of the satire mimic, must necessarily mirror its distorted nature. Even without its announced intention at the outset of each tract the title pages and appended list of ironic errata alert 'the learned reader' to the extended parody of disputation Marprelate develops to support his claim that others can also 'play the ignorant sots as well as you, Brother Bridges ... though, indeed, not so naturally, I grant' (p 171).

To capture this manner the satires develop several personae who purportedly epitomize Bridges's nature, although the ironic poses in *The Epistle* and *The Epitome* are neither consistently nor independently sustained. The voluble clown and the country simpleton most frequently characterize facets of the Marprelate manner. Like the professional fool who bounds about abruptly exclaiming at trivial incidents, the speaker often seems to alight literally on various aspects of the Anglican position and to express exuberantly his delight at his own antics. Bursting into gales of laughter or goading Bridges and the bishops with a whoop and a holler, he also plays the inflated buffoon overjoyed with his own wit and desirous of his onlookers' praise. When Marprelate detects what appears to be a patently false statement, he becomes 'a simple, ingram man' who in rustic dialect affects puzzlement and humble surprise. But he can also become an officious, pretentious upstart who tries to conceal his rusticity with an air of familiarity or with a formal speech filled with malapropisms. Under the guise of simplicity he recognizes the church ministers as familiar friends and treats them with apparent decorum, referring to dignitaries as Brother Canterbury, Mas Sarum, or Don John of London. Occasionally he lapses into suitable nicknames, greeting Thomas Cooper, the author appointed to uphold the establishment against the Martinists, as Tom Tub-Trimmèr or addressing the former apologist and now archbishop of Canterbury as Archbishop of Cant and His Grace of Cant. With a sly mispronunciation the various church divines become Doctors of Divility and Members of Conspiration.

In the later satires exclamations and affectations perfunctorily symbolize the Marprelate mode; in *The Epistle* and *The Epitome* they mime mannerisms found in Bridges's *A Defence*. As intentional parody they probably derive their inspiration partly from the dean of Sarum's tendency to begin sentences with 'A ha (brethren)' or 'Ha brethren.' Although this was a gesture of Christian kinship, the reformers resented being called 'our deare Brethren'; and they could not tolerate his apparent indulgence in frivolity. The divine, who in Travers's eyes behaved like a stage clown, becomes in Marprelate's imitation a self-dramatizing, irrepressible fool. Madcap, dramatic antics resembling those of the popular jester Richard Tarlton and rustic mimicry appropriate to the traditional country bumpkin of the Elizabethan stage cast the defender of Anglican polity into an ironically just role. The implications of this metamorphosis, particularly for an audience that found in Ephesians 5:4 a condemnation of professional jesters and actors, contribute to the success of the satires' mimetic criticism.

An audience schooled in rhetoric would further recognize that the foolish clowning and ignorant rusticity also violate commonly accepted rhetorical precepts. As Barrow's sermon indicates, both Aristotle and Cicero warn that jesting runs the risk of improper extremes; excessively employed it can 'become buffoonery or mere mimicking.'[35] Contemporary rhetoricians like Thomas Wilson might admit that methods chosen to 'make sport' have greater impact if 'the delight is vttered by countenaunce or by pointyng to some thyng,' but they generally heed Cicero's opinion that all 'unseemly language and offensive gestures' must be avoided.[36] Classical and contemporary books of rhetoric further recognize in their opposition to the buffoon that extremes of wit signify a boorishness commonly linked to the rustic. The standard contrast established in Cicero's discussion of urbanity has immediate parallel in the section on eloquence in *The Arte of Rhetorique*. Wilson warns his countrymen not to accept as 'a fine Englishmā, and a good Rhetorician,' anyone who exhibits a facile command of ostentatious diction, and he offers several illustrations of simple country folk who try to impress their betters with cultivated speech. Puttenham, who proscribes all patterns of speech found beyond a sixty-mile radius of London, agrees with Wilson's principle that rustic and 'affected Rhetorique' ignores the example of Tully's 'perfecte Oratour' who does not 'vse soche wordes, as fewe men doe vse, or vse them out of place, when an other might serue moche better.'[37] Marprelate's posture of the country upstart, as the antithesis of the ideal rhetorician, dramatizes Fenner's and Travers's complaints about wordmongering. The persona's embarrassing familiarity with his Anglican 'brethren' redefines their true status, and the frequent malapropisms and debasing allusions to their verbal chicanery insistently underscore the reality. The chief spokesman, also tacitly, becomes more than a simple fool; in joining his fellow churchmen as an 'illsample' of a rhetorician Bridges becomes one of those opponents of Renaissance humanism and education commonly known in the sixteenth century as followers of Duns Scotus, or dunces.

The Epitome promotes this association by introducing a persona in the pose of a frank, naive, and sympathetic critic. The speaker, who asks the reader to 'bear with my ingramness,' recalls the simple rustic of *The Epistle*; but his occasional lapses into rural dialect provide only a surface resemblance. Despite an earnest avowal, 'I am plain; I must needs call a spade a spade; a pope a pope,' his feigned ignorance thinly conceals a greater complexity. The mock bewilderment with which the 'poor gentleman' in the first paragraph wonders why so many search the country for a 'poor Martin' who is not lost is more playful and confident. Disregarding the 'Puritans and Precisians' as well as the Anglicans who he admits dislike his jesting, Marprelate toys confidently and obviously with the defenders of the established church. His pretence of emulating Bridges's incompetent criticism with an ironically ignorant appraisal of his own book[38] also reasserts the additional prerogative of *decorum personæ* to claim undeniable propriety. As the suitably dim-witted critic contends: 'The goodness and honesty of the matter he handled required such good and honest proofs as he brought. Let those that handle honest and godly causes labour to bring good proofs and a clear style. Presbyter John defended our church government, which is full of corruptions; and therefore the style and the proofs must be of the same nature that the cause is' (pp 124–5). Traditional criteria of evaluation are ignored in the auditor's effort to deal with Bridges's work on its own terms. His comments follow a basic pattern evident in the conclusion of his first appraisal: 'And therefore hath not the learned and prudent Master Dean dealt very valiantly (how wisely let John Cant. cast his cards and consider) in assaulting this fort of our precise brethren; which he hath so shaken with good vincible reasons, very notably out of reason, that it hath not one stone in the foundation more than it had' (p 123). The eager appreciation and the undercutting turn are one manifestation of the persona's irony; Marprelate also shows his intention through the commentator's ingenuous disclosures. By innocently offering his own damning accounts of why Bridges might have forced a point, or readily acknowledging Puritan arguments that could have proved damaging, Marprelate continues his indirect and purposely artless attack.

The transparent illusion of *decorum personæ* in *The Epitome* continues the manner characteristic of the other poses in the two-part satire. None of the masks assumes an identity separate from the author's, because Marprelate does not hesitate to shift his guise, blend several together, or step from behind his posture entirely to emphasize a point. His manipulation may be partly a necessary compromise with the pressures of hasty composition and the need for immediate impact, but the inconsistency of the personae also seems intentional. The ready, often flaunting juxtapositions of the personae not only contribute to the verve and jauntiness of the satires but also help sustain an unmistakable aura of deliberate dissembling. The imitations of Bridges, a divine who supposedly wrote much of his defence 'to playe and sport himselfe,' take the occasion to return a playful sport.

The satires' uniquely fictionalized contexts both facilitate and extend this irony. Through a semblance of summary and refutation common to written polemic, *The Epistle* and *The Epitome* transform the written page into a simulated debate in which Bridges and his allies apparently materialize to support their own cause. Marprelate never presupposes the presence of actual characters or designated settings, and the reproduction of passages from Bridges's work always suggests animadversion; nevertheless the Anglican defender reluctant to meet the reformers in open disputation suddenly appears as a participant in dramatic exchanges. By adapting the rhetorical technique of prevention, whereby an author commonly uses transitions such as 'but you will say' or 'I hear M. Doctor say' to anticipate rebuttal, the satires impart the illusion of real presence.[39] The alteration is often very simple:

For will my Brother Bridges say that the Pope may have a lawful superior authority over his Grace of Canterbury? I'll never believe him, though he say so. Neither will I say that his Grace is an infidel (nor yet swear that he is much better); and therefore Master Dean meaneth not that the Pope should be this High Priest.

No, Brother Martin, quoth Master Dean, you say true; I mean not that the Pope is this priest of Sir Peter. And I have many reasons why I should deny him this authority. (Pp 40–1).

The omission of the standard transition and the substitution of a direct reply simulate a confrontation in which Bridges seems for the moment actually present. Equally enlivened anticipations throughout the two-part satire together with the direct addresses and continual asides of the vibrant dramatic personae promote the fiction of actual encounter.

In transforming rigorous polemic into a dynamic medium which neither denies its affinity with the rhetoric of disputation nor conceals its dramatic fictions the satires manipulate Bridges effortlessly. In the midst of a discursive presentation of the dean's arguments Marprelate shifts media and dramatically interrupts: 'I was never so afraid in my life, that I should not come to an end till I had been windless. Do you not see how I pant?' (p 138). Or he simply presents a quotation from *A Defence* and adds in the margin: 'Wo, wo! Dean, take breath and then, to it again!' When he gets himself involved in a long digression which ignores the central issue, he stops and suggests: 'now alas, alas, Brother Bridges, I had forgotten you all this while. My brother London and I were so busy, that we scarce thought of you. Why could you not put me in mind that you stayed all the while?' (p 154). And in his most brazen moments Marprelate gives an obliging Bridges the opportunity to expose his own nature. Reacting partly to the dean's ability to weave the reformers' words into unexpected applications, the satires allow Bridges to make damaging disclosures. The point, as one of the marginalia observes, is apparent: 'Here is indecorum personæ in this speech, I know; for the Doctor should not give me this warning, but you know my purpose is to play the dunce after his example' (p 146). But the Anglican divine who confesses he dislikes syllogisms candidly reveals he is more than the ordinary fool: 'if the assumption or proposition be either more than I can prove, or be against myself, I will omit them. Pardon me, I pray you, my Masters, I will set down nothing against myself' (p 129). Against his expressed interest, yet with an inevitable predictability, he is by his very nature 'set down' as a hapless, inept, but sinister polemicist.

In *The Epistle* Marprelate enriches the dramatic immediacy with a larger cast of characters. Although the satire takes the form of a letter addressed to the members of Convocation, the speaker responds to the churchmen as if they were actually present. The invitation to draw closer at the climax of an attack, a pointed question directed to an individual, or a specific inquiry, 'Ha, ha, Doctor Copcot, are ye there,' seems more than an aside or a rhetorical question. In fact near the opening of the tract, as Marprelate concludes his initial argument indicting the Anglican bishops and their episcopal prelacy as petty popes and paltry antichrists, an audience actually appears: 'Therefore no lord bishop – "Now, I pray thee, good Martin, speak out, if ever thou didst speak out, that her Majesty and the Council may hear thee" – is to be tolerated in any Christian commonwealth' (p 23). The fervent intrusion heightens, of course, the conclusion; but the interruption is not in the persona's immediate character. A marginal comment, 'What malapert knaves are these that cannot be content to stand by and hear, but they must teach a gentleman how to speak,' suggests at least two distinct voices.

The auditors are at the same time Marprelate's *alter ego* and surrogates for the Anglican divines. Thus in the outburst which interrupts an argument espousing the equal authority of all priests an imaginary listener responds: 'Why, gentle Martin, is it possible that these words of the French *Confession* should be true? Is it possible that there ought to be an equality between his Grace and the Dean of Sarum, or some other hedge-priest?

Martin saith it ought to be so. Why then, Martin, if it should be so, how will the Bishops satisfy the reader on this point?' (p 27). The irony evident in this apparent confusion gains complexity with the re tort 'Alas, simple fellow, whatsoever thou art, I perceive thou dost not mark the words of the *Confession*.' Citing an exact quotation, the answer tacitly associates the bishops with the ignorant auditor for neither understands the obvious. The satire also utilizes a marginal objection to the speaker's sophistry to state outright, 'Why, sauceboxes, must you be prattling? You are as mannerly as bishops, in meddling with that [with which] you have nothing to do; as they do in taking upon them civil offices' (p 24). While Marprelate criticizes the bishops' manner, he employs the simple-minded questions of a commentator stationed in the margin or the inquiry of an imaginary auditor to enhance his argument. As he declares that bishops become antichrists when they abandon their callings, an onlooker interrupts in mock horror, 'Why Martin, what meanest thou? Certainly an thou takest that course but a while, thou wilt set thy good Brethren at their wits' end' (p 28).

Marginal comments and imaginary exchanges continue in *The Epitome*, where the roles of the participants are more precisely delineated. The voice in the marginalia is now unmistakably that of the speaker, who freely moves between the centre and the periphery of the attack. Often the satire feigns a neutral ground 'between my brethren bishops and my brethren the Puritans.' In the process of reviewing Bridges's book the dean and the Puritans face each other as they do over the question whether 'necessary to Salvation' means 'without which men cannot be saved.' ' "I mean even the same" saith Master Dean, "as it appeareth, page 60, ll. 21, 22 of my 'book.' " Then, we reply that nothing is of this necessity, but [except] only justifying faith, and we deny the sacraments to be of this necessity ... But, if you meant not this necessity, then we would know if you can tell yourself what you would have (forsooth, Brethren, a bishopric, he would have; and all such troublesome fellows as you are, banished the land). Ho, you mean such a necessity as every church is not bound to observe the same order upon this obedience' (pp 138–9). The persona also adds a marginal jibe to his parenthetical interruption, but Bridges and the Puritans appear to control a serious debate. By substituting the dean's summaries and paraphrases for actual quotations and by omitting the conditional phrases 'might say' or 'could argue' the satire creates a direct and immediate disputation which in actuality eluded the reformers.

The more straightforward animadversion of the fictionalized debates relieves the personae of involved polemic unsuited to their pretence of ignorance and allows them to pursue an interest in manner. Without upsetting the tracts' decorum Marprelate in his various guises presses Bridges and the bishops most seriously about their style. The satires' recourse to personal allegations, their development of the idea of blindness, and their incessant charges of solecism, ineloquence, and verbosity are based on the fundamental assumption that form and substance are inextricable. Because the bishops' position is substanceless, the personae allege, 'There be periods in this learned book of great reason, though altogether without sense' (pp 34–5). In Marprelate's interpretation any defence of the episcopal hierarchy must depend upon a sophistry bolstered by suspect language; 'truth,' he continually asserts, is 'the sole meaning that Master Doctor hath not at all thought of.' Without 'great reason,' though with their own sense, the satires insinuate their criticisms through dramatization, yet they never really meet the major tenets of Anglicanism. Marprelate advises further defenders of the established church to change their barbarously crude style by writing syllogistically and claims himself to be a master of the syllogism; he uses them, however, 'for recreation's sake.' In burying the bishops in an avalanche of absurd syllogisms, forcing a ridiculous analogical argument, or creating his own parody of a syllogistic mood, he maintains: 'I have set down nothing but the truth in the conclusion; and the syllogisms are mine own, I may do what I will with them, and thus hold you content' (p 25). The claim to truth, like the nature of the personae or the title of the second satire, retains a typical doubleness: as Marprelate concedes to Bridges, his 'syllogisms offended in form as yours doth; yet the common people ... will find an unhappy truth in many of these conclusions, when, as yours is, most false' (p 98).

Despite this conscious disregard for conventional methods of disputation neither *The Epistle* nor *The Epitome* disowns the idea of serious argument. Their principle of *decorum personæ* and the parody of Bridges's manner implicitly uphold an ideal which the reformers commonly argued would manifest 'the plaine and simple euidence of the trueth.' At the beginning of *The Epistle*, and as an essential complement to the basic fiction, Marprelate asks the members of Convocation 'to procure that the Puritans may one day have a free disputation with you about the controversies of the Church' (p 22). This request becomes part of the satires' contrapuntal movement. Although the major outlines of such a dispute are set down and the authority of the Bible is established, the *raison d'être* remains the desired exchange which must come about when the distortions and duplicity of superficial righteousness are dramatically exposed. Then the ideal, perceived in the first two satires mainly through its absence, can be realized.

The official response, issued in the January publication of *An Admonition to the People of England* by Thomas Cooper, the bishop of Winchester, and restated in Richard Bancroft's sermon on 9 February 1588/9, declined the request for public disputation; and within the month the Marprelate press printed another challenge. The broadside *Minerall and Metaphysicall Schoolpoints* is a brief and unimaginative satire consisting of thirty-seven propositions 'to be defended by the Reverend Bishops and the rest of my Clergymasters of the Convocation House,' yet the signs of the Marprelate manner are obvious even in this tract. The schoolpoints allegedly culled from the statements of Thomas Cooper and other prominent ministers supposedly represent the 'quintessence' of the established church, 'And withal, to the preventing of the cavils of these wrangling Puritans' (p 185). Wrenched from their context and distorted in their summary, the satiric schoolpoints nevertheless retain a characteristic ironic truth in the new, mocking inversion of a familiar argumentative form. Allowing for an ambiguity in the key word 'preventing,' the outlined defence contains several levels of irony. Marprelate would not seriously suggest that the bishops were able to prevent or to defeat the Puritans; but as his earlier satires show, the Anglican manner itself is sufficient to prevent or to anticipate the Puritan criticism. Either reading supports the basic desire for an open debate whose prospects are now differently assessed. At the conclusion of the list a final paragraph asks the reader if he knows any who would dispute the points,

that dare defend Christ Jesus and His prerogative, the truth of His word, the credit of St. Paul, the verity of the Apostles' Creed, her Majesty and her prerogative, and stand to the received truth in the Reformed Churches, and gainsay Popish errors; briefly, if thou know of any that dare defend the State of England, not to be so disordered, as before is set down (Article 29), and dare withstand the public general dishonour and slander of the whole English nation (Article 30), let him set up his name and we will send a pursuivant for him. Whosoever he be, the matters shall be according unto order quietly tried out between him and the bare walls in the Gatehouse or some other prison. (P 196).

The deflation captures the rhythm typical of the previous satires; in this conclusion, however, the tone is markedly different. The patterned syntax lends a hortative quality to a noticeably defensive posture, and a new bitterness emerges. His loyalty impugned and his hopes of public debate rejected, Marprelate begins to sound a more earnest note.

The alteration continues in *Hay any Worke for Cooper*, a reaction to Thomas Cooper's commissioned reply. Like the similarly addressed epistle in *The Epitome*, its introductory epistle to 'my Clergy Masters' begins with feigned amazement at the efforts made to locate Martin. But the playfulness of the persona is dominated now by a sharply ironic assertiveness. Outbursts from the threatening, self-congratulatory clown are still heard, and Marprelate does escape conventional seriousness with gestures such as 'Wo, wo! But where have I been all this while? Ten to one, among some of these Puritans. Why, Martin? Why, Martin, I say, hast thou forgotten thyself? Where hast'e been? Why man, 'cha' been a-seeking for a salmon's nest, and 'cha vownd a whole crew, either of ecclesiastical traitors, or of bishops of the devil' (p 257). These personae, however, appear more and more mechanical; and without the earlier tract's imaginary Puritan dialogues Marprelate is indeed caught among the Puritans directly espousing their arguments. Prolonged lapses into fervid seriousness reverberate with an Old Testament intensity: 'O cursed beasts, that bring this guilt upon our Estate! Repent, caitiffs, while you have time ... The living God whose cause is pleaded for will be revenged of you, if you give ear unto this slander' (p 241). Marprelate for the first time wagers his life that an open disputation will vindicate his cause.

The basis of this altered tone is an increasing sense of isolation. The growing opposition to his use of jest causes Martin some disappointment that none appreciates his expedient and reluctant introduction of laughter. Thomas Cooper's attack, of which only a quarter specifically deals with Marprelate, devotes much of its effort to refuting 'the slaunderous vntruethes, reprochfully *vttered by* Martin *the Libeller*.'[40] Cooper accuses Marprelate of base, improper detraction, and he fears the anonymous author 'will proue himselfe to bee, not onely *Mar-prelate*, but *Mar-prince*, *Mar-state*, *Mar-lawe*, *Mar-magistrate*, and all together, vntil he bring it to an Anabaptisticall equalitie and communitie.'[41] *Hay any Worke* denies this charge of disloyalty with repeated assertions that the word of God cannot be circumvented and that no monarch would wish to repudiate a polity which he realized had biblical sanction. Inverting the charge of treason, the satire passionately affirms a higher devotion to truth. In the name of love Marprelate proclaims: 'Shall I hear and see these things professed and published, and in the love I owe unto God's religion and her Majesty say nothing? I cannot; I will not; I may not be silent at this speech; come what will of it. The love of a Christian Church, Prince and State shall work more in me than the love of a heathen empire and state should do' (p 250).

The intensity of this commitment influences the satire's reliance on direct forms of attack. Accusing the bishops of hiring 'an unskilful and beceitful tubtrimmer' to barrel up their odious smells, Marprelate harshly ridicules the new defender Thomas Cooper. Never averse to scandal that might expose the bishops' hypocrisy, he shows no compunction about introducing slurs on Cooper's amorous wife. The merits of the bishop of Winchester are denigrated in a series of frequently applied epithets. Although at one point the satirist links Cooper and Bridges with the jester Tarlton, more commonly the satire hurls insults and tired jokes about their ears. The allegedly mad Cooper is repeatedly called an arrogant fool, a blockhead, block, or simply a 'sodden-headed ass.' With great contempt and less originality Marprelate snears: 'Because Dean Bridges durst not answer me, they have turned unto me, in his stead, a beast, whom by the length of his ears I guess to be his brother; that is, an ass of the same kind' (p 257).

The greater invective and longer periods of earnestness displace the principle of *decorum personæ* warranted by Cooper's relationship with Bridges. Marprelate unevenly makes good his boast that he has 'a good gift in imitation.' When he contends that Cooper's style is more verbose than Bridges's or promises by imitation to bring the bishop's statements 'into a marvellous good sense,' simple accusation and traditional refutation frequently replace the mimetic mode. A common dialogue form occasionally presents the illusion of Cooper's actual presence through direct address and imagined responses, but for the most part the cursory survey of the bishop's book departs less radically from traditional animadversion.

Earnestness does not, however, dispel jest. The more transparent speaker who reassures Cooper, 'Be not afraid, here be none but friends, man,' generates a vitality befitting the satire's greater urgency. Warning that his reasoning is crafty or congratulating himself on his syllogism's 'courteous' minor, Marprelate is capable of transcending the mounting pressures with self-possession and audaciousness. 'I will presently prove both major and minor of this syllogism. And, hold my cloak, there, somebody, that I may go roundly to work. For I'se so bumfeg the Cooper, as he had better to have hooped half the tubs in Winchester, then write against my Worship's 'pistles' (p 230). Jeering insolence modifies the boisterous clowning of the original personae and gives the jesting a brittle edge. Appraisal of Cooper's arguments and assessment of their alternatives also modulate the irony of the Marprelate manner towards a sarcasm that threatens to blunt much of the finer attack. But even as he claims 'I am not disposed to jest in this serious matter,' Marprelate reconfirms the value of laughter.

His greater disinclination to substitute jest for earnest becomes further apparent in *Theses Martinianæ*, a tract detailing 110 theses the Martinists are prepared to defend. All are serious propositions which the epilogue maintains have been either proved in *Hay any Worke* or will be evident in the forthcoming *More Worke for the Cooper*. Although their editor Martin Junior describes them as incomplete papers mysteriously dropped by a passer-by, this and the claims that his father has unaccountably disappeared and that a sea voyage has damaged the writings he left appear to be additional efforts to sidetrack the persistent searchers. Martin Junior's comments may in fact be an apology for a work beset with the increased difficulties of clandestine printing and the intensified searching of the authorities. In any case even with the brief lacuna in its preface *Theses Martinianæ* accomplishes its objective to uphold the Martinists' position until the more thorough answer to Cooper was completed.

The tract, as Martin Junior observes in his prologue, 'pretendeth the old man to be something discouraged in his courses.' Its opening words return to the criticism of Marprelate's satirical method and the growing disapproval from both the bishops' supporters and the Puritans. Admitting that now each side has become his adversary, Marprelate impatiently dismisses the Puritan critics as lukewarm believers and wearily concludes that the bishops may be incorrigible. Yet this disillusionment and despondency do not destroy the hope that motivates the tracts; paradoxically they intensify his desire for the cherished confrontation. The 110 theses he has gathered together detail an ecclesiastical corruption which the bishops 'in defence whereof, for their lives dare not they in any learned meeting or assembly dispute with me, or attempt to overthrow mine assertions by modest writings, handled anything scholar-like, that is, by good and sound syllogisms, which have both their *major* and *minor*, confirmed by the Word' (pp 304–5). The bishops, Marprelate passionately concludes, thrive on slander, lies, and vituperation; his own methods, he declares, are those of a man who 'could not do less' without betraying 'the truth of God, the laws of the land, and the doctrine of our Church.'

Through an ironic twist of events the fundamental contrast in manners was unexpectedly confirmed. After the great success of the first Marprelate satires Richard Bancroft licensed professional writers to supplement the ecclesiastical replies,[42] a decision which unwittingly played into Marprelate's hand by making the basic fiction of the satires a reality. The playwrights, rhymers, and pamphleteers who accepted the invitation to ridicule the Martinists obligingly proved the Marprelate thesis that the bishops' cause was best suited to jesters or the stage. As Martin Junior observes: 'they are marvellous fit upholders of Lambeth Palace, and the crown of Canterbury' (p 330). Mentioning by name only the more serious answerers

Leonard Wright and Richard Bancroft, the epilogue of *Theses Martinianæ* promotes the author of 'Mar-Martin' to the position occupied by Bridges and Cooper. Its mock biography of the doggerel poet offers the only obvious semblance of jest outside the convenient reversal that pre-empts the bishops' position by allowing the Martinists to advise: 'Suffer no more of these haggling and profane pamphlets to be published' (p 331).

The dramatic beginning of the next tract, 'Wo-ho then! And boys will now be a 'Pistle-making,' promises a return to the more familiar Marprelate manner which is never quite fulfilled. In *The Just Censure and Reproofe* Martin Senior tries to re-establish his patrimony with the reintroduction of marginal commentary and an imaginary context replete with direct addresses to his offspring Martin Junior. A long mock oration by Archbishop Whitgift to his pursuivants also captures the Marprelate genius for parodying an opponent's manner, although the author's wavering focus diffuses some of the satiric impact. Under the pretext of reproving Martin Junior for his unwise publication Martin Senior adds nine additional propositions he would defend, together with a rhyming retort to Mar-Martin and a formal accusation specifying prelatical corruption.

The Just Censure and Reproofe does not develop new directions; it reinforces the Marprelate position by drawing into more acute opposition the fundamental conflict of the Marprelate satires. In an attempt to unite all the Puritans in a common cause Martin Senior presents a petition for reform which he says a hundred thousand citizens will readily sign. Its four points succinctly restate the essence of *The Learned Discourse* and again demand a redress of the abuses and 'great ignorance' in the church through 'the quiet and orderly taking up of these controversies.' Martin Senior is certain that open disputation would manifest the truth; 'it would descrie our Bishops' English to be plain slander and treachery against the truth and the maintainers thereof, as indeed it is' (p 372). Bishops' English, or the distortion of language into unnatural and unintended meaning, aptly describes the literalistic play on words attacked in *The Epistle*, the ecclesiastical manipulation of double meanings exposed in *The Epitome*, and the bald-faced lie described as the 'Canterbury trick' in *Hay any Worke*. Incessantly the Marprelate tracts assert that a hierarchy built upon falseness must manipulate language to maintain an illusion of propriety; truth, on the other hand, need rely only on a language that 'simply and plainly' expounds the Word.

The final publication, *The Protestatyon of Martin Marprelate*, climaxes this fundamental belief. The discouragement Martin Junior noticed in his father gives way to a renewed resolve that 'feareth neither Proud Priest,

Antichristian Pope, Tyrannous Prelate, nor Godless Catercap; but defieth all' (p 393). Though he admits that the recent seizure of the printers and press has been a calamitous blow, Marprelate refuses to concede that the bishops will triumph. The tract tenaciously clings to the faith that only the Bible has the authority to determine victory or defeat, and this judgment can only be established in open disputation. Once again Martin offers his challenge: 'I, who do now go under the name of *Martin Marprelate*, do offer personally to appear, and there to make myself known in open disputation, upon the danger, not only of my liberty, but also of my life; to maintain, against all our bishops, or any else whosoever that shall dare in any scholastical manner to take their parts, the cause of the Church government' (p 401). But even as he makes his last effort to realize his ideal, he recognizes that the bishops dare not submit to any exchange other than one they can prosecute 'with slanders, ribaldry, scurrility, reviling, imprisonment and torture' (p 404).

A subsequent denunciation of the bishops in both their private lives and public offices completes Marprelate's essential criticism of their manner. The attempt in the last pages to summarize the satiric content of the ill-fated *More Worke for the Cooper* and the fleeting reintroduction of the rustic persona are intrusions from the past that seem out of place. The awkward reconstruction of the seized tract is tedious and anticlimactic, while its second-hand satire and token persona detract from the serious, personal tenor of *The Protestatyon*. In their evolution the satires have reached a point where sustaining the former attack against the bishops is neither possible nor necessary. The increasing dangers in operating a secret press together with the ever-growing numbers of anti-Martinist answers and the gradual shift towards earnest, direct confrontation render the jesting dramatic fictions inappropriate. In any case, the satires have sufficiently dramatized the need to confute the bishops; any further satire of their manner would be redundant.

Marprelate has achieved his ideal manner. His defiant demand for an ultimate confrontation assumes throughout the satires that a corrupt hierarchy cannot withstand the scrutiny of the reformers' truth; he now openly declares that their spirit ensures victory. 'We are sure to possess our souls in everlasting peace, whensoever we leave this earthly tabernacle; and in the mean time we know that an hair of our head cannot fall to the ground without the will of our heavenly Father' (p 398). His confidence in the hand of God rather than his certainty about the meaning of the contested biblical passages accounts for the belief that open disputation would vindicate the Puritan position. While the bishops may claim for themselves the external vestiges of authority, Marprelate shares the assurance of *The Learned Discourse* that an understanding of true polity is not dependent upon 'outward respectes but ... the reuelation of Gods spirit.'[43] The satires maintain that the bishops' distortion of the Word and disregard for the spirit force them inevitably to rely upon effusions of words and trappings of office. Marprelate's manner, like his lucid prose, repudiates verbiage and superficiality and embraces eloquence. His vision of style embodies Augustine's belief that 'The man whose life is in harmony with his teaching will teach with greater effect.'[44] The teacher who possesses this eloquence is not restrained by conventional propriety; he may, 'to secure compliance, speak not only quietly and temperately, but even vehemently, without any breach of modesty, because his life protects him against contempt.'[45] Marprelate agrees with the reformers that in open disputation 'any scholastical manner' will manifest the truth and spirit of the Word; but when the circumstances demand a departure from the norm, the 'manner' should also decorously sanction less traditional means. As he protests in his final defence of the satires, his methods transcend ordinary criticism, 'inasmuch as the end, wherefore I have taken this work in hand, was only the glory of God; by delivering of His Church from the great tyranny and bondage wherewith these tyrants do oppress the same. I dealt not herein, as the Lord knoweth, because I would please myself, or my reader, in a pleasant vein of writing. If that be the thing I sought, or seek, after, then let my writings be buried in the grave of all proud prelates; that is, never mentioned in the Church of God without detestation' (pp 406–7).

Cautious critics of the Anglican polity could not accept this vision of decorum. Josias Nichols's 1602 publication, *The Plea of the Innocent*, typifies the feelings of many who feared that the 'foolish iester' and his abusive attacks discredited the Puritan movement.[46] Among its most prominent leaders Thomas Cartwright in particular felt the need even some years after the publications ceased to apologize: 'I am able to produce witnesses, that the first time that euer I heard of *Martin Marprelate*, I testified my great misliking & grief, for so naughtie, and so disorderly a cause as that was.'[47] But as Matthew Sutcliffe quickly objected, Cartwright's apology did not repudiate the persistent report that he once said: *'seeing the Bishops would take no warning: it is no matter that they are thus handled.'*[48] The existence of these contradictory statements, whether Cartwright made them both or not, indicates a very real tension among the Puritans. Marprelate derisively complains in *Theses Martinianæ* that their quandary is one of reconciling matter and form. Like the eminent divine John Rainolds, who cannot defend Marprelate though 'if by the way, he utter a truth, mingled with whatsoeuer else, it is not reason that that, which is of God, should be cōdemned for that which is of man,'[49] Marprelate's contemporaries expressed their reservations by separating matter and manner. Ironically the satires themselves anticipate this separation in the literal-minded propriety of *decorum personæ* and in their expressed reluctance to jest: their author, however, is too sensitive not to realize that his unique arguments from circumstances take liberties with conventional assumptions. When he confronts this larger issue of decorum directly in the last tract, his higher Christian 'manner' is too radical for a Puritan movement not yet committed to the revolutionary course of the next century.

Supporters of the accused prelacy, of course, reacted much more negatively in their denunciations of the indecorous satires. Both the religious and the professional writers who came to the bishops' defence united in a general criticism of Marprelate's insensitivity to the inviolable boundary between allowable jest and earnest. Richard Harvey prefaces some of the most considered objections to the 'new Barbarisme' with the reminder that civility demands its forms and rules. 'Graue matters would be debated grauely; and who in learning or reason, can deny *Martin* to be a ridiculous mad fellowe, that handleth so serious matters and persons so ridiculously?'[50] Marprelate's decision to attire religion in motley particularly irritated sensibilities accustomed to ceremonial reverence, and writers as diverse as John Lyly and Matthew Sutcliffe criticized his crudeness. 'Forgetting the matter hee hath in hand,' they protest, 'hee holoweth, shouteth, and whoopeth like a man of Bedlem, and crieth, so, ho, ho. forgetting himselfe, he falleth in scorning, with termes vnwoorthie to be spoken, or written.'[51] They overlook the satires' charge that Bridges had originally initiated the jesting behaviour and they find no precedent for Martin's extremism except among the discredited writings of Lucian, Rabelais, and Beza. When ecclesiastical officials approved a counter-attack similarly reliant on jest, some authors like Harvey extend their disapproval to these jesters as well.[52] Other ministers and professional writers excuse their responses with the argument, 'if these fellowes take to themselues libertie to *degorge* their filthy stomackes against the Church; I trust none will be offended with them, that haue written in defence of the Church and state.'[53]

The displeasure with Marprelate's indecorous method, and even the paradoxical acceptance of its use against him, reflects a sensitivity to the importance of Christian charity. Bishop Cooper's official reply to the 'vntemperate, vncharitable and vnchristian' satires first criticizes the transgression of this virtue, and the writers who follow continue in their own way to ask: 'Is this the honest nature, charitable disposition, and curteous behauiour, beseeming a ciuill religious Gentleman?'[54] Deriding the arrogance of Marprelate's behaviour, they counsel that humility, meekness, and love are fundamental to Christian respect. The discretion these virtues foster might sanction gentle admonishment, though the truly fervent 'woulde rather sigh in their hearts and groane in their consciences, and pray vnto God in the spirit of mildenes, to take away such blemishes from the face of his Church.'[55] The ideal of charity, however, might do no more than cover a multitude of faults. As *Hay any Worke for Cooper* sarcastically demonstrates in a parody of mild exhortation, reform would be slow in coming. Discrepancy between ideal behaviour and urgent necessity also forces some proponents of the establishment, and of charity, to agree with Richard Bancroft that against malefactors consumed in their own self-love and intent upon harm it is 'very fit they be rapt on the shinnes.'[56]

The labels of backbiter, libeller, and slanderer which accompanied the demands for charitable Christian civility indicate a wide apprehension of the satires' willingness to ridicule the clergy. Although it is suggested that Marprelate laughs at the ministers because he cannot refute their doctrines, the citing of long lists of biblical and patristic authorities who condemned reproachful attitudes towards the clergy reveals a more basic abhorrence of disrespect.[57] Marprelate is warned that any criticism of divinely annointed men inevitably entails blasphemy, for as the gospel of Luke teaches, 'if any one despiseth his preachers and messengers, he despiseth him, and ... he which despiseth him despiseth the father which sent him.'[58] The anti-Martinists further insist that improper reverence for ministerial authority threatens the sanctity of the church and the security of the realm. Within the Anglicans' carefully ordered and divinely authorized polity the office cannot be separated from the man nor a part isolated from the whole. Ridicule directed against an individual clergyman reflects on the doctrine of the entire church, and questioning ecclesiastical authority endangers the monarchy that provides temporal authority.[59] Even when the possibility of faults among the clergy is considered, replies to the Marprelate tracts refuse to allow a private individual the right to criticize the clergy openly or to intrude freely into public affairs. In their reverence for authority and in their fear of disorder they urgently conclude: 'christian charitie will hide the blemishes and faultes of their brethren, and specially of the preachers of the gospell sincerely teaching Gods trueth.'[60]

Because Marprelate cannot concede that the established clergy inherently merit respect, a different idea of love governs his conception of decorum. In the course of ridiculing the ecclesiastical dignitaries with the accounts of *The Epistle*, he assures the members of Convocation, 'I make not your doings known for any malice that I bear unto you, but [for] the hurt that you do unto God's church' (p 79). Playfully suggesting that the facts he presents and their publication under his own name prevent any charge of libel, he more earnestly argues that his disclosures relate only 'What you have not blushed to commit in the face of the sun, and in the justifying whereof you yet stand ... to the dishonour of God, and the ruin of His Church' (p 81). Rather than charitably overlook these public miscarriages of office, he, with his love for truth, is compelled to expose those who subvert a ministry which he claims has no biblical authority. The satires' relentless stripping away of illusion pursues an ideal that Marprelate believes all would see if only they had the opportunity to view it. A conspiracy of silence, like the metaphoric blindness in the satires and like the bishop's coopering of the stench, condones a greater evil. The active love that *Hay any Worke* poses against Cooper's charitable passivity advocates an ultimate good which Marprelate assumes justifies any violation of conventional decency.

This unyielding commitment to an ideal, which Marprelate refers to as love and his critics attack as presumptuous malignity, is characterized in one contemporary manuscript as zeal. In a work unpublished until 1641[61] Francis Bacon groups Marprelate and his more extreme adversaries together and opposes their zeal with a 'character of love' that disavows religious satire or jest and allows only 'reverent and religious compassion towards evils, or indignation towards faults.'[62] The love envisioned in *An Advertisement touching the Controversies of the Church of England* demands a compassionate understanding and a moderate compromise from those on each side of the divided issue. In Bacon's assessment of the controversy crucial questions of dogma and liturgy are not in dispute; 'we contend about ceremonies and things indifferent; about the extern policy and government of the church.'[63] Fearing that modest differences may be amplified into violent faction, he offers a delicately balanced solution with concessions designed to soothe intemperate passions. For Bacon the present church is an established fact, and the lives of its bishops should be above human judgment. By compassionately and moderately exercising their powers they in turn should avoid the abuses of a rigid authority bound to the letter of the law or custom; indeed Bacon believes much present dissatisfaction would be removed if the bishops were inspired 'with a fervent love and care of the people; and that they may not so much urge things in controversy, as things out of controversy, which all men confess to be gracious and good.'[64] The discontented critics, to whom legitimate grievances are conceded, should likewise realize that their temptation to claim 'light and perfection' also fosters rigidity and intolerance. With a precise formulation of the disagreements and an honest recognition of their own shortcomings both sides might peacefully resolve their differences; for then, Bacon concludes, knowledge and love would dispel implacable zeal.

The compromise Bacon proposes can be pursued only through private conferences; he has no sympathy for the zealous methods of either Marprelate or his imitators. While he recognizes that people will uphold their firmest beliefs with passionate conviction, he cannot accept the debasement of religion implicit in the stage antics and jesting of the present controversy. 'To search and rip up wounds with a laughing countenance; to intermix Scripture and scurrility sometime in one sentence; is a thing far from the devout reverence of a Christian, and scant beseeming the honest regard of a sober man. *Non est major confusio, quam serii et joci; there is no greater confusion, than the confounding of jest and earnest.* The majesty of religion, and the contempt and deformity of things ridiculous, are things as distant as things may be.'[65] Emphasizing the first quotation from Proverbs, Bacon approves Thomas Cooper's decision not to answer a fool in like manner; he also agrees with him that attacks on individuals have no place in substantive discussions of significant matters. In his total repudiation of the Marprelate manner Bacon further questions the usefulness as well as the propriety of laughter. The wisdom of Job in matters of grave and important judgments, he interprets, 'saith, *If I did smile, they believed it not*: as if he should have said, If I diverted, or glanced unto conceit of mirth, yet men's minds were so possessed with a reverence of the action in hand, as they could not receive it.'[66] The urgency of the circumstances and the ramifications temporally and eternally require reverence, not ridicule. When the instinct to laugh defies this more noble obligation, it must not seek public expression.

Confronted with even stronger disapproval and threatened by a new decree designed to suppress his publications, Marprelate found little support for his unique mixture of jest and earnest. The stereotype of the scurrilous rebel, which became a reality for many in the next century, and the image of the blasphemous jester, still current into the nineteenth century, obscured the serious nature of the satires. Marprelate openly acknowledges his expedient motives, yet the tracts nevertheless integrate laughter into a consistent vision of manners with far-reaching importance. Compared to the tiresome, quibbling ingenuity of the pasquils or 'playne Pierses' written in response, and unlike its own brittle ridicule of 'Mar-Martin' at the end of *The Just Censure and Reproofe*, Marprelate's characteristic wit vitalizes his serious purpose. Certainly the magnitude of his accomplishment increases with awareness of the difficulties and dangers faced by those involved in the Martinist venture, but the literary achievement remains in any case unmistakable. The poignant moments of self-doubt in *Theses Martinianæ* or *The Protestatyon* and the passionate outbursts in *Hay any Worke* are those of an intensely committed author who manages through imaginative satiric jest to give literary and philosophical shape to a range of emotional responses. The wide popularity of the Marprelate tracts suggests that many Elizabethans did appreciate the satires even though they were not disposed to approve of them. Francis Walsingham, in a letter probably written by Francis Bacon, explains the only reaction he thought could be taken:

When they descended into that vile and base means of defacing the government of the church by ridiculous pasquils; when they began to make many subjects in doubt to take an oath, which is one of the fundamental parts of justice in this land and in all places; when they began both to vaunt of the strength and number of their partisans and followers, and to use comminations that their cause would prevail though with uproar and violence; then it appeared to be no more zeal, no more conscience, but mere faction and division; and therefore, though the state were compelled to hold somewhat a harder hand to restrain them than before, yet it was with as great moderation as the peace of the church and state could permit.[67]

Fifty years later, when turbulent civil war favoured a renewed interest in the literature of jest and earnest, the pseudonym of Marprelate would again appear.[68] While his manner would not be duplicated, the power of laughter he had demonstrated and the vision of zeal he had begun to formulate would be realized by other writers.

Marprelate offered a memorable illustration of the potential for religious satire. His unique interpretation of *decorum personæ* and his uncompromising insistence upon true charity promoted a new satiric mode based essentially upon character. In the earlier tracts the mimicry of Bridges and the Anglican prelacy seems to determine this focus, but throughout the satires Marprelate recognizes the central importance of his specific ethos. Although his cause may be partisan, he appeals in the later tracts to all who share his fundamental love for truth. This commitment, above all else, justifies expediency. When developed by embattled seventeenth-century pamphleteers, zealous charity receives still further emphasis. Then the most significant of these writers, John Milton, responds to Bacon's criticisms of religious jest and defends the propriety of zeal. In doing so he builds upon the precedent of the last Marprelate tracts to justify manner in terms of the religious satirist himself.

4

John Milton *contra* Hall

REVIEWING THE CAUSES that prevented the establishment of true Christian discipline in Elizabeth's reign, John Milton notes in *Of Reformation* the 'greennesse of the Times.' Cautious counsellors and moderate prelates, he contends, were unprepared or unable to extirpate completely the popish errors reintroduced by Mary. Worldly clergy eager to thrive in privileged positions promoted the fear that attacks upon their prelacy would infringe upon the royal prerogative, and repression in the name of order frustrated religious reform. 'From that time follow'd nothing but Imprisonments, troubles, disgraces on all those that found fault with the *Decrees* of the Convocation, and strait were they branded with the Name of *Puritans*.'[1] The succeeding decades of Stuart rule had not outwardly altered the Anglican polity, but to Milton in 1641 the course of history promised 'after many a tedious age, the long-deferr'd, but much more wonderfull and happy reformation of the *Church* in these latter dayes' (1, 519). The Long Parliament assembled after Charles's disastrous Bishops' Wars had already condemned Strafford to the block and imprisoned Laud in the Tower; pending before the Commons was the Root and Branch Petition of fifteen thousand Londoners demanding the destruction of the episcopal polity. Reflecting some years later on the monumental reform debated by parliament during this period, Milton writes that he was irresistibly drawn to follow the 'true path' to human liberty. 'Since, moreover, I had so practiced myself from youth that I was above all things unable to disregard the laws of God and man, and since I had asked myself whether I should be of any future use if I now failed my country (or rather the church and so many of my brothers who were exposing themselves to danger for the sake of the Gospel) I decided, although at that time occupied with certain other matters, to devote to this conflict all my talents and all my active powers.'[2] His vision of Christian truth and duty prompted Milton to publish within the next year five antiprelatical tracts. A 'grim laughter' characteristic of his most satiric vein augments the earnestness with which Milton first anonymously and then openly committed his talents to the vindication of the new epoch.

While all of the tracts resort to satiric laughter, the two that are part of the Smectymnuan controversy most consciously and thoroughly develop attacks dependent on ridicule. *Animadversions upon the Remonstrants Defence against Smectymnuus*, the first of the pamphlets to associate Milton with the five Puritans pseudonymously entitled Smectymnuus, appeared soon after his initial prose publications *Of Reformation* and *Of Prelatical Episcopacy*. The refutation of arguments based on antiquity, self-interest, and political necessity in *Of Reformation* and the ostensibly reasonable criticism of specific Anglican defenders in *Of Prelatical Episcopacy* give way in this third tract to an often abusive animadversion on Joseph Hall's *A Defence of the Humble Remonstrance* (April 1641). Bishop Hall, whose support of episcopal government and liturgy in *An Humble Remonstrance to the High Covrt of Parliament* prompted the Smectymnuan *An Answer* (March 1641), had perhaps set the tone with his forceful counter-attack. By the end of July, probably after the Puritan divines replied with *A Vindication* and before Hall continued in *Short Answer*, John Milton came to the support of the Smectymnuan tract which his former tutor Thomas Young played a prominent part in writing and whose postscript he himself probably contributed.[3] Now more deeply and personally involved in the growing controversy, he signed his name for the first time to the more dispassionate statement of his position, *The Reason of Church-Government*. Several months later *An Apology against a Pamphlet Call'd A Modest Confutation* (April 1642) completed his antiprelatical satires with vigorous attack on the unknown author who had impugned both the personality and the manner displayed in his animadversion on Hall. Although the five tracts vary considerably in form, the result is an impressive body of prose. Milton's style, 'hardly prose and not quite English,' and his personal impersonality[4] distinguish the tracts from the growing number of pamphlets produced throughout the turbulent 1640s; yet their technique and their vision are unmistakably indebted to contemporary attitudes. The two Smectymnuan tracts particularly reveal Milton's ability to invigorate the conventional. In a recognized form of disputation his satiric laughter transcends the forces that shape its expression.

Milton describes the nature of this laughter in the paragraph prefacing *Animadversions*. Addressing himself to the 'softer spirited Christian' who possesses a 'tender and mild' conscience, he apologizes for the manner forced upon him by circumstances. At the conclusion Milton assures his audience,

although in the serious uncasing of a grand imposture (for to deale plainly with you Readers, Prelatry is no better) there be mixt here and there such a grim laughter, as may appeare at the same time in an austere visage, it cannot be taxt of levity or insolence: for even this veine of laughing (as I could produce out of grave Authors) hath oft-times a strong and sinewy force in teaching and confuting; nor can there be a more proper object of indignation and scorne together then a false Prophet taken in the greatest dearest and most dangerous cheat, the cheat of soules: in the disclosing whereof if it be harmfull to be angry, and withall to cast a lowring smile, when the properest object calls for both, it will be long enough ere any be able to say why those two most rationall faculties of humane intellect anger and laughter were first seated in the brest of man.   (I, 663–4)

Like the rest of this remarkably rich and complex paragraph the images and themes in this sentence realize their fullest dimensions in the major movements of the satire; immediately striking, however, is Milton's attitude towards laughter. The relationship between laughter and truth is the same as that expressed in the Marprelate tracts, though now the stress is on 'teaching and confuting.' The sentence links laughter with austerity and anger rather than with levity and insolence; its epithets yoke grimness and lowering with laughter and smiles. But the most provocative juxtaposition occurs in Milton's statement that laughter and anger are the 'two most rationall faculties of humane intellect.' Renaissance treatises on psychology often state that laughter and anger both may stem from indignation or scorn, and some writers trace a common origin to the spleen; however they do not describe them as 'rationall faculties.' Within the various systems of faculty psychology both are passions more appropriately related to the motions of the sensitive soul, and in general usage the opposition between reason and anger or reason and laughter is well established.[5] Milton's deliberate association of laughter and anger with reason may be based on Aristotle's notion that only man can laugh and that anger may be both voluntary and involuntary; in any case he gives laughter and anger exalted status. Reason it would seem expresses itself most forcefully and spontaneously through its most 'rationall faculties,' laughter and anger; conversely, according 'grim laughter' a 'strong and sinewy force in teaching and confuting' also implies that laughter and anger most powerfully influence reason. Either way, the context and language of the sentence place this form of laughter most favourably in an alliance with reason and the human intellect.

Milton's elevation of laughter derives its impetus partly from the commitment pressed upon him. Although different attitudes towards jest cannot be rigidly ascribed to either Anglican or Puritan positions, the prefatory comments in *Animadversions* resemble those of a zealous reformer. John Bastwick, for example, answers *'exceptions made against his Letany'* with the parallel proposition that 'there is no iust cause why any should blame mee for mingling *ioca serijs et seria iocis.'*[6] Bastwick claims that precedent for the use of 'pleasant and merry' laughter can be found in 'all the famous writers of all ages,' yet like Marprelate and Milton he is reluctant to cite authorities. A quotation of Elijah's retort against the worshippers of Baal and an allusion to *The Beehive*, also referred to by Penry, constitute Bastwick's only evidence. More concerned with laughter's effectiveness, the imprisoned doctor candidly admits: 'for these *three score yeares* and vpward there haue been *thousands*, that haue writ with all maner of grauity and humble lowliness calling for reformation, and yet nothing hath been listned vnto, but for their paines they haue beene Seuerly punished, and miserably vndone by the *Prelats.'*[7] Sensitive to the public Bastwick bases much of his apology upon pragmatic arguments stressing rhetorical usefulness. Some attempt is made to justify laughter through a passing reference to a principle of stylistic diversity, and a quibbling manipulation of words tries in the manner of Marprelate to shift the responsibility for humour onto Anglicans who 'make playes of honest men' in their own sermons; these efforts, however, are secondary to a fundamental desire to reach the widest audience and to expose the greatest corruption. The refrain that runs throughout the *Letany*, 'from plague pestilence and famine, from Bishops Priests and Deacons good Lord deliuer vs,' is the zealous writer's foremost concern; and the need to defend ridicule under these circumstances seems from Bastwick's treatment, more obviously than in the Marprelate tracts, a constraint met on the whole somewhat mechanically. Despite a similar urgency to deliver the English nation from the bondage of prelacy, Milton displays a much greater sensitivity to the implications of religious ridicule. When an anonymous confutant questions the brief apology for laughter advanced in *Animadversions*, the last of the antiprelatical tracts confronts the objections with a vigorous, thoughtful defence of 'grim laughter.'

In answer to the accusation that he offers no authority for his 'scurrilous jests,' Milton supplies his own version of acceptable precedent. The confutant, who begins his criticism with a witty fabrication of his unknown adversary's personality, provokes Milton's defence with his perfunctory dismissal of all religious laughter. Challenging the suggestion that Solomon countenances the manner of *Animadversions* and refusing to hear any argument Milton can produce from his serious authors, the anonymous writer instead quotes from a newly published essay by Francis Bacon. He reproduces from Bacon's comments on the Marprelate controversy the warning that 'to turn Religion into a Comedy or Satyr, to rip up wounds with a laughing countenance, to intermixe Scripture and scurrility sometimes in one sentence, is a thing far from the devout reverence of a Christian, and scant beseeming the honest regard of a sober man.'[8] Against the pre-eminence of Bacon, and in support of his earlier assertions, Milton sets the authority of the Book of Proverbs. Conveniently overlooking the preceding verse, he argues that laughter provides a means to answer '*A Foole according to his folly.*' Besides forcing a foolish person to acknowledge his folly, the scorn inherent in laughter teaches others to avoid the same behaviour. This didacticism motivated the prophet Elijah's mockery; and this derision marked the martyrs' response to their persecutors. It also characterizes Milton's retort: 'Now may the confutant advise againe with Sir *Francis Bacon* whether *Eliah* and the Martyrs did well to turne religion into a Comedy, or Satir; *to rip up the wounds* of Idolatry and Supersitition *with a laughing countenance*' (1, 903). Adding a secular authority on 'wit and morality' to the 'pious gravity,' the paragraph counters Bacon's quotation with Horace's famous statements, '*– laughing to teach the truth | What hinders?*' and '*– Jesting decides great things | Stronglier, and better oft then earnest can*' (1, 904). Cicero and Seneca, he adds, may also be cited; but Milton refrains from adding further reference.[9]

The reluctance to offer more than the conventional authority summoned against Bacon is consistent with Milton's conception of 'grim laughter.' The antiprelatical tracts maintain that any authority offers only another easily distorted opinion whose value must be assessed in terms of each new context. Citing sanctioned precedent only begs the central question of religious ridicule. Horace, Cicero, and Seneca, among others, can bear witness to laughter's value, yet Milton recognizes that the 'bounds, and objects of laughter' finally determine the relevance of any generality. He dismisses Francis Bacon and accepts writers who do not countenance laughter's indiscriminate use, because Milton believes religion is not the 'object' of laughter. *An Apology* significantly alters Bacon's quotation by adding '*to rip up the wounds* of Idolatry and Superstition *with a laughing countenance.*' Later Milton unfairly accuses Bacon of libel and wrenches his example of Job to suggest that the biblical figure favoured laughter;[10] the present interpolation, however, is neither specious nor concealed. The confutant is reminded in the next paragraph that religion can never be wounded by disgraceful treatment of the prelates 'since religion and they surely were never in such amity.' Balancing the defence's opening lines from Proverbs with a not dissimilar verse from Sophocles' *Electra*, Milton neatly shifts responsibility: '*Tis you that say it, not I, you do the deeds, / And your ungodly deeds finde me the words*' (1, 905). The verbal 'stripes' Milton administers to the prelates to cure the religion they have harmed are in keeping with the accepted image of 'satyr' as a beneficial scourge, and decorously observe the classical authorities who regularly prescribe laughter as a means of exposing base error.

Milton has no doubt that he is correct. The 'guiding *Genius*' of the classical philosophers and the 'reason' of the stoics have their counterpart for Christians in 'an inward witnesse, and warrant of what they have to do, as that they should need to measure themselves by other mens measures how to give scope, or limit to their proper actions' (1, 904–5). *Reason of Church-Government* more specifically defines the only guides in the controversy against the prelates to be conscience and 'preventive fear.' The recognition and fulfilment of truth, the duty of one's covenant with God, demand in Milton's view continual self-scrutiny. All of the tracts, particularly the last two, emphasize that self-respect is merited only when the individual knows he is worthy of redemption. Distinctions of time, person, and place then yield to the manifestations of the ultimate authority: 'lest any one should be inquisitive wherefore this or that man is forwarder then others, let him know that this office goes not by age, or youth, but to whomsoever God shall give apparently the will, the Spirit, and the utterance' (1, 875). The tracts, in short, assume the standard of decorum outlined in Richard Greenham's contempoary discussion of 'the gouernment of the tongue': 'if we do it in a single heart, and euen because we loue Gods word, and in zeale of Gods glorie: we may boldly speake, committing the success which on vs (if we obserued all circumstances) did not depend, to the omnipotencie of God, to the blessing of Christ, and to the working of the holy spirit; for we being neither God, nor Christ, nor Angels, must not thinke to preuaile of our selues, by our speeches.'[11]

Milton implies this sense of decorum when he cites the precedent of Elijah to counter objections to his 'grim laughter.'[12] Throughout the seventeenth century Elijah's reproof of the Baalites in 1 Kings 18 remains the most documented illustration of divinely sanctioned ridicule and an important exemplification of zeal. Men reluctant to criticize the extremeness of someone like Henry Barrow because they 'know not

what particular motion of the Spirit guided him so to write' cite the
parallel of Elijah's unrestraint,[13] and they use his example to distinguish
between the gentleness and meekness desired in civil behaviour and the
religious manner which 'in the cause of Christ, in the cause of religion ...
must be fiery and fervent.'[14] In a previously published commentary on the
confrontation between the Old Testament prophet and the priests of Baal
Bishop Hall himself points out: 'Graue and austere *Elijah* holds it not too
light to flout their zealous deuotion; he laughes at their teares and playes
vpon their earnest ... Scornes and taunts are the best answers for serious
Idolatry; Holiness will beare vs out in disdainfull scoffes, and bitternesse
against will [sic] superstition.'[15] The prophet chosen by God to reform
Israel's declining religion exemplifies, for other Anglicans, 'the dutie of a
faithful Minister of God' and the zealous manner necessary when the
faithful are beguiled 'away from the living God to dumb and dead Idols.'[16]
Puritan writers share much the same understanding of Elijah's 'iron-like'
disposition, though they, of course, define contemporary idolatry differently when they cite the 'spirit of Elias' to contend that 'True zeale drives
on the work of Reformation so as it leaves not the least remnants of *Baal*.'[17]

Milton's memorable image of zeal captures this spirit. 'Times of opposition' and the 'proud resistance of carnall, and false Doctors' warrant, he
argues in *An Apology*, a passionate manner. 'Then Zeale whose substance is
ethereal, arming in compleat diamond ascends his fiery Chariot drawn
with two blazing Meteors figur'd like beasts, but of a higher breed then any
the Zodiack yeilds, resembling two of those four which *Ezechiel* and S. *John*
saw, the one visag'd like a Lion to expresse power, high autority and
indignation, the other of count'nance like a man to cast derision and
scorne upon perverse and fraudulent seducers' (1, 900). The two beasts
who draw Milton's figurative chariot over the proud and unrepentent
'Scarlet Prelats' are appropriately among the four surrounding the throne
seen in Revelation by those zealous individuals who avoid the errors of the
Laodiceans. Symbolic of the power and wisdom of 'ministring spirites,' the
leonine and human figures embody the mysterious and awesome might
given in Revelation to the divine ministers or angels of God.[18] Their Old
Testament counterpart is implicit in the further personification of zeal as
the 'invincible warriour' who drives the fiery chariot. When Milton likens
this majestic image to the 'true Prophets of old' and to 'Christ himselfe,'
the association with the spirit of Elijah seems unmistakable. In Elijah's
miraculous translation 'Fire fitly answered the heroick spirit of Elijah, who
was enflamed with an holy zeal. Chariots and horses set forth the ready
and speedy ministry of Angels, Psal. 68.17. and fire sets forth their zeal,

Psal. 104. 4.'[19] This idea of militant zealousness particularly suits Milton's conception of an embattled 'warriour Zeale' since the fiery chariot suggests the additional commonplace that 'Elijah did more for the strength and defence of Israel's church and commonwealth by doctrines and prayers than all their forces of chariots and horsemen.'[20] Contemporary Englishmen involved in their own epic conflict recognized that the 'successful reformer,' like Luther, must be in the tradition of Elijah.[21] They also agreed that individuals chosen to 'fit' people 'for the Kingdom of Christ, ought to be men of Elijah's temper, for through zeal and integrity, for courage and fidelity to resist a declining generation, to contend with the greatest decliners, and freely to reprove the sins of the time; for such a one was Christs fore-runner, he was Elijah the Prophet, as coming in his Spirit and power, Luke 1. 17.'[22]

References in the antiprelatical tracts to John the Baptist and Martin Luther confirm the desirability and nature of a zealous ridicule which embodies the prophet and the angel found in the figurative Zeale and the fiery Elijah. The reformer destined by divine choice to enlighten the nation fulfils a role traditionally associated with the biblical prophet when he fearlessly and righteously exposed 'Idolatry and Superstition.' Citing the example of Luther, Milton further argues that 'morall and generall observation' rather than 'revelation' may also inform the 'judgement' that guides a harsh, uncompromising zeal. Those who assault 'men carnally wise' without the divine inspiration granted to Elijah have their own source of spiritual guidance; they remain angels like the prophet's antitype, John the Baptist, who signifies for Milton the ministering spirit.[23] All who fulfil the spirit of Elijah become, in one sense, ministers or preachers of the gospel who lead their people towards their religious destiny. Guided by the examples of the 'true Prophets of old' and of 'Christ himselfe,' their means, as well as their inspiration, are complexly varied.

Righteous indignation and scornful superiority constitute Milton's zealous spirit. The parliament that Milton says broke the calm smile they maintained throughout the Bishops' War and 'laught such weake enginry to scorne' and the faithful who would burst their midriffs if they could not laugh at the pompously garbed clergy express a laughter epitomized in Milton's derisive 'Ha, ha, ha.' Taken out of context, as the outburst sometimes is in modern studies, the laugh appears crudely brutal; within the incremental movement of the satire the three words are a fit response to proven absurdity. The satires imply that anyone who would use his reason must respond in like manner, for anger and laughter are the 'most rationall faculties.' The individual who follows a reason guided by conscience, the Bible, and divine spirit may 'safely imitate the method that God uses; *with the froward to be froward, and to throw scorne upon the scorner*, whom if any thing, nothing else will heale. And if *the righteous shall laugh at the destruction of the ungodly*, they may also laugh at their pertinacious and incurable obstinacy, and at the same time be mov'd with detestation of their seducing malice' (1, 875).[24] The tracts pursue a taunting ridicule of the 'toothlesse satyrs' Hall wrote when he was younger, and they insist that 'grim laughter' must bite out the evil to cure it. But Milton has no illusions that the proud, obstinate prelates who have closed their minds to any form of reason and become immune to all remedy will respond to his ridicule. In an important distinction between teaching and exposing he recognizes that his satire must uncover the disease of prelacy for the instruction of others. '*Eliah* mockt the false Prophets' not to exhibit his wit or humour 'but to teach and instruct the poore misledde people' (1, 903). Flailing the degenerate with contempt is done so that all who see may experience a therapeutic scorn even though the laughter never penetrates to its insensitive victim. The bystander, who justifies such mockery, is a central focus in *An Apology*.[25]

In teaching through exposure by zealous laughter, the satires are themselves a lesson in decorum. To the accusation that Hall had been treated by '*a scurrilous* Mime, *a personated, and (as himself thinks) a grim, lowring, bitter fool*,'[26] Milton replies in *An Apology* that 'his foolish language unwittingly writes foole upon his owne friend, for he who was there *personated*, was only the *Remonstrant*; the author is ever distinguisht from the person he introduces' (1, 880). The distinction recalls Martin Marprelate's principle of *decorum personæ* by suggesting that the satires tailor their laughter to Bishop Hall's example. Earlier the *Sixth Prolusion* makes a similar distinction between the author and the demands of the occasion, and later in the Salmasian controversy *A Second Defence* again blames its frivolity on the need to suit Alexander More's nature.[27] Explaining that the 'impetuous folly' of the bishop's 'quips and snapping adagies' presumptuously dismisses the Smectymnuan's unassailable wisdom, *An Apology* claims the right to answer Hall and his defender with 'as little lightnesse as the Remonstrant hath given example.' Milton, however, does not attempt to mimic his opponents in the manner of Martin Marprelate. Dispelling the notion that critics of prelacy are 'grosse-headed, thick witted, illiterat, [and] shallow,' the satires demonstrate the correct way to exploit jest and earnest. Laughter, the confutant is schooled, does not express itself in the 'sucking Satir' of Hall's juvenalia; and the 'mere tankard drollery' in the bishop's utopian *Mundus Alter et Idem* debases the gravity of a form nobly upheld by Plato, More, and Bacon. Before hurling about accusations of miming and quoting Bacon's pronouncement on religious laughter, the confutant is advised to look 'where neither reproofe nor better teaching is adjoyned' (1, 882). Milton insists that his own satires observe a strict fidelity to traditional decorum; they do not, like Hall's or the confutant's misconceived wit, blatantly and pointlessly violate the circumstances and obligations of just enlightenment. Committed to the reformer's plain dealing and convinced that he possesses truth, Milton preempts the only right to decorum. With a consistency that may at first seem contradictory he uses laughter; the satires are their own justification.

They establish 'lawfull reason' for their decorous jest at the outset of the attack against Hall. Besides its brief apology for a Miltonic laughter the preface to *Animadversions* establishes a fundamental opposition. Without mentioning Hall by name Milton proposes the necessity and authority to suspend sometimes the restraints of Christian charity. At a time when both divine and human forces are prepared 'to explode and hisse out of the land' everything related to prelacy, those who glibly defend the enemy of truth and peace deserve to be roughly 'bespurted' with their own 'holy-water.' The precepts of Solomon on folly and the reaction of Christ and his followers to their detractors authorize vehement correction, particularly when a haughty enemy of religion deceitfully uses 'no common Arts.' Forced out of his 'hold in Scripture' and deprived of divine commands, Hall becomes a foe who seeks cover in the 'rouling trench' of apostolic tradition and 'creeps up by this meanes to his relinquish't fortresse of divine authority again; and still hovering betweene the confines of that which hee dares not bee openly, and that which he will not be sincerely, traines on the easie Christian insensibly within the close ambushment of worst errors, and with a slye shuffle of counterfeit principles chopping and changing till hee have glean'd all the good ones out of their minds, leaves them at last, after a slight resemblance of sweeping and garnishing under the sevenfold possession of a desperate stupidity' (1, 663). Against a decadent dissembler who destroys for selfish, materialistic reasons men 'cannot be blam'd though they bee transported with the zeale of truth to a well heated fervencie' (1, 663). Zealous love for the souls of others in itself justifies extremeness, but this noble passion becomes especially commendable when the 'false trade of deceiving' is exposed 'not without a sad and unwilling anger, not without many hazards, but without all private and personall spleene, and without any thought of earthly reward, when as this very course they take stopps their hopes of ascending above a lowly and unenviable pitch in this life' (1, 663).

The lawfulness of zeal is apparent in the main body of the satire when Hall becomes the 'false Prophet' personified. *Animadversions* relentlessly reveals his true identity through the 'uncasing of a grand imposture.' In denying him the charity that the bishop complained could not be found among 'furious and malignant spirits,' Milton demonstrates that in his own zealous love there is 'nothing disagreeing from Christian meeknesse.' The attention given in the preface to a selfless love expressed without animosity and at apparent personal sacrifice is expanded most directly in the personal disclosures of *Reason of Church-Government* and *An Apology*; it remains, however, always implicit in the ensuing satire of *Animadversions*. Although the assault on the hapless Hall dominates the tract, Milton recognizes that the nature of his zealous scorn presupposes the ideal love minimally outlined in the preface.

These prefatory references to the satirist's ethos help vindicate zeal,[28] for Milton and his contemporaries understood that 'true zeale' is easily abused whenever the ethical view of the satirist weakens. The biblical sources summarized in Richard Greenham's 'Of Zeale' include most prominently Revelation 3: 'when after the Church of Laodicea for her lukewarmnes, is threatened to be spued out of the Lord his mouth, it is added, be zealous and amend: where we see zeale to be opposed to lukewarmnes, which is too temperate an heate for the profession of the Gospell.'[29] The fire of zeal, its 'proper tongue,' is also described in Hebrews 10, and additional directions are indicated in 1 Corinthians, 'which in our common translation we reade, *Follow after loue & couet spiritual gifts*, &c. the naturall text hath, *Be zealous after the more excellent gifts*. And Rom. 12. *Be feruent in spirit. i.* let God his spirite kindle in you a fire which may flame out of you.'[30] Zealots opposed to the Anglican notion of decency derived from Corinthians 'Let all things be done decently, and in order' commonly deride this moderation as the lukewarmness of Laodicea; they do not, however, advocate radical extremes. They might in fact agree with the Anglican churchman Edward Boughen that a decency synonymous with reason and order does not condone laughing and jeering at any 'not of our owne *cut*.'[31] Thomas Brightman, for example, condemns Martin Marprelate; and other writers sympathetic to zeal also warn against the excesses of Martinists, Brownists, or Papists.[32] They object that these writers are 'very hotte indeede,' and they conclude that lies, slander, railing, or 'cursed speaking, and the like' are really the signs of the devil.[33] Paradoxically, discussions of zeal stress instead discretion, boldness, and compassion. Hasty and unexamined zeal may kindle fervour without accompanying meekness, and sharp attacks on anything beyond the sin itself lack the 'blessed temperature' which mingles grief and compassion with zeal.[34] To maintain the delicate balance between 'frantic fury' and 'moathy-pollicy' zeal must be discreet, circumspect, and judicious. Only the individual who is confident that his boldness is selfless and impartial and pursues a great good 'may take all liberty hee can in reproouing, as occasion is offered, and his calling admitteth.'[35] And even then commentators who admit that zeal cannot defer to persons, place, or time circumscribe only tentatively a spirit which, guided by a thorough knowledge of the self and the Word, is 'both meek and gentle as a dove, and earnest, and zealous, and hot as fire.'[36]

While not reluctant to extend the limits of acceptable zeal, Milton recognizes the importance of these traditional sanctions. In the first of his tracts, the temperate *Of Reformation*, his justification for vehement language is similar to that of Greenham or Burges. Dealing 'plainely and roundly,' he proposes to write 'neither out of malice, nor list to speak evill, nor any vaine-glory; but of meere necessity, to vindicate the spotlesse *Truth* from an ignominious bondage, whose native worth is now become of such a low esteeme' (1, 535). To this catalogue of major prerequisites for zeal *Of Prelatical Episcopacy* adds expediency. 'It came into my thoughts to perswade my selfe, setting all distances, and nice respects aside, that I could do Religion, and my Country no better service for the time then doing my utmost endeavour to recall the people of GOD from this vaine forraging after straw, and to reduce them to their firme stations under the standard of the Gospell' (1, 627). A nobly conceived battle for truth may be undertaken only after the careful self-scrutiny from which all 'true Zeale' originates. When necessity once more forces Milton to re-enter the fray and rout Hall from his 'rouling trench,' his motivations, however sincere, also resemble the conventional. The unification of 'Christian meeknesse' and 'well heated fervencie,' the 'sad and unwilling anger,' the impersonal rancour, and even the tantalizing reference to the deferral of unexplained aspirations are standard in the literature of zeal. But the involved syntax and complex diction create a dimension missing from either the apologies in the previous tracts or the expositions in the various commentaries. The elaborate clauses and the periodic structure that suspend resolution reflect the searching, sensitive mind drawn almost inevitably into the zealous commitment so fundamental to the satires. Before the reader has an opportunity to judge the pressing circumstances, individual epithets and clusters of images manœuvre his sympathies towards the acceptance of an apparently unavoidable conclusion.

The preface completes this manipulation in the final sentences addressed now to the 'ingenuous Reader.' Anticipating the objections to his 'close and succinct manner of coping with the Adversary,' Milton proposes to lead his reader around the 'labyrinth of controversall antiquity' in the 'speediest way to see the truth vindicated, and Sophistry taken short at the first false bound' (I, 664). The imagery of the journey or quest reinforces the contrast between the straightforward, sincere satirist and his devious, sophistical opponent. As the plain-dealing spokesman for truth, Milton has no leisure for a fictional vehicle that might detract from the exposure of error. In this pursuit the remonstrant will be forced to recognize that 'as oft as hee pleases to be frolick and brave it with others,' he will achieve 'no gaine of money, and may learne not to insult in so bad a cause' (I, 664). Ostentation, mirthful insult, and usury are among the vices linked in the satires with a corrupt prelacy; they will, Milton assures his honest reader, receive their just and forthright assessment.

The attack that follows is deceptively simple. A series of statements and refutations indicates the form common to much animadversion. Beginning with a sentence-by-sentence scrutiny and then gradually overlooking larger and larger sections of the bishop's arguments, *Animadversions* presents excerpts from Hall's *A Defence of the Humble Remonstrance* in a dialogue between the remonstrant and his answerer which makes no pretence to any dialectical development. Not reluctant to edit for his own purposes, Milton summarizes statements, expurgates prejudicial words, or shifts the sequence to achieve a more economical, favourable presentation. *An Apology* considers this general strategy a sound military tactic. Rather than confront Hall's array of 'specious antiquity,' its attack follows 'some kinde of military advantages to await him at his forragings, at his watrings, and when ever he felt himselfe secure to solace his veine inderision of his more serious opponents' (I, 872). Although the increasingly sporadic attack in *Animadversions* may actually reflect Milton's flagging interest in the bishop's tract, the explanation does loosely fit the pattern of the satire. The first significant breaks in the consideration of Hall's comments avoid issues related to tradition, while the lengthy middle sections which Milton ignores contain arguments heavily dependent upon ancient authorities. In seizing the opportunity to educate the bishop in the proper use of laughter or to make longer pronouncements of his own beliefs Milton spurns the bishop's position with contempt. A sense of the original can be reconstructed sometimes from closely analysed sections of Hall's tract if the reader patiently reintegrates the remonstrant's dialogue, but often the prelate's statements remain cryptically isolated. Despite the formal structure with its pretext of dialogue the bishop has no active role. He exists to be used in a consciously crafted lesson in 'plaine dealing' zealous laughter.

The design of this instruction significantly extends the dramatic mode exploited in the Marprelate satires. Like Martin, Milton departs from traditional polemic,[37] flouts the seriousness of his adversary, and prompts the charge 'scurrilous Mime.' He, however, retains the semblance of animadversion without the earlier satirist's egregious playfulness. While both authors fabricate new characters for their opponents, Milton's distortion creates a more complete and insidious antagonist than that developed in the Marprelate tracts. His own identity as satirist also remains clearer in the dramatic confrontation with the redefined Hall. The character he projects may be just as consciously crafted as the personae of Marprelate, but Milton never departs from its consistency or lessens its central importance. His satire begins where the Marprelate tracts end: greater focus is placed on the persona of the satirist embattled in a critical confrontation.

The fictions that sustain his imaginative interpretation of this conflict unify the abrupt and apparently discordant opening of the satire's assault. With the simple transition, 'But now he begins,' Milton heaps scorn upon selected sentences from Hall's opening paragraph. In their original context the excerpts help support the bishop's confidence that his cause possesses both truth and justice. Against his adversaries Hall had proclaimed: 'were they as many Legions as men, my cause, yea Gods, would bid me to meet them undismaid, and so say with holy *David, Though an hoast should incamp against me, my heart shall not feare*: The truth of God, which I maintaine, shall beare me up against the discouragements of my confessed weaknesse.'[38] Omitting the essential references to truth or justice and reproducing incomplete sentences, Milton quickly inverts the remonstrant's efforts to establish his integrity. Hall's claim to be one against many is ridiculed with the charge that he brings 'a hot sent of your more then singular affection to spirituall pluralities' (1, 665); and his use of the proverbial 'legion,' misconstrued to mean the devil, becomes an illustration of the bishop's contemptuous 'esteeme' for other men. Repeating three times Hall's phrase 'My cause, yea Gods,' the satire completes its own version of Hall's character. Isolated from its context and emphasized through repetition, the bishop's choice of words becomes vulnerable to Milton's sarcasm: 'Ere a foot furder we must bee content to heare a preambling boast of your valour, what a St. *Dunstane*, you are to encounter *Legions*, either infernall or humane' (1, 665). Hall's cause is vanity and self-preservation, not divine majesty or spiritual salvation; the boastful valour is only anxiety 'lest you should lose that superfluity of riches and honour which your party usurp' (1, 665). Accused of deceit, greed, and hypocrisy, and denied the selfless ideals of a Christian minister, Bishop Hall is scornfully dismissed. 'You are not arm'd *Remonstrant*, nor any of your band, you are not dieted, nor your loynes girt for spirituall valour, and Christian warfare, the luggage is too great that followes your Camp; your hearts are there, you march heavily. How shall we think you have not carnall feare while we see you so subject to carnall desires' (1, 666).

The military overtones of Milton's satiric imagery underscore the remonstrant's deficiency. The ideal of the Christian soldier emerges naturally from the consideration of heroic valour and draws the satire's quibbling retorts into a rich cluster of allusions. Antithetical to the vaunting St Dunstane and the 'carnall' prelatical forces, the portrait of the true spiritual warrior anticipates the later image of the 'warriour Zeale' and recalls both St Paul's Ephesians and Spenser's *The Faerie Queene*. The theme of Christian warfare also figures prominently in seventeenth-century religious literature where military imagery rivals the journey motif as the favourite Puritan conceit.[39] Both are united in the preface's quest for truth and in the satire's vision of England 'standing on the shoare of that red Sea into which our enemies had almost driven us' (1, 706). The militaristic metaphor, the association of the man of words with the man of arms, is especially congenial to Milton's conception of a momentous struggle which demands men of Elijah's spirit who fearlessly assert the word of God. Indeed the archetypal imagery of Christian warfare enlarges a polemical skirmish into an epic strife that both articulates and transcends the immediate issues of liturgy and polity.

The opposition pits error against truth. From the perspective introduced in the preface and applied in the opening attack Hall seems a cowardly champion of prelacy who shirks an inevitably fatal combat. Deprived of his scriptural 'hold' and unarmed for Christian warfare, he can only sneak towards the divine 'fortress' of authority, ambush the unwary, or flaunt his pretensions of valour. His own castle of Anglicanism, which *Of Reformation* depicts as 'the painted Battlements, and gaudy rottennesse of Prelatrie,' separated by its bulwarks from its own laity, is the refuge of falsehood.[40] To maintain and to extend their tyrannical control the prelates willingly 'rout, and dis-aray the wise and well-couch't order of Saint *Pauls* owne words' and make them 'rampe one over another, as they use to clime into their Livings and *Bishopricks*' (1, 708–9). But the ineptitude of Hall's verbal fencing and the scattered words shot from his harquebus suggest to Milton that 'your Castle cannot hold out long.' The prose prophet who believes he will soon see his enemies engulfed in another Red Sea contents himself with the public exposure of prelates 'thus unvisarded, thus uncas'd.' In his next tract Milton specifically equates 'good warfare' with the Presbyterian discipline that arrays its forces in a cubic formation, 'the main phalanx, an embleme of truth and stedfastnesse' (1, 789); his weapon in *Animadversions* remains more consistently the divine scriptures. Like Elijah, a man inspired to scorn false prophets, Milton conveys the assurance of divine authority measured against scriptural truth. At an epic turning-point, a moment which resembles Chrysostom's time 'of battell, & fight, & watching, & warding, and arming & of standing in battell raie,' Milton disagrees with the patristic writer that 'The time of laughter can haue no place here, for laughter pertaineth unto the world.'[41] Armed with 'this weapon' of heavenly origin, in the 'spirit of Elias' he opposes the lukewarm and idolatrous defenders of prelacy. Called from his private affairs to take up the cause of truth, he further resembles a Spenserian hero without allegorical trappings committed to a battle that will end in 'the serious uncasing of a grand imposture.'

He will win the conflict because the remonstrant is unprepared as well as unwilling to meet him in open combat. Encumbered with his worldly possessions and unarmed for Christian warfare, Hall appears in the satire's initial scrutiny undieted and ungirt for a struggle of such significant dimensions. Other contemporary reformers frequently level charges of luxury and intemperance against the Anglican prelates, but the accusation has special significance in these satires. In addition to making the obvious criticisms of excessive worldliness, Milton accuses the ministers of 'seeking to effeminate us all at home' (1, 588). *Of Reformation* insists that an England that must vigorously maintain its liberty and strive for its potential greatness cannot sacrifice its '*manhood* and *grace*' to clergy who enfeeble the body and cow the spirit. *Reason of Church-Government* envisions both national and religious service that demands 'the right possessing of the outward vessell, their body, in health or sicknesse, rest or labour, diet, or abstinence, whereby to render it more pliant to the soule, and usefull to the Common-wealth' (1, 754). This blending of the individual and the state, the temporal and the eternal, informs the tracts' guiding spirit of militant Christian humanism. Without compromising any of these essential values Milton proclaims a harmony of ideals at once classical and Augustinian. The physically fit and spiritually attuned individual will prove his ultimate worth in a state of readiness. He will express a unity enabling him to emerge victorious from the unrelenting struggle. But the Christian who ignores the manna of doctrine and feeds 'otherwhere on meats not allowable, but of evill juice' may disorder 'his diet, and spread an ill humour through his vains immediatly disposing to a sicknesse' (I, 846).

Because he believes his cause to possess the manna of 'incorruptible Doctrine' and the healing 'salve' of incontestable discipline, Milton naturally desires to restore to health a nation gravely threatened by the disease of Anglicanism. Not all cures, however, are easy. While the tracts admit many Christians can be nurtured with doctrinal manna, they also realize the necessity for harsher medicines. Hall himself and many of the prelates he represents may be incurable, but the dissection of their diseased beings must be rigorously undertaken none the less. Satire by its very nature, Milton chides Hall, is not toothless, and evil must be given no quarter. Although Milton does not pretend to write formal satires, the popular figure of the barber-surgeon fits the tracts' emphasis on a 'saving med'cin' that will restore clear eyesight and will purge the festering prelatical diseases. Together with the figure of the embattled warrior prophet, this image provides the satirist with a distinctly religious posture with larger, traditional literary associations. Both fulfil contemporary understandings of satiric decorum.

This view of the relationship between satirist and adversary governs the basic attack. The prelates, whose favourite weapons are slander and sophistry, have entrusted a diseased institution to the defence of their most able champion. Without the armour and skill of the Christian warrior and sapped of his manly vigour, however, Hall becomes the deceptive, wily militarist outlined in the preface; Milton, on the other hand, represents the forces of truth expertly supported with 'plain-dealing.' Thus the satire's first exchange dismisses Hall's correction of the Smectymnuans' improper inflection of the word *Areopagi* as a pedantic itch more suitable to the 'capricious *Pædantrie* of hot-liver'd Grammarians' (I, 666). Although not above similar criticism, Milton in defence of the Smectymnuans contrasts the damaging image of the pretentious Hall with a patriotic appeal to a native, lucid English that need not accept any 'harsh forreigne termination.' He then deflects Hall's complaint about libellous writing by retorting: 'it shew'd but green practise in the lawes of discreet *Rhethorique* to blurt upon the eares of a judicious *Parliament* with such a presumptuous and over-weening *Proem*: but you doe well to be the Sewer of your owne messe' (I, 667). Neither this diversionary reply nor the subsequent demand to know when the 'Prelaticall troop' suddenly developed their displeasure with libelling directly meets Hall's objection; the point is swept aside. The allusion to the 'messe' and the intrusion of the word 'troop' introduce earlier connotations of diet and warfare in an already biased contrast between the excesses of Hall and the composure of parliament. In inverting the bishop's point as readily as he had turned his image Milton makes Hall the only violator of decorum; he agrees with Marprelate that the prelates defended by the bishop are the only enemies of honest truth. Fearful that their armour will be 'uncased,' they have reduced the nation with their gags and purgatives to a 'broken-winded tizzick' that requires the harsh anatomies performed by 'free-spoken, and plaine harted men.'

Throughout the satire's subsequent dissections the diagnosis demands a 'physick' which must be administered 'for plainnes sake.' Milton appeals in its opening movement to the patriotic and religious sympathies of the individual and allies the 'Pharisaicall' Hall with the forces of superstition, hypocrisy, and chaos. Called a Roman partisan, a 'Simon Magus,' and a common circus juggler, the bishop appears a 'subtile *Janus*' who would trick the people into forfeiting their liberties. The alternatives leave the bystander little choice but to judge Hall 'either grossly deficient in his principles of *Logick*, or else purposely bent to delude the *Parliament* with equivocall Sophistry, scattering among his periods ambiguous words, whose interpretation he will afterwards dispence according to his pleasure; laying before us universall propositions, and then thinks when he will to pinion them with a limitation' (1, 694). Carefully chosen verbs continually support the impression that the remonstrant's tracts 'sift' and 'shuffle' meanings through his 'sophisticall boulting hutch,' 'riot' and 'clap' scriptural words together to force an interpretation, support the 'motley incoherence of a patch'd Missal' with similitudes incongruously 'thwact together,' employ all arts to 'heave and hale' his '*Polyphem* of Antiquity to the delusion of the Novices,' and nonsensically 'cramme' his views into the Word by applying his 'cramping irons to the Text.' If this arrogation of absolute authority remains unchallenged, it will engender blind and unwavering obedience to the prelates' whims; however in the present 'age of ages,' where parliamentary actions promise the 'resurrection of the State,' Milton confidently believes that 'God is manifestly come downe among us, to doe some remarkable good to our Church or state' (1, 703). All those who accept the 'better enlight'ning' of human reason, Scriptures, and the 're-ingendring Spirit of God' will see through this prelatical deception. Milton may not finally remove the 'pearle' in the eyes of prelacy, but he can make the people laugh derisively at the false prophets of Baal who would mislead the chosen people. Divine truth needs only the 'clearest and plainest expressions.'

Forthrightly he exposes the duplicity of the prelacy and their defender with a scornful vigour untypical of contemporary polemicists. The vivid epithets and descriptions applied to Anglicanism show a prophet intent upon exposing the true nature of evil. Language that might offend delicate sensibilities must be employed to make the essence of falsehood graphic. John Bastwick, who had earlier 'come to prophesy,' explicitly condemns men clerically garbed with 'foure square COW TVRDS upon their heads' and resembling a diabolical force unloosed from hell to 'beshit vs all – pho how they stinke';[42] but Milton's language possesses considerably more zest. Deriding the 'dissembling *Joab*,' 'mysticall man of *Sturbridge*,' or '*Ephesian* Beasts' with 'Samaritan trumpery' or 'Rabbinical fumes,' his inventive epithets appeal to the intellect as well as the emotions. While the image alone of divines who 'keep back their sordid sperm begotten in the lustinesse of their avarice' (I, 722) stands out, its derisiveness does not depend entirely upon the suggestion of perversity or the line's consonance. Themes and images in the satire combine to give momentum and direction to an attack that unifies individual retorts into a forceful whole.

The satire gradually develops the early vision of an oppressive, corrupt 'Pseudoepiscopy of Prelates.' Where Marprelate supports a similar charge with specific illustrations gathered from lists, anecdotes, and gossip, Milton relies upon his richly poetic language. Images of commercialism and money accompany the figurative emphasis of the preface on veneers and counterfeiting and announce the satire's preoccupation with a depraved, deceptive ministry. Repeated throughout the satire, they relate to various images of clothing, disease, and sight. Together with references to prostitution and blatant sexuality, the imagery underscores the great disparity between the external and its reality. This fundamental tension, which the tracts describe as the duality of inner and outer, embodies a lukewarmness irreconcilably opposed to zeal. More consistently than Marprelate, Milton asserts that Anglicanism wallows in indulgent luxury only superficially concealed by vestiges of respectability. Hall's efforts to reconcile substance and form, described as the 'odde coinage' that 'no mintmaister of language would allow for sterling,' assume a tolerance Milton will not grant. *Animadversions* insists that substance that may have some apparent holiness 'is but the matter; the forme, and the end of the thing may yet render it either superstitious, fruitlesse, or impious, and so, worthy to be rejected. The Garments of a Strumpet are often the same materially, that cloath a chast Matron, and yet ignominious for her to weare' (I, 686). In the satire's repudiation of Hall's arguments for the Anglican liturgy and episcopacy, allusions and images structurally reinforce the relentless exposure of prelacy's 'grand imposture.' Individually and woven together, they form an attack that completes its pattern in a series of increasingly striking designs.

Midway in the satire the tempo reaches the first of these climaxes. Shorter answers and specific charges give way to lengthy passages of a different tenor. Milton approaches the ideal of teaching inherent in the informing vision of his satire with declarations of his own beliefs. The poetic prose blends exposition and prophecy with satiric attack to extend the thematic implication of the imagery. Issues of knowledge and self-fulfilment supplant questions of liturgy, and the underlying concern with time and timelessness becomes increasingly significant.

Milton repudiates the guidance of the 'old wayes' with a wisdom based upon the perfect instruction of the Bible. The 'old paths' dimly marked among the myriad volumes of antiquity mislead their followers from the desired goal of complete fulfilment. Rapidly shifting imagery contends that people who 'bind' themselves to the unwieldy rule of tradition stand immobilized before a lifeless deity 'that like a carved Gyant terribly menacing to children, and weaklings lifts up his club, but strikes not, and is subject to the muting of every Sparrow' (1, 699). Its massive, powerless form may delude some ignorant Christians into submission, but the prelates' godlike effigy cannot mislead those guided by the rule of Scriptures. With the 'harmonious *Symmetry* of complete instruction' the individual may clearly see 'a perfect man of God or *Bishop*,' and with this 'weapon' he can destroy the false gods of prelacy. The Christian nurtured in this wisdom possesses a unity and harmony paradoxically absent in the order and continuity reverenced in Anglicanism; he can easily overcome the sterility that has reigned throughout the decline from the patristic golden age to the present era of mud and straw.

In the current period of pagan worship, where whining prelates urge parliament to protect their 'Flesh-pots of *Egypt*' and lament the loss of former luxury, Milton further counsels: 'Open your eyes to the light of grace, a better guide then Nature' (1, 702). True sight looks beyond the silver and gold ages of Constantine and the patristics to the 'meane condition' chronicled in the gospels. Here it would see directions for the 'true *Bishop*' who contents himself with the knowledge that materialistic values can only harm the man of God. Stressing his belief that precept and practice must be harmonious, Milton cannot imagine any 'sound Doctrine' or resolution to the present controversy from men who perpetuate a corrupt legacy. The superstition and malfeasance that moulded the traditions and institutions of the reigning bishops create in Milton's view only the ill-gotten gains which support the pompous edifice of prelacy. If these 'benefits' claimed by the prelates are to have any value and if the curse of their patrimony is to be alleviated, their wealth must be given to the 'places and meanes of Christian education,' and all ministers must again become 'faithfull labourers in Gods harvest.'

Animadversions prophesies that episcopacy will be driven from the land. Milton scorns Hall's arguments from tradition as little more than the 'fleshly apprehension' of an idolatrous man 'destitute of better enlight'ning,' and insists that these 'tatter'd Rudiments' should already have been cast aside by the English people 'after the many strivings of Gods Spirit.' The images of light and dark, vision and blindness, are the framework of Milton's exhortation of reverence and purification. In this present 'age of ages' Britain has emerged with divine guidance from the fourscore years spent in 'our wilderness since Reformation began'; under the 'speciall indulgent eye' of divine destiny the moment of purification and renewal is at hand. Once before, suffering the obdurate 'blindnesse' of the people, providential forces sent a 'healing messenger to touch softly our sores, and carry a gentle hand over our wounds.' Gradually lifting 'our drousie eye-lids' with the light emanating from the earlier reformers and removing the 'inveterat scales from our nigh perisht sight,' divine providence prepared the nation for 'the sudden assault of his reforming Spirit warring against humane Principles, and carnall sense' (I, 704). The conflict of the Reformation, which Milton also describes in terms of 'spiritual preparatives, and purgations,' 'melted' the bonds of traditionalism and 'fleshly reasonings' with the 'morning beam of *Reformation*.' After this 'earely thaw,' however, the English people have again been 'clamm'd and furr'd' with the prelatical 'levin' and may lose their sun forever and 'freeze at noone.'

Fearful of this possibility, yet confident that it will not happen, Milton concludes his prophecy with a prayer to the divine image, 'ever-begotten light.' The prose poem expresses his gratitude to the force that has already 'open'd' the oppressive times and restored unrestricted breathing. In a language charged with biblical overtones, particularly from Revelation, Milton praises the enlightening truth which has dispelled the 'vaine shadow of wisdome' and exposed the 'false *Prophets*.' Driven in fearful confusion by the brightness of the divine cloud, they have left behind a corruption to be purified by 'thy beamy walke through the midst of thy Sanctuary' (I, 705–6). Imploring divine immanence not to leave the nation to perish in the wilderness it deserves, the prayer promises that, when England stands triumphant on the edge of its Red Sea, its author will offer a more elaborate 'Song to Generations.' Now in this epochal moment when the 'Kingdome is now at hand, and thou standing at the dore,' intense yearning finds its expression in the powerful plea, 'Come forth out of thy Royall Chambers, O Prince of all the Kings of the earth, put on the visible roabes of thy imperiall Majesty, take up that unlimited Scepter which thy Almighty Father hath bequeath'd thee; for now the voice of thy Bride calls thee, and all creatures sigh to bee renew'd' (1, 707).

The final image in this remarkably poetic movement appropriately expresses Milton's sense of prophetic expectation. Turning away from a moribund past graphically represented in the satire's imagery and imitating 'the Prophets' in a fervent 'hymne in prose,'[43] Milton anticipates the kingdom foreseen by John the Divine. While he never explicitly defines the nature of Christ's reappearance, like the radical millenarians who preached before the Long Parliament, Milton links immediate religious reform with an inevitable New Jerusalem. The light of divine splendour finds its counterpart in a majestic figure whose power and manhood ensure that the nation will never again flee the field of Christian warfare. His bride, represented by both the chosen people and their prophetic spokesman, similarly conveys rebirth. Unlike the Anglican whore of Babylon who breeds only illegitimate offspring, the chaste bride who longs for her forthcoming marriage evokes the ideal union of Christ and his church found in numerous contemporary interpretations of the Song of Songs and of Revelation. Indeed the exultant vision of *Animadversions* expresses the same promise contained in a translation commissioned by parliament of Joseph Mede's *The Key of the Revelation*: 'The marriage of the Lamb, and that Emperiall kingdome of the Almighty Lord God, both begin after the destruction of Babylon, where the seventh trumpet beginneth.'[44] The harmonious individual and the spiritual and national body he helps constitute are prepared to embrace this new era of grandeur.

This readiness and the expectation of its fulfilment determine the next climactic movement in *Animadversions*. After the soaring prophetic heights reached in the visionary prayer the prose subsides momentarily to a series of fine distinctions concerning disputed biblical passages. From particular textual exchanges, where images of warfare represent the semantic conflict, Milton moves towards issues that are for him more fundamental. While biblical authorization of desired polity is certainly

important, contested questions about the proper edifice are less attractive
to him than an understanding of its actual function. Straining and
quibbling with the meanings of single scriptural words, he becomes
eloquent when he seizes the opportunity to discourse on the essence of
priesthood. True ministerial calling depends upon an 'inward calling of
God' rather than an 'outward signe or symbol.' Against Hall's arguments
for ordination and jurisdiction Milton cites the apostolic eminence derived solely from 'their powerfull preaching, their unwearied labouring in
the Word, [and] their unquenchable charity' (1, 715). Where the empty
ceremony of ordination can create nothing, the ordinary minister 'ma-
nures' his authority with this same apostolic love for the souls of others
and with his own diligent efforts. Only love and merit empower him 'to see
to the thriving and prospering of that which he hath planted' (1, 716).
Animadversions likens this care of souls to a garden tended by a skilful,
hardworking servant. When a 'strange Gardener' unaccustomed to
labour and ignorant of gardening challenges his right to nurture the
flowers, the honest worker politely refuses to surrender his care of the
garden. But the intruder insists that his dignity alone allows him to assume
the gardener's duties, and to receive for his unwelcome efforts ten times
the ordinary wages. 'The Gardener smil'd and shooke his head,' the
parable concludes, 'but what was determin'd I cannot tell you till the end
of this Parliament' (1, 717).

Unlike the prophetic exhortation of the 'hymne in prose,' the homely
parable resembles the figurative lessons of the gospels. In emulating the
method of instruction practised by Christ, whom he believes to be the
greatest of teachers, Milton introduces a didactic voice different from that
of his derisive satire yet compatible with his role and vision. The zealous
spirit of reformation implicit 'in teaching and confuting' readily blends
excoriation, hymn, and parable with the sanction of biblical precedent.
Prior to the parable, moreover, Milton reminds Hall that the 'Prophetick
pitch' relies on 'types, and Allegories' to signify its meaning. A counterpart to the symbolic bride, the figurative gardener recalls the satire's
interest in proper nurturing and complements its expectation. Besides
the strong suggestions of an Eden lost through years of prelatical ministry, the metaphorical garden gains significance from the numerous biblical references to cultivation and the satire's promise of a New Jerusalem.[45]
England will have its paradise when the truth implanted in the people is
allowed to flourish. Too often the biblical lessons on husbandry that
ensure such fruition have been lost to 'blind and undiscerning Prelates.'

Professing that the 'greatest gaine' any teacher can realize is 'to make a

soule vertuous,' Milton enlightens his audience with a further development of the satire's imagery. The 'root of all our mischiefe' appears to him
an inordinate desire for worldly power that subverts the ideals of ministry
into ambition, pride, and self-gratification. Universities that should prepare men to toil in the 'Vineyard' have instead 'poyson'd' and 'choak'd' the
crystaline springs of knowledge and have bred a 'brood of flattering and
time-serving priests.' Prelacy attracts people who 'gorge' their insatiable
'belly-cheere' with the riches of the church and repulses the clear-sighted
who have been 'nurst' with the knowledge that the 'greatest fruit and
proficiency of learned studies' is to condemn such debasement. Divines
'moulded and bred up' in the expectation of their own advancement will
undoubtedly engender 'a baseborn issue of Divinity like that of those
imperfect, and putrid creatures that receive a crawling life from two most
unlike procreants the Sun, and mudde' (1, 720). The hypocritical or
foolish divines who masquerade behind pretensions of knowledge, 'sow-
ing the World' with idle speculation, can edify no one. While the 'plaine
unlearned man' fulfils himself and inspires others with his own 'light,' the
ostentatious divine conceals his avarice by 'painting his lewd and deceitfull
principles with a smooth, and glossy varnish in a doctrinall way' (1, 720).
Only the 'true' minister sent into the divine 'Harvest' will not neglect or
abuse learning. Encouraging others with his own example and wisdom, he
pursues a calling Milton considers to have no parallel. As the 'messenger,
and Herald of heavenly truth' he resembles the creative force of divinity
infusing 'spirit and likenesse' in the creation of faith and bursting into the
'chill and gloomy hearts of his hearers, raising out of darksome barren-
nesse a delicious, and fragrant Spring of saving knowledge, and good
workes' (1, 721). If he does not enjoy the public offices which the Anglicans
fear are being unjustly denied to their ministers, this in Milton's view is
inconsequential. His gifts of wisdom and doctrine enable him to be a
teacher to all the august bodies of the state; rather than simply restraining
men from evil, his 'perswasive power' cultivates goodness through instruction. After the example of Christ, who himself entered temporality
'to bee a teacher,' the divine calling tolerates no worldly compromise yet
promises unlimited self-fulfilment. He who nurtures souls to this fruition
will not resemble lusty prelates who with their 'sordid sperm' futilely instil
their ideas 'into that lump of flesh which they are the cause of' (1, 722). He
will create and inhabit a golden world which the lengthy passage from
Spenser's *Shepheardes Calender* describes as a time that 'was once, and may
again returne.' The bounty of this pastoral realm, however, is not further

described; 'without the Prelates,' Milton cuttingly concludes, 'the courses are so many and so easie, that I shall passe them over' (I, 724).

The final sections of the satire move from the prophetic mode and its visions of instruction and rebirth into a series of direct rejoinders. Milton selects brief segments from the remonstrant's many statements and relies on the scornful quip to dismiss them. The imagery of nourishment and breeding in the final pages complements the garden metaphor, and the brief answers retain the satire's preoccupation with deception, but the effect is anticlimactic. After the intensity with which Milton espouses his own beliefs, his harshness and perhaps impatience reflect a lack of interest in much that *A Defence of the Humble Remonstrance* develops in its last sections. Even Hall's criticisms of the Smectymnuans' postscript, which Milton probably wrote himself, fail to open a more impassioned vein. Closing its attack with retorts characteristic of the blunter satire, *Animadversions* dismisses Hall for the last time with the hope that he will receive 'a more profitable, and pertinent humiliation, then yet you know, and a lesse mistaken charitablenesse, with that peace which you have hitherto so perversely misaffected' (I, 735).

Despite the manner in which it ends *Animadversions* returns to the theme of charity in a satisfying resolution. By not succumbing to the mechanical form inherent in polemical exchanges Milton transforms conventional disputation into an imaginative, unified satire. Consistent imagery and a conscious ethos form a continuity which distinguishes the satire from the myriad other animadversions published during the civil crisis. Although the tonal variations occasionally seem less controlled than the tight thematic unity, the informing vision is never compromised. Extremes ranging from poetic flights of inspiration to derisive sallies of scorn and indignation are characteristic of a zeal which uniquely adapts established religious and literary precedents to the medium of pamphlet warfare. When an unknown challenger criticizes the achievement as an '*immodest and injurious Libell*,' Milton's defence indicates what *Animadversions* demonstrates: the implications of the use of zealous ridicule are most carefully considered.

An Apology against a Pamphlet Call'd A Modest Confutation of the Animadversions upon the Remonstrant against Smectymnuus appropriately assumes a different satiric stance. For the first time in the controversy Milton responds to a direct and personal attack which forces him into a defensive posture. Without relinquishing his aggressive charges against the 'false Prophets' or abandoning the 'dissection' and 'strokes' of the physician-satirist, in this satire Milton refocuses the perspective of *Animadversions*. Although images of disease, clothing, diet, and warfare remain integral to the satiric unity, they do not structure impassioned expressions of the satire's ideals. Instead the centre of importance, and the subject of considerable imagery, remains the embattled satirist, John Milton. The arguments he advances in support of his religious ridicule and, more importantly, the prominence he now gives to his character are essential to the apologia.

The greater emphasis on the satirist is apparent in the opening paragraph of *An Apology*. Unlike the general statements at the beginning of *Animadversions*, Milton's prefatory comments retain the first person to suggest his undisguised involvement. 'I resolv'd,' Milton emphatically begins, to uphold the position 'where I saw both the plain autority of Scripture leading, and the reason of justice and equity perswading' (1, 868). In responding to a zeal too often confused by his lukewarm contemporaries with choleric indiscretion he adds: 'I could not to my thinking honor a good cause more from the heart, then by defending it earnestly' (1, 869). A necessity dictated by Scripture, reason, and honour does not, of course, negate personal initiative; it does, however, absolve the satirist from any charges of self-interest. He may proceed with a personal defence, indeed 'must be forc't to proceed,' even though he admits that silence is ordinarily the most effective response to false accusations. Expounding the wisdom of passivity in a mounting series of parallel sentences, Milton nevertheless abandons his reluctance to break 'Silence, and Sufferance' and accepts a transcendent obligation. 'When I discern'd his intent was not so much to smite at me, as through me to render odious the truth which I had written' (1, 871), he writes, activity and passivity simultaneously claimed his allegiance. Viewing himself now 'not as mine own person, but as a member incorporate into that truth,' Milton recognizes he has no choice but to accept the duty 'not to leave on my garment the least spot, or blemish in good name so long as God should give me to say that which might wipe it off. Lest those disgraces which I ought to suffer, if it so befall me, for my religion, through my default religion be made liable to suffer for me' (1, 871). His course and even his very words predetermined, the satirist accepts a position that paradoxically raises the self in the very act of minimizing the person.

This selfless individuality is more than a rhetorical ploy to enhance the satirist's dignity and to excuse his self-indulgence. The burden of apologizing for his scornful treatment of Hall obligates Milton to a defence premised largely upon this conception of integrity. He begins his answer to his adversary's criticisms of manner with an apparent denial of total responsibility. Explaining that he was in fact provoked into use of harsh ridicule, Milton follows Marprelate's strategy and shifts the blame for his style partly onto Hall. Throughout the satire he will continue to insist that his answers have 'as little lightnesse' as those of the remonstrant. Because the bishop's folly was directed against the sound arguments of the Smectymnuans, Milton also justifies his reaction with Gregory Nyssenus's excuse: 'it *was not for himselfe, but in the cause of his brother; and in such cases,* saith he, *perhaps it is worthier pardon to be angry, then to be cooler'* (1, 873). Milton's strongest defence, however, rests upon divine authorization. Biblical precedent sanctions the harsh exposure of obstinate, false teachers; and the 'office' to disclose these deceivers 'goes not by age, or youth, but to whomsoever God shall give apparently the will, the Spirit, and the utterance' (1, 875). Later in the satire Milton further argues that, in the cause of truth, words 'like so many nimble and airy servitors' effortlessly come to the command of the educator and 'fall aptly into their own places' (1, 949). But the licence and the means of speech are not absolutely preordained. 'True eloquence,' which the satire equates with total commitment to truth, begins with oneself. Although he willingly shares the burden for his manner with divine guidance and with the mitigating circumstances of person, place, and time, Milton recognizes at the outset that 'regenerate reason' always guides the 'most eloquent' expression. Without reservation he declares in the second paragraph of *An Apology*: 'So that how he should be truly eloquent who is not withall a good man, I see not' (1, 874).

While the idea is common to a long tradition of writers,[46] the relationship between morality and eloquence becomes increasingly important in the antiprelatical tracts. By the time he wrote *Reason of Church-Government* Milton had accepted the biblical and classical notion that 'manlike' persuasion appeals through the medium of 'true eloquence the daughter of vertue' (1, 746). The arguments in this tract justifying the sanctity of individual judgment and the belief fundamental to all the tracts that conscience and self-knowledge are essential to any meaningful action are again apparent in the final satire. Truth is best evaluated by its threefold guide: follow the Scriptures, scrutinize the behaviour of the teacher, and live an irreproachable Christian life. *An Apology* also affirms that an author who hopes to achieve praiseworthy goals 'ought him selfe to bee a true Poem, that is, a composition, and patterne of the best and honourablest things; not presuming to sing high praises of heroick men, or famous Cities, unlesse he have in himselfe the experience and the practice of all that which is praise-worthy' (1, 890). Milton's famous disclosure specifically refers to future literary ambitions deferred by the current urgency, yet it applies in principle to the prose he deliberately minimizes. The apology for his zealous manner becomes indistinguishable from the issue of true eloquence; both assume a mutual relationship between truth and personal character. Before Milton can claim the elevating provenance of either truth or zeal he must demonstrate his righteousness; once zealously committed to truth, this 'honest estimation' must remain above suspicion or 'it would but harme the truth.'

Milton asserts his right to uphold truth and to expose the prelatical deceivers in the famous autobiographical disclosures offered before he begins the section-by-section analysis of the *Modest Confutation*. Applying to himself the instruction set forth in *Reason of Church-Government*, he understands that justice to others begins with justice to oneself. The confutant's fabrications of a 'loytering, bezelling, and harlotting' youth, a sudden expulsion from the university, and a London life of dissipation particularly exacerbate him, but Milton insists he would suffer the slanderous libels if the cause of truth were not weakened by his silence. The necessary digression, which prompts him to show 'in a way not often trod' that his figurative inner and outer garments are spotless, is expressly designed to 'gaine beliefe with others' that he merits his position as a spokesman for truth. The testimonials and facts concerning his outer identity and his private thoughts form a harmony consciously opposite to the emerging character of the confutant. Contrasting starkly with the superficial caricature of ambitious deception, Milton's revelations more than coincidentally develop details integral to the tracts' informing vision.

The autobiographical apology begins with repudiation of the imaginary life the confutant invented for the author of *Animadversions*. Milton responds to the accusations contained in the several sentences prefaced to the reader of *Modest Confutation*, quibbling with the confutant's language and turning back upon his accuser the allegations of debauchery. The life he recounts in his lengthy defence, however, contains surprisingly few biographical details, for much of the apology deals with his attitudes towards his early experiences. But among the opinions expressed about his life at the university and in London Milton volunteers several personal facts with satiric implications. Assuring the reader that his past has been neither riotous nor disreputable, he alludes to many testimonial letters from university friends. The 'ingenuous and friendly men' described as the 'countnancers of vertuous and hopefull wits' are also the valued community of readers with whom Milton allies himself in the satire. To help them realize what was so apparent to those who knew him personally, he then reveals a daily regimen that begins before the sounds of dawn call others to work and ends only when the mind is surfeited. 'Then with usefull and generous labours preserving the bodies health, and hardinesse; to render lightsome, cleare, and not lumpish obedience to the minde, to the cause of religion, and our Countries liberty, when it shall require firme hearts in sound bodies to stand and cover their stations, rather then to see the ruine of our Protestation, and the inforcement of a slavish life' (1, 885–6). While Milton may very well have lived this life at Horton and in London, his recollection stresses precisely the values idealized throughout the antiprelatical tracts. The imagery of diet and warfare expresses the themes of fulfilment and freedom that constitute the harmonious union of personal, national, and religious destiny envisioned in the heroic Christian warrior. All that Hall and the Anglican prelates are seen to oppose, Milton appears to fulfil.

The extent to which the satirist embodies his own ideal becomes more apparent in the disclosure of his 'inmost thoughts.' Milton admits to the sympathetic reader that the love of learning and the welcome recreation of reading encouraged within him the hope that one day he might win literary acclaim. With this aspiration and an 'honest haughtinesse' he formulated his belief that only an author who is himself 'a composition, and patterne of the best and honourablest things' (1, 890) can successfully write about the heroic. Central to this nobility are the virtues of love and chastity. The love that *An Apology* declares divinely begets in the soul knowledge and virtue also engenders the zeal essential to their uncompromising development. Chastity's importance, graphically expressed in the fervent prayer of *Animadversions*, justifies the belief that unchastity in man 'who is both the image and glory of God' must be 'much more deflouring and dishonourable' (1, 892) than in woman. For Milton the chastity of a prophet who awaits the appearance of the celestial bridegroom or of the church that nurtures herself for her divine spouse 'a pure unspotted virgin'[47] symbolizes disciplined readiness which, together with love, promises to transform the vision of a new age into a reality. A conventional sign of undefiled harmony, chastity supports in the tracts the paradox that both exalts individuality and merges it into a larger rhythm. The chaste man, *An Apology* adds, possesses a special power to sing the praises of divine grandeur; the values of chastity, in addition, help create this glory within the flux of time.

The character Milton establishes through these private revelations consciously differs from the satiric depiction of the confutant's nature.

Declaring that 'he shall be to me so as I find him principl'd,' Milton depersonalizes his adversary. Confronted indirectly through his tract, and not through dialogue as in *Animadversions*, the unnamed assailant is made either indistinguishable from the remonstrant or an upstart 'lozel Bachelour' as it suits Milton's purpose. Deliberately avoiding direct references to the confutant, the textual scrutiny as well as Milton's own apology addresses instead a select audience of bystanders. The slight implies that the anonymous objector is beneath the most minimal courtesy and suggests that he is impervious to any form of rational enlightenment. Milton reminds his readers in the opening paragraph that the punishment of postlapsarian man is a great difficulty 'now to know that which otherwise might be soone learnt'; in the tract's closing paragraph he summarizes for them the satire's additional wisdom that 'false Prophets' and 'arch deceavers' are totally unreceptive to knowledge: 'And if yee thinke that soundnesse of reason, or what force of argument soever, will bring them to an ingenuous silence, yee think that which will never be' (1, 953). Among the hopeless, the confutant must be 'discover'd and laid open' for the edification of others sensitive enough to 'laugh at their pertinacious and incurable obstinacy, and at the same time be mov'd with detestation of their seducing malice' (1, 875).

Against Milton's personal image of virtue and truth *An Apology* presents an arrogant dissembler deficient in all of the qualities the satires propound. Chastity and love, which in the figurative description are differentiated from 'a thick intoxicating potion which a certaine Sorceresse the abuser of loves name carries about' (1, 892), confront a similar seduction in the confutant. Characterized as a deceiver, the defender of Hall and Anglicanism is wedded to a 'decency' that hides the splendour of the Bible in garish trumpery, bewitches unsuspecting Christians with her 'whoorish cunning,' and transforms the unwary into '*Iudaizing* beasts' with her 'sorcerous' doctrines of formality. A seventeenth-century Simon Magus, Chaldean, or Empirick, the confutant is also seen as a charlatan who deludes others with his bogus powers. Additional comparisons to a wizard, a gypsy, and a soothsayer extend the image of a fraudulent 'Alchymist of slander' who poisons the faithful with concoctions of falsehood palmed off as quintessential truth. Scornful charges of divining, soothsaying, and figure-casting reflect Milton's displeasure with the satiric portrait of himself sketched in *Modest Confutation* and forward the theme of false prophecy. The ideal of the zealous prophet inspired by truth is debased in the confutant to a 'transcendent Sage' consumed with rapturous madness and with the 'lascivious promptnesse of his own fancy.' A big, blunted, and lumpish being who guilefully shifts his shape, he appropriately remains in Milton's rendition a nameless adversary, a blurry likeness of Hall and Anglican prelacy.

This 'whole lumpe,' which cannot endure the scrutiny of either eye or judgment, impresses its form on all the pages of *Modest Confutation*. More insistently than in *Animadversions*, Milton demonstrates the classical idea that style expresses the man. Vivid epithets and verbs capture the false qualities of a creature made to appear a 'cursing *Shimei* a hurler of stones.' From his 'stufft magazin' the confutant 'blunders' and 'flings out' his venomous defamation. Sobbing mottoes in convulsive fits of agonizing wit or belching Jesuitical sedition, this 'obscure thorn-eater' adds his noxious effusions to the 'old vomit' of prelatical traditions. His 'ging' of 'maim'd' words and his 'mincing,' 'warping' distortions are characteristic when he 'labours to cavill' or 'falls to glozing.' His empty style, 'girded with frumps and curtall gibes,' can only 'vapour' sound reasoning away or leave the path of common expression to 'tread the aire' with cloudy transmigrations. The satire forthrightly determines that this is the slovenly reflex of a 'malevolent Fox' or simply 'plaine bedlam stuffe.'

In characterizing the confutant's manner *An Apology* extends the premise of *Animadversions* that truth requires no adornment. The 'dust and pudder' of insubstantial prelatical antiquity mask its corruption with barbaric latinizing and 'finicall goosery' to encourage 'Scholastick foppery' and 'itching pedantry.' Milton contrasts this view of narrow, constricting traditionalism with his own understanding of a vibrant style. Although he is once again not above Marprelate's tactic of ridiculing his opponent as a 'hip-shot *Grammarian*' and as a tormentor of semicolons, he mixes his criticism of flaccid syntax and dull expression with a technical, stylistic vocabulary. By calling attention to an atticism he has just written or to the antistrophon of his adversary, Milton consciously demonstrates his mastery of classical rhetoric. His discourse on the proper etymology of satire and his renewed attack on the frivolity of Hall's *Mundus Alter & Idem* further suggest great sensitivity to formal demands. When challenged to defend his satiric manner, it has already been seen, Milton marshals authorities from both classical and religious traditions in a learned defence that reveals a strict sense of decorum.

Milton invokes the principle of decorum in *An Apology* and berates the confutant for his impropriety in the belief that decorum and merit are inextricably one. When he laughs at the confutant's 'language of stall epistle non sense' and calls him a sonneteer, or chides him about toothless satires, Milton ridicules the discrepancies in his opponent's literary values.

Just as surely as a 'sucking Satir' contradicts true satire, the nature of Hall and Anglicanism, he implies, renders attempts to praise them no better than a patently insincere epistle or sonnet. Milton also has no compunctions about ridiculing the remonstrant and the confutant, for he believes no other course would suit the degree of their folly. Inherently his satiric attack maintains the unquestioned assumption that the conflict he is engaged in polarizes good and evil. Although prelacy may hide its decadence behind obscuring tradition and surface decency, the subversion of Christianity must be apparent to anyone who would see. Endowed with the sight of divine inspiration and dedicated to truth, Milton claims the prerogative of forthright speech which was given to the prophets he admires. Anything less than a vigorous enlightenment would compromise truth.

An Apology personifies the inseparable union of truth and eloquence in the prose prophet John Milton and complements the more impersonal tenor of Animadversions. The ethical and rhetorical proofs that justify a harsh, unrelenting style are familiar to the seventeenth-century understanding of zeal, and some would reappear when events forced other pamphleteers to realize that 'presbetry is but prelacy writ large.' Milton's achievement, however, lies in his ability to develop the passionate commitment seen in Marprelate's final tracts into a sustained vision of religious ridicule. The indignation that offended the confutant, and still dismays some who would rather remember only the great poetic accomplishments, soars above the crude outbursts of Bastwick and unremitting vituperation of Thomas Edwards. Milton understood that zeal, etymologically linked in the seventeenth century with the hissing of coals, was commonly described as the extreme heat of the affections, but he also knew that the fire 'wrought in the heart of man by the holy Ghost'[48] both consumes and creates. The zealous indignation burning in Animadversions and An Apology tempers scornful laughter, fervent prophecy, and intimate disclosure into an impressively wrought whole, resplendent with patterns of imagery which oppose the decadence of prelacy with the renewal of Puritanism and juxtapose the false prophecy of the deceptive divine and the true prophecy of the militant satirist. True to their spirit, the satires mix the sublime and the ridiculous without compromising their fidelity to aesthetic and religious values.

Only recently has this accomplishment been appreciated.[49] The 'diverse learned and judicious men' who, Milton assures his readers, 'testified their daily approval' did not publicly record their reactions to the antiprelatical tracts;[50] and the anonymous supporter of Bishop Hall alone voiced serious disapproval. Later, after the epochal moment had been lost and England had restored its former polity, Milton was openly derided for his involvement in the Smectymnuan controversy. Englishmen anxious to reassert the supremacy of Anglicanism and fearful of future upheaval found little sympathy for any expression associated with enthusiasm and opposed to reason. In a reactionary atmosphere that only reluctantly forgave Milton's involvement in the revolution the zealous vision of the tracts was discredited. Often the criticism is no more than blindly partisan emotion, as in the instances of several detractors who ironically linked the tracts and their author with Andrew Marvell's *The Rehearsal Transpros'd*.[51] At best they saw in the satires of both authors a common departure from the expectations of animadversion and a vision dependent upon literal-minded decorum. None of them understood or appreciated Milton's incorporation of classical and religious satiric precedents into the impressive figure of the prose prophet. Nor did they recognize the integral role the drama of character or personation plays in the tracts' conception of decorous jest. They could not or would not consider the remarkable artistic integrity with which immediate issues of passionate confrontation are transformed into memorable satires, because perhaps in part they failed to see many of the same achievements in *The Rehearsal Transpros'd*, a satire whose distinctive development of character and mode embodies a sense of manners appropriate to the Restoration temperament.

5

The Rehearsal Transpros'd

REFLECTING ON THE TURBULENT ERA that failed to fulfil the promise envisioned in Milton's tracts, Andrew Marvell observes: 'I think the Cause was too good to have been fought for. Men ought to have trusted God; they ought and might have trusted the King with that whole matter.'[1] This famous and perplexing opinion carries the assurance of time. 'Even as his present Majesties happy Restauration did it self,' Marvell retrospectively views the course of history, 'so all things else happen in their best and proper time, without any need of our officiousness' (p 135). But when the design of providence and the lessons of time are ignored, as they appeared to be in a new ecclesiastical attempt to dictate royal policy, patriotic and humanitarian men cannot remain passive. Faced with a decision comparable to those analysed in 'An Horatian Ode' and 'Upon Appleton House,' Marvell yielded with ostensible reluctance to the forces of necessity that 'should tempt me from that modest retiredness to which I had all my life time hitherto been addicted' (p 169). The publication of *The Rehearsal Transpros'd* in 1672 and the appearance of the second part in the next year represent Marvell's first involvement in polemic prose. Likened by contemporaries to both Marprelate's tracts and Milton's antiprelatical writings, *The Rehearsal Transpros'd* immediately captured the attention and admiration of an age that consciously valued wit.[2] Today Marvell's poetry overshadows his prose, but the two-part prose work remains a complex, imaginative illustration of the sophisticated, even whimsical laughter that characterizes a serious satire.

The object of ridicule is Samuel Parker, an energetic and rising young minister Marvell had met earlier at John Milton's London residence. Parker, originally a staunch Presbyterian, joined the Church of England shortly after Charles II ascended the throne; soon he began to advocate publicly that all Englishmen follow his example. Expanding a position moderately expressed in 1666 in *A Free and Impartial Censvre of the Platonick Philosophie*, Parker three years later forcefully proposed an Erastian absolutism in *A Discourse of Ecclesiastical Politie*. Encouraged by Simon Patrick, whose dialogues between a Conformist and a Nonconformist were attracting wide attention, Parker advances the thesis that it is 'absolutely necessary to the Peace and Government of the World, that the Supreme Magistrate of every Common-wealth should be vested with a Power to govern and conduct the Consciences of Subjects in Affairs of Religion.'[3] When the Nonconformists led by John Owen tried to refute the arguments for religious conformity, he retaliated with his 800-page *A Defence and Continuation of the Ecclesiastical Politie* (1671), which was followed in 1672 with a briefer but more virulent attack prefaced to an edition of Bishop Bramhall's *Vindication*. Consistently and rather repetitiously the tracts pursue the same arguments with an increasingly extreme ideological obsession. In fact the vigour and the fervour with which Parker espouses Anglicanism and attacks all nonconformity caused doubt about his real motives; Marvell, among others, shared the widespread belief that Parker was an opportunistic turncoat.[4] Whether personal animus or private ambition motivated his pronouncements on ecclesiastical polity, their extremism is remarkable even in the Restoration atmosphere of growing conservatism. Writers unsympathetic to Parker's Hobbesian position quickly decried his intolerance, and, according to a contemporary account, 'As to the *Church of England* few of them approved the Style ... and fewer his *Doctrines*: He was in the *Pulpit* declaimed against as the *young Leviathan*.'[5] It is Parker's uncompromising absolutism which determines Marvell's satiric strategy in *The Rehearsal Transpros'd*.

Marvell ignores the philosophical validity of Parker's proposal for ecclesiastical polity and directs his attention to a contradiction in the arguments for absolute religious conformity. Throughout his lengthy tracts Parker associates Nonconformists with 'the Genius of Enthusiasme or opinionative Zeal' and derides their ardour. All excess is personally abhorrent, but instances of zeal in particular provoke in him a fearful hatred of disruption and a conservative rage for order. In his opinion, 'Zeal is a fire in the Soul, which unless qualified and slaked by meekness and a calmnature, doth not only prey upon the mind, and devour its intellectual Powers, and enflame all the Passions, but its rage breaks forth, and sets whole States and Kingdoms into a combustion, and reduces the whole World to Ashes.'[6] Certain that the magnitude of this threat warrants the sternest measures, Parker argues that zealots should be liable to the 'Correction of the Publick Rods.' He makes only one exception: using the precedent of Christ's attitude towards the buyers and sellers in the temple, Parker maintains there is 'one single Instance, in which Zeal, or a high Indignation is just and warrantable; and that is when it vents it self against the Arrogance of haughty, peevish, and sullen Religionists, that under higher pretences to Godliness supplant all Principles of Civility and good Nature.'[7] The distinction is crucial, for it justifies the manner in which the tracts are written. Believing that 'nothing but Zeal can counter Zeal,' Parker argues at great length that harsh ridicule is both necessary and 'so farr from being a criminal Passion, that 'tis a zeal of Meekness and Charity.' Ultimately he asserts in his 'Preface' to Bishop Bramhall's *Vindication*:

No Argument in so palpable a Cause can be duly urged to its proper Head, without some Satyr and Invective; so far is it from being any excess of temper, that 'tis downright Dulness and want of Wit, not to expose their Persons whilst we confute their Principles: for how is it to be avoided, but that such Men must appear contemptible to all Mankind, that have so little Wit to believe, or so much Confidence to maintain such monstrous and thick Absurdities? ... It is not only fit, but necessary to take down such an aspiring Mind from its heighth and loftiness, to take off all his demure and hypocritical Disguises, and to shew him to the deluded People in his own Colours; and if it be possible to disabuse them, by letting them see that the only thing that lies at the bottom of all his *Tumultuatingness* of Spirit, is Pride and Ambition.[8]

The concern with affectation and hypocrisy also prompted Simon Patrick to contend: 'I do not make my self merry with any mens Sins: but at their little foolish Affectations, how can one chuse but smile';[9] though he and the other Restoration divines who oppose their reason and judgment against the Nonconformists' imagination and senses are closer to the moderate position of Isaac Barrow than to the sweeping licence of Samuel Parker. Because Parker is certain that he represents the truth, that his intentions are perfectly clear, and that his criticisms 'proceed not from Passion or Revenge, but from an upright and composed Mind, that upon mature Judgment chuses this way of procedure as most proper and rational,'[10] he has no qualms about aggressively belittling character in increasingly laboured and needless assaults. He fails to consider that his own form of zeal could be confused with the object of his attack, the 'Non-sence and Enthusiasm' that, uncontained, 'run stark mad with zeal and reformation.' Marvell, however, does not.

Reacting specifically to what he sees as Parker's arrogant and presumptuous witlessness, Marvell focuses the first part of *The Rehearsal Transpros'd* on this offensive manner. Parker later rightly complains in his *Reproof* that his 'Grand Thesis' has been ignored, but he never does receive an explicit statement of Marvell's attitude towards a desirable ecclesiastical polity. Although the second part of the satire admits that the ruler 'hath some Power, but not all Power in matters of Religion' (p 193), the immediate concerns of compassion and expediency determine Marvell's initial reaction. Like Samuel Rolle, who undertook the refutation of Simon Patrick in *A Sober Answer To the Friendly Debate*, Marvell attacks scorn and ridicule as anachronistic and incongruous behaviour in an Anglican divine. Without specifically using Rolle's objection that zealous reviling by embattled men of passion should not be confused with the present scornful attacks by men '*at ease* ... of those that did never *persecute* you,'[11] the first part of *The Rehearsal Transpros'd* exposes Parker's malicious, self-serving arrogance. Marvell sidesteps the question of the lawfulness of zeal with the declaration that he could 'overload' Parker with authorities and examples disproving its desirability; he stresses instead the harm that needless railing engenders. He agrees with John Owen and other temperate Restoration writers that 'mutual forbearance to each other'[12] offers the best assurance of public tranquillity. After all that the Nonconformists have endured and suffered, the satire urges that they be extended the compassionate toleration of simple decency and Christian charity. Further intemperate and vitriolic railing such as Parker advocates only undermines the Anglican cause it allegedly advances and incites renewed danger of persecution and bloodshed.

At greater length in the beginning of the second part Marvell stresses the social responsibility violated by Parker's invective. Writers, he observes, respond to several primary motivations: they can follow their ambition to strive for fame, or they can follow charity, the only other motive for writing, to delight and to profit mankind. If an author accepts his awesome responsibilities, ' 'tis necessary that he be copious in matter, solid in reason, methodical in the order of his work; and that the subject be well chosen, the season well fix'd, and, to be short, that his whole production be matur'd to see the light by a just course of time, and judicious deliberation' (p 160). This sense of decorum respects a fundamental connection between the inviolability of individual reputation and the stability of society. In Marvell's view a human desire to protect one's self-image first motivated man to seek the ordering force of government, and any civil institution that cannot in turn ensure security abrogates its rationale for existence. Rather than risk disturbing this order, ' 'tis better that evil men should be left in an undisturbed possession of their repute, how unjustly soever they may have acquired it, then that the Exchange and Credit of mankind should be universally shaken, wherein the best too will suffer and be involved' (p 161). The clergy particularly warrant what Marvell considers discretion, decency, and conscience, because of all men they have in their care an even more basic moral order. 'Being Men dedicate by their Vocation to teach what is Truth, what Falshood, to deter men from vice, and lead them unto all virtue; 'tis expected from them, and with good reason, that they should define their opinion by their manners. And therefore men ought to be chary of aspersing them on either account, but even reflect upon their failings with some reverence' (pp 162–3).

The conclusion agrees in principle with the Restoration attitude seen in Barrow, Falkner, and Rapin; but in practice Marvell's position confirms a belief fundamental to Marprelate and Milton. Although Marvell expresses greater toleration for the clergy's failure to fulfil their teachings, he too refuses to condone ministers who have forgotten their humanity, their gospel, and 'that Humility, that Meekness, that strictness of Manners and Conversation, which is the true way of gaining Reputation and Authority to the Clergy; much less can they content themselves with the ordinary and comfortable provision that is made for the Ministry: But, having wholly calculated themselves for Preferment, and Grandeur, know or practise no other means to make themselves venerable but by Ceremony and Severity' (p 107). The criticism contains none of the revolutionary zeal of the earlier satirists, yet the passage reflects the values of Marprelate and Milton. Each writer understands that the close relationship between the precepts and the manner of the clergy cannot tolerate pretence or empty office. They agree with Milton that true ministerial calling depends upon inner worth rather than 'outward signe or symbol.' Thus, despite repeated assurances that he most reluctantly has undertaken his course, that he would rather rely solely on reason, and that he will in any case scrupulously limit the extent of his laughter, Marvell follows the example of the earlier satirists and promises to pursue Parker 'till I have laid hand on him, and deliver'd him bound either to Reason or Laughter, to Justice or Pity. If at any turn he gives me the least opportunity to be serious I shall gladly take it: but where he prevaricates or is scurrilous (and where is he not?) I shall treat him betwixt Jest and Earnest' (p 187). The appropriateness of a duality also characterized as 'merry and angry' depends upon an expediency and decorum consistent with Marprelate's and Milton's apologies. In Marvell's opinion an attack that subjects even a man of the clergy to ridicule can be 'not only excusable but necessary' when a minister publicly abuses his trust. Clergymen such as Parker who betray their ideals in the forum of publication place themselves beyond private admonishment and prudent silence. 'In this Case it is that I think a Clergy-man is laid open to the Pen of any one that knows how to manage it; and that every person who has either Wit, Learning or Sobriety is licensed, if debauch'd to curb him, if erroneous to catechize him, and if foul-mouth'd and biting, to muzzle him' (p 164).[13]

The decision to combine ridicule and serious animadversion develops out of traditional rhetoric the ironic vindication pursued by Marprelate and Milton. The appeal to wit and humanitarianism would have impact particularly in a Restoration court attracted to fashionable raillery and drollery; Marvell's paraphrase of the rhetorical commonplace, however, contains a significant re-emphasis. The metaphorical language seems to echo Cicero's *De oratore*: 'That which is solid and sharp, being imp'd by something more light and airy, may carry further and pierce deeper, and therefore I shall look to it as well as I can, that mine Arrows be well pointed, and of mine own whetting; but for the Feathers, I must borrow them out of his Wing' (p 187).[14] The distinction upholds Marvell's pose of the reluctant wit while playing on the meaning of 'light and airy'; it also suggests with an ironic half-seriousness that laughter at Parker's sweeping proposals for ecclesiastical polity is inevitable. The ideas are laughable, but in another sense they also thrive on laughter. Parker does, in fact, promise in the preface to *A Discourse of Ecclesiastical Politie* to use his own 'comical humour and pleasantness,' and in addition to his defence of zealous ridicule he also appends to *A Defence and Continuation of the Ecclesiastical Politie* a long letter from Simon Patrick supporting with conventional arguments the use of laughter in religious disputation.[15] In the body of this tract he further defends Patrick's method against the criticism levelled by John Owen that laughter may weaken or dispel reason. Unable to dismiss satisfactorily Owen's citation of the harm caused by Aristophanes' ridicule of Socrates, Parker clings to his belief that falseness should be made to appear ridiculous: 'if Men Publish Sense, all the World can never make them ridiculous; if Non-sense, they make themselves so; ... if they are exposed in a Fools Coat, 'tis with one of their own making.'[16] With poetic justice Marvell therefore shifts the onus for wit onto his opponent. The laughter in *The Rehearsal Transpros'd* remains premised upon an unexpected extension of decorum in the manner of Marprelate and Milton: 'For, as I am obliged to ask pardon if I speak of serious things ridiculously; so I must now beg excuse if I should hap to discourse of ridiculous things seriously. But I shall, so far as possible, observe *decorum*, and, whatever I talk of, not commit such an Absurdity, as to be grave with a Buffoon' (p 49).

The satiric plan employs the literal-minded decorum central to the earlier satirists. Parker complains in his answer to the first part of *The Rehearsal Transpros'd* that Marvell's decision 'to treat me according to *Decorum*, i.e. like a Buffoon' resembles 'the very same Request word for word that Martyn-Mar-Prelate has often put up to his Readers to be allowed the same freedom with his *Nuncka John* the Arch-Bishop of Canterbury.'[17] But the new version of *decorum personæ* – which strikes Parker as the ridiculous, libellous play of a monkey – does not develop the dramatic mimesis of the Marprelate tracts in the same way. While both satirists claim the prerogative of laughter from the example of their opponents, Marvell's imitation in *The Rehearsal Transpros'd* neither attempts Marprelate's sustained parody nor pretends that the persona matches the character of the adversary. Marvell's calculated foolery develops elements of Marprelate's playfulness with the licence Milton derives from the proverbial wisdom that a fool should be answered accordingly. Because Parker's manner and propositions are variously ridiculous, they warrant and even supply a suitable ridicule which never obscures Marvell's own character. Without succumbing to the antics of Marprelate's clowning or 'losing' himself in his fiction, the speaker in Marvell's satire consciously and directly embodies the manner appropriate to acceptable laughter. He agrees with John Humfrey that Parker's conduct poses 'a villainy to Religion, an indignity to humane nature, [and] a breaking the hedge of what is Sacred, laying open the inclosures of all modesty and civility';[18] and like Milton, he proposes to educate his adversary in the proper conduct of religious ridicule. While he keeps the tension between jest and earnest always in perspective, his metaphorical pretence to an absolute distinction between solid sharpness and airy lightness suits a manner based upon the Christian humanism of Marprelate and Milton. The expression, however, remains distinctly his own urbane humour.

Its mode depends upon a decorous distortion of animadversion. Both its critics and its admirers sense but do not fully recognize the transformation when they agree that the immediate popularity of *The Rehearsal Transpros'd* stems from Marvell's cleverness at 'Raillery à la mode.' As an unknown contemporary notes in a tract with this title, Marvell's 'extraordinary fancy' and 'Wiredrawing Wit' were widely appreciated among the devotees of the '*New Canting Drolling Way*.'[19] Although Samuel Parker does not object to a similar quality in Simon Patrick, he loudly protests that Marvell sacrifices all seriousness 'to picqueer at single words in Introductions and Transitions, and animadvert upon them with the Similitude, the Aphorism, the Rithm, the Story, and the Parenthesis.'[20] Marvell's humour still impresses modern scholars as unmethodical, *ad hoc* wit[21] that ranges widely in its allusiveness and strains conventional notions of relevance. Parker's continual reference to John Owen only by his initials, for example, occasions whimsical punning about secret motives behind the use of J.O., while his geographical error in the location of Geneva leads to a lengthy explanation characterized by anagrams, allegories, and banter. In obscuring the substance of Parker's main points Marvell refuses to be drawn into remote theorizing, where Parker's temperament and philosophy hold the advantage; instead he appears content to carp at the peripheral. But the fanciful, almost burlesque wit of deflation, not unlike the 'nimble sagacity of apprehension, a special felicity of invention, a vivacity of spirit and reach of wit' valued by Isaac Barrow and his contemporaries, is only part of Marvell's intention. More extensively than either Marprelate or Milton, Marvell develops or 'personates' the character of his adversary: 'it being so necessary to represent him in his own likeness that it may appear what he is to others, and to himself, if possibly he might at last correct his indecencies' (p 185).

The nature of the joke becomes clear in the satire's first part. Conforming to the subtitle's promise to present *Animadversions Upon a late Book, Intituled, A Preface Shewing What Grounds there are of Fears and Jealousies of Popery*, Marvell takes his structure from Parker's 'Preface' to Bramhall's *Vindication*. A loosely sustained metaphor of the journey defines his involvement in an endless maze and his walk in a Bedlamite garden. The pursuit along the trail of the prolix writer follows the basic outline of his 'Preface' with occasional digressions into random wandering, though the animadverter's recourse to quotation and refutation provides obvious guidance. Six essential arguments from Parker's earlier works summarized in 'several Aphorisms or Hypotheses' and an extended reproduction of an opposite and admired view from John Hales's *A Tract Concerning Schisme* add substantially to the specific issues; however the effect is not that of traditional polemic. Although Marvell seriously considers the baselessness of Parker's fears and the dangerous impracticality of his proposals, he quotes Parker's major points without rebuttal. His primary focus, seen in the consuming interest in Parker's motives for undertaking the tracts, is the character of the upstart divine. Just as Milton understood that integrity must finally vindicate his use of zealous ridicule,

Marvell realizes that Parker's right to appropriate zeal depends upon his character. Offended by Parker's arrogant maliciousness and certain that he presents a cure far more deadly than the disease, Marvell follows his opponent's lead and submits him to an anatomy of 'Pride and Ambition.' Parker, a disputant so concerned with exposing the character of Nonconformist zealots, is beaten at his own game when *The Rehearsal Transpros'd* amusingly redefines him as an epitome of all that his writings seem to oppose. Once the metamorphosis is complete Marvell can in the final pages quote with impunity the warning from Francis Bacon familiar to both the Marprelate and Smectymnuan controversies: 'But to leave all reverence and religious compassion toward evils, or indignation towards faults, and to turn Religion into a Comedy or Satyre, to search and rip up wounds with a laughing Countenance, to intermix Scripture and Scurrility sometimes in one Sentence is a thing far from the devout reverence of a Christian, and scant beseeming the honest regard of a sober man' (p 324).

The characterization stems essentially from the personality Parker reveals in his tracts. In the opening page of *A Discourse of Ecclesiastical Politie* its author purports to be a model of judicious decorum. Pretentiously he proclaims: 'But I will assure thee, the Author is a Person of such a tame and softly humour, and so cold a Complexion, that he thinks himself scarce capable of hot and passionate Impressions.'[22] The ingenuousness is designed to reinforce the justice of his observations and to dramatize the gulf between his own moderation and the fanaticism of the Nonconformists, but the conviction in Parker's tone suggests that his statements are more than simply rhetorical strategy. In a tract written several years earlier the same man had declared he was 'too simple or too serious to be cajol'd with the frenzies of a bold and ungovern'd Imagination'; he also confesses, 'I am neither valiant nor miserable, and am as yet in my green and unexperienced years, and have tasted less of sensual delights, then (I believe) any one plac'd in the same capacities and circumstances with my self (for I have hitherto scarce employ'd any of my senses, but that of seeing).'[23] Again the phrasing, the exaggeration, and the personal nature of the revelations have an embarrassing frankness which suggests their author's earnestness. Biographical information also supports this interpretation, for even biased contemporaries admit that the young Parker was a serious-minded man 'with a high profession of piety.'[24] Statements of a similar kind in the other tracts reveal a certitude which comes close to disagreeable self-congratulation. Even in his earlier and more moderate pronouncements Parker simply takes himself too seriously: the man 'hardned enough to be proof against the poison of Asps, the Stings of

Vipers, and the Tongues of _____'25 is incapable of any laughter outside his own conception of heavy-handed, scornful ridicule.

The opening pages of *The Rehearsal Transpros'd* capitalize on this inability to cope with either casualness or a less serious laughter and initiate a jestful inversion of character. In a manner reminiscent of Milton's *Animadversions* Marvell isolates a statement from Parker's copious writings and reinterprets it as an index to his personality. The quotation is the concluding sentence to the preface of *A Defence and Continuation of the Ecclesiastical Politie*: 'But to conclude, if this be the Penance I must undergo for the wantonness of my Pen, to answer the impertinent and slender Exceptions of every peevish, and disingenuous Caviller; Reader, I am reformed from my incontinency of scribbling, and do here heartily bid thee an eternal Farewell.'26 In context the exaggerated conclusion is a rhetorical statement designed to emphasize the onerous burden of contending with disputants beneath answer, but the tone and wording are quite differently interpreted in *The Rehearsal Transpros'd*. Marvell accepts the statement at face value and ironically suggests that the writing of still another attack in the 'Preface' is an apparent contradiction. Like the Nonconformists whom he accuses of hypocritical exaggeration, Parker does not mean what he says, and 'his Modesty is all impudent and counterfeit: Or, if he will acknowledge it, why then he had been before, and did still remain upon Record, the same lewd, wanton and incontinent Scribler' (p 3). Rather than decide which is more probable, the ensuing satire accepts both. Wantonness and incontinency, characteristics far from the image Parker tries to establish, are unexpectedly seized upon as common denominators in this new characterization of Parker as a prolific pamphleteer indifferent to either 'Truth or Eternity.'

Beginning innocuously, Marvell turns to the tract in question, the 'Preface' to Bishop Bramhall's *Vindication*, and starts to examine the 'Story' behind its publication. Again he chooses part of the argument – Parker's explanation that a bookseller in possession of Bramhall's work 'was very solicitous to have it set off with some Preface' – and infers a very different motivation. Insinuating that the 'young Priest' would compromise even the highest principles for the opportunity to promote himself, Marvell adds: 'And yet our Author is very maidenly, and condescends to his Bookseller not without some reluctance, as being, forsooth, first of all *none of the most zealous Patrons of the Press*' (p 4). Without pursuing the contradiction in this false modesty the satire shifts to droll commiseration about the difficulties encountered in publication; the brief characterization, however, is significant. The double meaning of 'maidenly' – a play on the word 'solicitous' and an allusion to Parker's character – tacitly recalls the ethos of the previous tracts and interjects a sexual overtone. After his aside on the perils of publication, which obliquely comments on Parker's official role as licenser for theological publications, Marvell returns to this point and continues: 'But, next of all, our Author, beside his aversion from the Press, alledges, that *he is as much concerned as* De-Wit, *or any of the High and Mighty Burgomasters, in matters of a closer and more comfortable importance to himself and his own Affairs*' (p 5). While Parker does not explain what 'comfortable importance' commands his present attention,[27] Marvell volunteers three possibilities. He rejects, however, concerns about salvation and promotion, for Parker is certain of the one and has taken steps through his writing to assure the other, and takes up the third suggestion, a woman. Marvell argues that this must be the real explanation and 'a sufficient excuse from writing of Prefaces, and against the importunity of the Book-seller. 'Twas fit that all business should have given place to the work of Propagation. Nor was there any thing that could more closely import him, than that the Race and Family of the Railers should be perpetuated among Mankind' (p 6). Like the others, this conjecture underlines the conceit which, Marvell then concludes, is responsible for the courteous 'Civility' Parker ultimately displays towards his bookseller's importunities. Still another dimension of character emerges, however, in Parker's capitulation of the bookseller: 'And so, not being able to shake him off, *this*, he saith, *hath brought forth this Preface, such an one as it is; for how it will prove, he himself neither is, nor (till 'tis too late) ever shall be a competent Judge, in that it must be ravish'd out of his hands before his thoughts can possibly be cool enough to review or correct the Indecencies either of its stile or contrivance*' (p 6). As part of the opening remarks Parker's exaggerated apology for any errors in the text is not particularly unusual. It seems to Marvell, however, more '*extempore*' than any Nonconformist divine might attempt; in an extrapolation that extends the sexual satire he puns: 'Some Man that had less right to be fastidious and confident, would, before he exposed himself in publick, both have cool'd his Thoughts, and corrected his Indecencies: or would have considered whether it were necessary or wholsom that he should write at all ... But there was no holding him. Thus it must be, and no better, when a man's Phancy is up, and his Breeches are down; when the Mind and the Body make contrary Assignations, and he hath both a Bookseller at once and a Mistris to satisfie: Like *Archimedes*, into the Street he runs out naked with his Invention' (p 7). Hardly a staid image, this undignified picture of Parker completes the characterization developed throughout both parts of *The Rehearsal Transpros'd*. Undermining the pompousness and moral authority of this 'wanton and incontinent Scribler,' Marvell fancifully suggests that beneath Parker's exaggerated assumption of righteousness and civility lurks the nature of an enthusiast.

Pretending that 'Never Man certainly was so unacquainted with himself,' the hyperbole of *The Rehearsal Transpros'd* introduces Parker to his real self: the next paragraph promptly announces 'This is *Bayes* the Second.' Marvell thus allies his attack on Parker with *The Rehearsal*, a newly published play acclaimed among the wits of town and court,[28] and exploits an unmistakable satiric counterpart in the play's portrayal of the principal creator of heroic drama, John Dryden. Caricatured in the person of Bayes, Dryden is transformed by the Duke of Buckingham and his associates into a fanciful fool and an ambitious hack addicted to nonsensical outbursts of high-flown rhetoric. He becomes the archetypal poetaster unconcerned with reason, wit, or pleasure; his ideal of art, he proudly boasts, is even more important than money: 'Now, I gad, when I write, if it be not just as it should be, in every circumstance, to every particular, I gad, I am not able to endure it, I am not my self, I'm out of my wits, and all that, I'm the strangest person in the whole world. For what care I for my money? I gad, I write for Fame and Reputation.'[29] As Johnson and Smith realize when they are privileged to view a rehearsal of his latest play, the vain Bayes has completely isolated himself and his art from the world of reality. Blinded by his own pride and ambition, he is certain that his method alone constitutes true drama. The heroic plays he creates are therefore his inspiration, and he proclaims: 'I despise your *Johnson*, and *Beaumont*, that borrow'd all they writ from Nature: I am for fetching it purely out of my own fancie, I.'[30] The result is a ludicrously absurd world where bombastic puppets worry about trivia and all important issues are translated into the author's ruling monomania that values the 'one quality of singly beating of whole Armies, above all your moral vertues put together, I gad.'[31] A similar madness, *The Rehearsal Transpros'd* proceeds to demonstrate, motivates the outpourings of Samuel Parker.

Once more Marvell's wit sees another side of Parker's admission that 'he knows not which way his Mind will work,' and he compares Parker in turn to Bayes, his actors, and the principal character Prince Volscius. The introduction of *The Rehearsal* obscures the distinction between a serious religious work and a frivolous play within a play to provide a metaphor for the satire's fundamental metamorphosis. Marvell's fusion of contemporary drama and animadversion capitalizes on the resemblance between Parker's arguments for ecclesiastical polity and their *alter ego*, the popular farce ridiculing heroic drama. The transformation enables Marvell to summarize and dismiss cavalierly Parker's major points as plays; his individual tracts are also suitably characterized. The 'Preface,' for instance, is compared with the prologue of the drama satirized in *The Rehearsal*, and Marvell is quick to point out that the resemblance is such that 'indeed like *Bayes* his prologue, that would have serv'd as well for an Epilogue, I do not see but the Preface might have past as wel for a Postscript, or the Headstal for a Crooper ... For, as they are coupled together, to say the truth, 'tis not discernable, as in some Animals, whether their motion begin at the head or the tail; whether the Author made his Preface for Bishop *Bramhal's dear sake*, or whether he published the Bishop's Treatise for sake of his *own dear Preface*' (p 9). Similar analogies in both parts of the work offer a form of continuity and a semblance of unity; but Marvell is not consistent in his equation of Parker's polemics and the farcical drama, nor does he really superimpose on them the structure of *The Rehearsal*. The relationship, for the most part, functions as allusion rather than illusion; its nexus remains essentially that of character.

The redefinition of character presupposes the principle of decorum at work in the earlier satires of Marprelate and Milton. According to Marvell, the unexpected appellations of 'the second Bayes,' 'Necessity Bayes,' or simply 'Mr. Bayes' are given to the author of the anonymously published works because Parker too appears 'a lover of Elegancy of Stile' enamored with his own writing, and because both authors reveal a similar disposition 'in their expressions, in their humour, in their contempt and quarrelling of all others, though of their own Profession' (p 9). To the charges of arrogant incivility Marvell then adds: 'And, lastly, because both their Talents do peculiarly lie in exposing and personating the Nonconformists' (pp 9–10). Later the second part of *The Rehearsal Transpros'd* objects to the absence of 'good manners' in the methods Parker approves and contends, 'when *Ecclesiastical Politie* march'd *Incognito*, and Theology went on mumming, it was no less allowable for any one to use the license of Mascarade to show him, and the rest of 'm the consequence of such practice' (p 166). While Parker's tracts rely neither upon drama nor even a loosely conceived comedy, his specific approval of the satiric dialogue Simon Patrick employs and his own recourse to ridicule render him vulnerable to the same kind of accusation Marprelate levelled against Bridges almost a century earlier. Marvell will suit the occasion with appropriately theatrical style, and he too will, in the manner of Marprelate and Milton, personate his adversary; in the process, he adds, the audience will see how any popular farce can be used for merriment without succumbing to Parker's profane wit. Like Milton, he proposes to educate his adversary in the proper development of religious ridicule.

Parker represents in this metamorphosis into Bayes all that most disturbs Marvell. Early in his first important pronouncement on religious conformity, *A Discourse of Ecclesiastical Politie*, Parker singles out the would-be wits of the town and brands them as 'wild and hare-brained' irreligious zealots. Even more virulently than Buckingham, Parker expresses the Restoration fear of atheistic wits seen in Isaac Barrow's sermon and particularly in Joseph Glanvill's warnings. They appear to him 'A sort of Creatures that study nothing but Sloth and Idlenes, that design nothing but Folly and Extravagance, that aspire to no higher Accomplishments than fine Phrases, terse Oaths, and gay Plumes, that pretend to no other stock of Learning, but a few shavings of Wit gather'd out of Plays and Comedies; and these they abuse too, and labour to pervert their chaste Expressions to Obscene and irreligious purposes; and *Johnson* and *Fletcher* are prophaned, as well as the Holy Scriptures.'[32] These 'Proud' and 'Ambitious' fools feed on the errors of fashionable philosophies and parade a wisdom 'pick'd up at Plays, out of the stiff Disputes of *Love and Honour*.'[33] But unlike the innocuous Bayes, they display a sensual appetite and a blasphemous 'aftergame of their Debauchery' that jests with the sacred. When these wits reappear at the conclusion of the 'Preface' Parker reduces the issue of ecclesiastical polity to a choice between loyalty or faction and laments that only the established church offers sanctuary for the 'old Probity and Integrity of our Nation' against the assaults of its twin enemies, the 'Fanatick Rage' of the Nonconformists and the 'base-natured Atheism' of the stylish wits.[34] Should these zealots unite, he warns, the consequences for England would be dire. The cataclysm does not occur, however, when the two forms of zeal unexpectedly and ironically meet in Marvell's fictitious transformation of the ecclesiastical legislator.

The accusation of enthusiasm implicit in Marvell's characterization of Parker as Bayes becomes explicit when the prefatory comments and a brief consideration of Bishop Bramhall's basic thesis give way to a burlesque biography of the career leading to the publication of the 'Preface.' The portrait of 'over-weening Presumption and preposterous Ambition' which superficially traces Parker's actual career is based on the character of the typical Nonconformist preacher Parker himself describes at length in *A Defence and Continuation of the Ecclesiastical Politie*. Unusually severe, Parker's description goes much further than an emphasis on pride and fancy. The zealous minister he portrays is a mountebank who disguises his ignorance behind a facade of seriousness and a facility for canting. His empty speech and his sanctimoniousness often further more insidious ends. Besides seeking personal aggrandizement, the hypocritical Nonconformists win converts to a religion which is a 'vizor to maintain their pride, their peevishness and their wantonness.' Parker states that this is apparent in any number of instances, yet his sweeping condemnation ends evasively: 'How my Character suits with their Humour, I must leave to your own Experience and Observation; though I could give you a sufficient Catalogue.'[35] Marvell finds only one character who fits this catalogue, as is apparent in his delightfully absurd and witty caricature of Samuel Parker. An early education that only slightly expanded the aspiring minister's skill in rhetoric and greatly increased his giddiness and pride accounts for a vanity not unlike that found in the stereotype of the ignorant Nonconformist preacher. Parker's premature exposure to *Don Quixote* agitated 'a medley in his brain-pan,' and although he gains an advantageous polish by reading and seeing 'the Playes, with much care and more proficiency than most of the Auditory' (p 30), his fortunes are those of an aspiring Nonconformist. Like the zealot, Parker ingratiates himself with a wealthy family, becomes a nobleman's chaplain, and soon achieves great acclaim among the ignorant domestics. Spellbound by his demagoguery, 'They all listened to him as an Oracle: and they allow'd him by common consent, to have not only all the *Divinity*, but more wit too than all the rest of the family put together' (p 30). With tongue in cheek Marvell suggests that this great accomplishment further aggravates a melancholy fancy and pride, and soon a deep-seated sensuality emerges. Parker's success with women matches the fears expressed about the lascivious Nonconformist ministers, and 'The innocent Ladies found a strange unquietness in their minds, and could not distinguish whether it were Love or Devotion' (p 30). However, Parker's conceit is greater than his passion, and he is unable or indisposed to do little more than 'speculate his own Baby in their Eyes.' But initial success convinces him that the entire world can be his: with aspirations even more grandiose than those of the most deluded zealot he succumbs to unbounded fancy and begins his pompous pronouncements on ecclesiastical polity.

The mock biography of Parker demonstrates, in other words, a remarkable similarity to the pattern of enthusiasm developed ten years earlier in Henry More's *Enthusiasmus Triumphatus; Or, A Brief Discourse of the Nature, Causes, Kinds, and Cure of Enthusiasm.* Anglican rationalists, eager to revitalize the long confrontation with the Puritan sects, had already introduced More's analysis of religious enthusiasm into their satiric attacks,[36] and Samuel Parker in particular recognizes the value of bolstering tired clichés about Puritan hypocrisy with new emphasis on the delusion and madness inherent in zealous fanaticism. Although he never acknowledges More by name, in his analysis of enthusiasm's physiological, 'mechanical' nature in *A Defence and Continuation of the Ecclesiastical Politie* he admits that 'there are some Treatises that give a more exact and consistent Hypothesis of Enthusiasm than any *Des Cartes* has given of the natural Results of Matter and Motion.'[37] In transposing Parker's observations about zeal to the fictional survey of his life and qualifications, Marvell achieves a close parallel to More's influential portrait of enthusiasm.

This unconventional application of *Enthusiasmus Triumphatus* figures prominently in Marvell's account of the divine's mercurial rise from attaining additional livings and local fame to gaining public recognition. Never very far from total instability, the giddy young man is overwhelmed with his own success as a wit. 'This thing alone elevated him exceedingly in his own conceit, and raised his *Hypochondria* into the Region of the Brain: that his head swell'd like any Bladder with wind and vapour. But after he was stretch'd to such an height in his own fancy, that he could not look down from top to toe but his Eyes dazled at the Precipice of his Stature; there fell out, or in, another natural chance which push'd him headlong. For being of an amorous Complexion, and finding himself (as I told you) the *Cock-Divine* and the *Cock Wit* of the Family, he took the priviledge to walk among the Hens' (p 30). The vivid description of pride and the sexual slur, echoing Parker's own description of John Owen as 'the Cock of the Congregation,'[38] underscore the self-importance of the upstart divine in a manner that matches Henry More's diagnosis of the religious enthusiast:

The *Spirit* then that wings the *Enthusiast* in such a wonderful manner, is nothing else but that *Flatulency* which is in the *Melancholy* complexion, and rises out of the *Hypochondriacal* humour upon some occasional heat, as *Winde* out of an *Aeolipila* applied to the fire. Which fume mounting into the Head, being first actuated and spirited and somewhat refined by the warmth of the Heart, fills the Mind with variety of *Imaginations*, and so quickens and inlarges *Invention*, that it makes the *Enthusiast* to admiration *fluent* and *eloquent*, he being as it were drunk with new wine drawn from that Cellar of his own that lies in the lowest region of his Body, though he be not aware of it.[39]

Showing that mounting vapours do indeed have great powers, Marvell transports Parker to even further heights; 'and like the Bishop over *Maudlin Colledge* Altar, or like *Maudlin de la Croix*, he was seen in his

Prayers to be lifted up sometimes in the Air, and once particularly so high that he crack'd his Scul against the Chappel Ceiling' (p 31). Like a broken mirror, the fractured skull multiplies the vanity and imagination inherent in his vaporous, melancholy complexion; and Parker, following the pattern of More's enthusiast, is seized by an uncontrollable desire to express his newly acquired powers in a book about ecclesiastical polity. *Enthusiasmus Triumphatus* warns that in this state alteration of the 'Blood and Spirits' will magnify the imagination, but the enthusiastic minister is so engrossed in his writing 'that he sate up late at nights, and wanting sleep, and drinking sometimes Wine to animate his Fancy, it increased his Distemper' (p 31). The little understanding that remained quickly vanishes in his uncontainable joy at the book's reception among the gallants and its billing with the latest drama. To make matters worse, the newly famous zealot is hit with a 400-page book, dropped on his head by John Owen. 'And so in conclusion,' the biography ends, 'his Madness hath formed it self into a perfect *Lycanthropy*. He doth so verily believe himself to be a Wolf, that his speech is all turn'd into howling, yelling, and barking: and if there were any Sheep here, you should see him pull out their throats and suck the blood' (p 32). The transformation of Parker into a wolf collapses the figurative into the literal once more to dramatize his dangerous, predatory writing. Henry More observes that vapours rising into the brain, a primary cause of enthusiasm, stimulate the imagination to produce 'distempers of the Mind, whereby men imagine themselves to be *Wolves, Cats,* or *Doggs.*'[40]

Throughout the first part of *The Rehearsal Transpros'd* the parallel with the zealot, like the link with Bayes, stresses the 'Extravagance and Rapture' of an incurable enthusiast who believes that he alone is competent to legislate authority. At no time does the satire acknowledge Parker's self-description of sweet reasonableness and propriety; it insists that the author is deluded, deranged, and demented. Marvell refuses to see any virtue in either his method or his ecclesiastical policy and repeatedly contends: ' 'Tis just your way of writing all along in this matter. You bring nothing sound or solid. Only you think you have got the *Great Secret*, or the *Philosophers Stone* of Railing; and I believe it, you have so multiplied it in *Projection*: and as they into Gold, so you turn every thing you meet with into Railing' (pp 116–17). The fantasy world of Parker parallels the lunacy of Bayes: complex problems of church and state are reduced to a rigid battle line between Conformists and Nonconformists where, in place of pompous rant, pitched battles, and heroic Drawcansirs, Parker stridently urges relentless persecution to resolve the conflict he has worried into existence. This desire for a Hobbesian uniformity – expressed in an incessant concern with the 'Vulgar Rout,' 'Common Herd,' 'tyranny,' 'anarchy,' 'Spiritual Pride,' 'sullen Humour,' 'Duncery,' and 'Sectarian Madness' – conforms in its excessiveness to the pattern of religious enthusiasm described in *Enthusiasmus Triumphatus* as 'political enthusiasm.'

Such bloated and high-swoln *Enthusiasts*, that are so big in the conceit of their own inward worth, ... fancy themselves either *equal* or *superiour* to Christ; whom notwithstanding God has declared *Supreme Head* over Men and Angels. And yet they would disthrone him, and set up themselves, though they can shew no Title but an unsound kind of popular Eloquence, a Rhapsodie of slight and soft words, rowling and streaming Tautologies, which if they at any time bear any true sense with them, it is but what every ordinary Christian knew before; but what they oft insinuate by the bye, is abominably false, as sure as Christianity it self is true.[41]

Although this description was obviously never intended to be applied to an Anglican minister, *The Rehearsal Transpros'd* sees that it precisely recounts Parker's egotistical intolerance. The similarity is perhaps most apparent when Marvell comments on his opponent's fanatic Erastianism: 'I cannot but wonder, knowing how amibitious Mr. *Bayes* is of the power over words, and jealous of his own Prerogative of refining Language, how he came to be so liberal of it to the Prince: Why, the same thing that induced him to give the Prince a power antecedent and independent to *Christ*, and to establish what Religion he pleased, &c. Nothing but his spight against the Non-conformists' (p 104). The elaborateness with which Marvell taunts his adversary is a major source of the satiric ridicule in his analysis of Parker's writing.

Cast as another Bayes and typed as a deranged megalomaniac, Parker finds his ruling passion highlighted in a series of military allusions. Capitalizing on his adversary's penchant for martial terminology,[42] Marvell expands the traditional metaphor of verbal warfare. By substituting a word or recasting a phrase the satire redirects Parker's rhetorical thrusts to show how he charges his cannon, ranges his forces, and designs to blow up both the nation and his enemies. But the bursts of passionate railing are never assigned a dignity greater than burlesque seriousness. In emphasizing his ruling passion for pitched conflict, the first part of *The Rehearsal Transpros'd* likens Parker to a chimerical champion steeped in the lore of *Don Quixote* who enters the lists against imaginary enemies. His grandiose visions of conquest are in reality a tilting at windmills in a realm which, like the province of Bayes, is filled with absurd activity that appeals only to those who, lacking hobbyhorses, 'climb up first to get down one of the old Cuirasses, or an Habergeon that had been worn in the dayes of Queen *Elizabeth.*' The result is a frantic inanity: 'Great variety there was, and an heavy doo. Some clapp'd it on all rusty as it was, others fell of oyling and furbishing their armour: Some piss'd in their Barrels, others spit in their pans, to scowr them. Here you might see one put on his Helmet the wrong way: there one buckle on a Back in place of a Breast. Some by mistake catched up a Socinian or Arminian Argument, and some a Popish to fight a Papist. Here a Dwarf lost in the accoutrements of a Giant: there a *Don-Quixot* in an equipage of differing pieces, and of several Parishes. Never was there such Incongruity and Nonconformity in their furniture' (p 120). Unlike the imagery of warfare in Milton's tracts, which is an expression of serious moral battle, Marvell's descriptions caricature Parker's actions. He is, in the satire's judgment, a self-aggrandizing, pernicious man consumed with an insane, messianic mission; and his narcissism is more and more unmistakably that of a most enthusiastic zealot. Indeed the best gloss of his character is Parker's own account of the prototypical Nonconformist: 'What else I say can be the humour of these mens Consciences, but a proud Impatience of all controul, and a restlessness against all Authority, till themselves may have it at their own disposal ... There is a passionate, untutor'd, and impetuous Conscience, that becomes rude and insolent from the sense of its own Integrity, and because 'tis confident in the goodness of its intentions, it is furious and ungovernable in the Prosecution of its ends.'[43] But Marvell's burlesque version of Parker recklessly challenging the imaginary forces of disruption and triumphantly parading captured Nonconformists behind his chariot refuses to consider Parker seriously. Marvell's satiric fictions show his urbane and moderate audience that the ecclesiastical politician is only a threat if his monomaniacal vision is taken seriously.

In hoisting Parker with his own petard *The Rehearsal Transpros'd* weaves into the military terminology a complex of sexual allusions. Not surprisingly Parker's tracts oppose excessive emotion in any form; sensuality, however, receives specific attention, 'For religion is pure, cleanly and spiritual; but an intemperate sensuality is nasty, sottish, and makes the mind of man cheap and foolish, and unapt for any thing that is Manly, Generous, and Rational, and so is the greatest Impediment to all the ends and Exercises of Religion.'[44] Parker naturally associates passionate sensuality with zealousness, and he emphasizes his own temperance. Judged by his own standards, the interpretation given in *The Rehearsal Transpros'd* to the phrase 'wanton and incontinent' develops an ironic contradiction underscored in the allusions to 'comfortable importance.' Although Marvell only indirectly mentions Parker's imminent marriage to Rebecca Pheasant with a pun – 'I know no Dainty wanting, or that could have pleased his Tooth so well, except the Leg of a Pheasant at the *Dog* and *Partridge*' (p 92) – he brazenly intrudes the italicized words '*comfortable importance*' to insinuate Parker's preoccupation with sexual matters. The recurrence of the phrase forces the impression of enthusiasm and gives further dimension to Marvell's remark 'Thus it must be, and no better, when a man's Phancy is up, and his Breeches are down.'

Marvell's interruption of the recapitulation of an argument with an allusion to sensuality and his use of sexual diction to summarize Parker's points increase the humorous debasement. 'The more hidden and lurking fumes of Lust,' More emphatically reiterates in *Enthusiasmus Triumphatus*, are often characteristic signs of the political enthusiast. These 'venereous fumes,' which Robert Burton also mentions in *The Anatomy of Melancholy* and Samuel Parker himself delineates in his description of the Nonconformist minister, are in More's analysis influenced by the hypochondriacal humor. Alone 'this *Flatulencie* ... solicits to lust'; and when the vapours mingle with the other humours, 'all the imaginations of *Love*, of what kind soever, will be farre more lively and vigorous, more piercing and rapturous, then they can be in pure *Sanguine* it self.' The enthusiast with this complexion will then mistake his 'no better than *Poetical* fits and figments for divine Inspiration and reall Truth.'[45] Parker agrees, and without being similarly explicit he echoes the earlier treatise in his belief that the essense of religious enthusiasm is an unbalanced humour that 'inflames them with Raptures and Exstasies of Joy; their hearts overflow with content, and their Mouths with exultation; they feel themselves strangely enlarged in duty, their affections warm, and expressions fluent; they admire their own freedom and eloquence of speech, and delight to be streaming forth in Torrents of Prayer and Devotion. And withal they usually grow amorous, and vent their swelling spirits in affections of love and fondness.'[46] A comparable behaviour, quite unmistakable in the mock biography of Parker's rise to notoriety, dominates his effusive outpourings; and Marvell's analysis continually implies that all his religious tracts reveal these characteristics.

More than egregious insult or convenient stylistic satire, this representation undermines a value essential to both Parker's self-identity and his vision. All of his tracts against the Nonconformists maintain that religious differences are often merely a matter of expression. At one point Parker even asserts that 'the most material difference between the sober Christians of the Church of *England*, and our modern Sectaries, [is] That we express the Precepts and Duties of the Gospel in plain and intelligible Terms, whilst they trifle them away by childish Metaphors and Allegories, and will not talk of Religion but in barbarous and uncouth Similitudes.'[47] This criticism of figurative language, which leads him to demand an act of parliament to prevent preachers from using 'folsom and lushious Metaphors,' is rooted in a common Restoration distrust of fancy. As a leading exponent of the plain style Parker believes that metaphoric language is a vehicle of 'wanton & luxuriant fancies' that defy reason and, 'instead of real conceptions and notices of Things, impregnate the mind with nothing but Ayerie and Subventaneous Phantasmes.'[48] Fanatic enthusiasm, he frequently reminds the Nonconformists, invariably resorts to cant and similitudes.

The Rehearsal Transpros'd finds Parker guilty of the same vices. Actually Parker's style, particularly in the earlier tracts, is usually tight, forceful, and direct; but Marvell has the uncanny ability to locate the most telling lapses and to build from them a satire far more complex than mere stylistic ridicule. The first attack, which ridicules Parker's praise of Bishop Bramhall's noble character, demonstrates his approach. The main point seems to be the excessiveness of the panegyric: 'By the Language he seems to transcribe out of the *Grand-Cyrus* and *Cassandra*, but the Exploits to have borrowed out of the *Knight of the Sun*, and *King Arthur*. For in a luscious and effeminate Stile he gives him such a *Termagant* Character, as must either fright or turn the stomach of any Reader' (p 11). This characterization recalls Bayes's obsession with the world of romances and identifies Parker's own penchant for the chimerical and the self-indulgent. Marvell dismisses the eulogy as ridiculous and chides the Anglican minister for his indecorous rhetoric; then he takes the opportunity to remark once more on Parker's supposedly amorous character: 'I shall say nothing severer, than that our Author speaks the language of a Lover, and so may claim some pardon, if the habit and excess of his Courtship do as yet give a tincture to his discourse upon more ordinary Subjects' (p 13). When he later adds that Parker's fanciful distraction may also represent a greater interest in *Don Quixote* than in the Bible, the satiric inversion seems complete; however the humour and its significance are not. Parker's 'language of a Lover' resembles the expression of both Bayes and the irrational Nonconformists. In a similar manner the suggestion that Parker's real forte is the romance implies that he is like those enthusiasts whose 'whole business of Religion is transacted in their Imaginations'; furthermore, Parker as a writer of romances indulges in a form of literature ridiculed by Parker the author of the polemical tracts.[49] Recast into a role opposed to his self-image, Parker is an ironic mockery of himself: 'I have no where played with Phrases, nor argued from Met-aphors and Similitudes; and if any of my Words may happen to be fine, they are none of them empty; and the most pompous and lofty Expressions contain under them Notion, and Thing enough to fill out their Sense, and warrant their Truth.'[50]

The satire continually tests this assertion. When the man opposed to 'wanton and lascivious allegories' compares Calvin to 'a mighty bramble on the South side of Lake Lemane,' Marvell seizes upon the similitude and interprets Parker's meaning literally. In the process 'Allegorical Elo-quence' is reduced to absurdity and exuberant fancy and wit are exposed. Often Marvell simply makes his point in passing. For example, Parker's conclusion to the 'Preface' includes the unfortunately phrased apology, 'I never intended to have been so tedious; but so many warm and glowing Meditations started up in my way, as without much musing made my Heart burn, and the fire kindle; and that has heated me into all this wild and rambling Talk, (as some will be forward enough to call it).'[51] Marvell unhesitatingly ignores the intent of the passage and offers it as proof that indeed Parker is a 'hot-headed Incendiary; and a wild rambling talker' (p 74). He creates similar evidence with repeated allusions to the tracts as a gazette; for he assumes that the reader remembers Parker's declaration that the 'Masterpiece of Nonconformist wit' is 'to make Satyrical Remarks upon the GAZETS and publick Narratives.'[52] If the tracts do not provide ready ammunition, Marvell follows Marprelate's lead and imagines his adversary's most guarded thoughts. Thus the polemicist is made to con-fess: 'In all matters of Argument I will so muddle my self in Ink, that there shall be no catching no finding me; and besides I will speak alwayes with so Magisterial a Confidence, that no modest man (and most ingenious per-sons are so) shall so much as quetch at me, but be beat out of Countenance: and plain men shall think that I durst not talk at such a rate but that I have a Commission' (p 72).

This last fiction in its obviousness suggests what the first part of *The Rehearsal Transpros'd* confirms again and again. By transposing the Samuel Parker of history into the fanatical enthusiast of *The Rehearsal Transpros'd* Marvell probes the tenuous borderline between zeal and madness. Giddy flights of imagination and uncontrollable fancy result, Marvell pretends, in a florid verbiage which often rivals the incoherence of ecstasy. Fre-quently the excessive outbursts reflect turbulent confusion in a maze of muddled ideas, and 'All that rationally can be gathered from what he saith, is, that the Man is mad.' The ecclesiastical politician who runs amuck in the manner of a 'raging *Indian*,' or erupts into a 'furious Debauch' against foreign churches, or claws and tears at all opposition displays a 'beastly railing unbecoming any man, much more a Divine' (p 71). Spewing out distortions and roaring against imaginary dangers, Parker surpasses the conventional enthusiast; railing for him 'is not onely the most material and useful part of his Religion, his Reason, his Oratory, and his Practise; but the ultimate end of this and all his other Books' (p 72). As a hopelessly deranged fool who believes in the quintessential power of railing, he tries to achieve his grand scheme; and when this does not succeed, there is only one other solution, persecution.

A religious fanatic far more dangerous than the Nonconformists he hoped to suppress, the Parker reconstructed from his tracts either wilfully or helplessly breaches a fundamental civility. In Marvell's various interpretations he has succumbed to an 'Arrogance and Dictature' or a 'disturbance and dispondency of mind' that have obliterated all desire to 'know or care how to behave himself to God or Man' (p 23). The satire's continual references to discourtesy, insolence, and malice express a concern with manners apparent in the attention given to the word 'civil.' Later Robert Ferguson also contends that Parker's excessive 'Pride, Petulancy, Wrath, Rancour, Revenge, Scurrility, Reviling and Railing' 'do ill become the extraction and civility of a Gentleman.'[53] Marvell's interpretation, however, develops a more basic understanding of civility. In response to Parker's excoriations of immodest people who persist in 'rudeness and incivility' towards the established church, Marvell inverts the accusations of ill-nature and proposes that Parker does not understand the real meaning of civilized behaviour. The divine's preoccupation with absolute conformity and his respect for the external signs of authority reveal 'no *Idea*' of the 'wisdom' history teaches. The suggestion in *The Rehearsal Transpros'd* that war may be attributed to 'Corruption of Manners' contains a certain amount of rhetorical hyperbole, but the view is consistent with Marvell's belief in the social importance of manners. Parker is advised that he should have learned from the previous decades of civil disruption the folly of narrow-minded vision and the importance of tolerant coexistence. In his preoccupation with himself the divine cannot realize that civility demands from people a sensitivity to the larger welfare of the state.

John Hales and Charles II represent the satire's vision of true civility. The contrast with Parker drawn after the extensive quotation from Hales's discussion of schism invites a choice between diametrical behaviours: 'The one to uphold his *Fiction*, must incite Princes to Persecution and Tyranny, degrade Grace to Morality, debauch Conscience against its own Principles, distort and mis-interpret the Scripture, fill the

World with Blood, Execution, and Massacre; while the other needs and requires no more but a peaceable and unprejudicate Soul and the native Simplicity of a Christian-spirit' (p 83). Marvell cannot condone a reactionary withdrawal into rigid intolerance even though he has experienced the turmoil of civil war. His ideal of Christian charity finds greater fulfilment in the higher wisdom with which Charles II placed the nation above his sense of personal injustice and forgave those who had brought about his father's death and his own exile. This magnanimity entails an understanding of respect which Marvell finds absent in Parker's preoccupation with brittle titles and unbending rights. 'If Kings do, out of discretion, connive at the other infirmities of their People; If great persons do out of civility condescend to their inferiours; and if all men out of common humanity do yield to the weaker; Will your Clergy only be the men, who, in an affair of Conscience, and where perhaps 'tis you are in the wrong, be the onely hard-hearted and inflexible Tyrants; and not only so, but instigate and provoke Princes to be the ministers of your cruelty' (p 111)? The answer to this question is a foregone conclusion when reason and sensibility are absent.

Against such blatant disregard for the propriety basic to a harmonious Christian society Marvell's ironic indirection appeals to urbane wit and judgment. Sacrificing neither composure nor perspective, he pursues public invective in a droll manner that offers an alternative to the railing found in Parker. Marvell's urbanity blends Aristotelian *eutrapelia* with Horatian ease as it fulfils many of the ideals expressed in Barrow's sermon. Implicit in its detached, ironic circumspection is a social ideal first formulated by Aristotle and restated by Restoration contemporaries such as Barrow who value discreet banter and light raillery as signs of a sophisticated and responsible demeanour. In contrast to Parker's intense emotionalism Marvell's wit and humanitarianism add intellectual depth to his ridicule. Unlike his opponent's attacks, in which laughter signifies a distasteful vanity and a reactionary intolerance, Marvell's humour illustrates the capacity to entertain both ideas and people. It demonstrates the common sense and charity necessary for the continued well-being of a society forced by the great upheavals of civil war to recognize that uniformity can never again be possible. By exposing the extremism of Parker's rancour while avoiding the endless wrangling and potential disruption of conventional disputation, Marvell suits his ridicule to the occasion. Like Dryden he knew the difficulties in making 'a man appear a fool, a blockhead, or a knave, without using any of those opprobrious terms'; indeed Dryden could well have spoken for Marvell when he remarks: 'If I had railed, I might have suffered for it justly; but I managed my own work more happily, perhaps more dexterously. I avoided the mention of great crimes, and applied myself to the representing of blindsides, and little extravagancies; to which, the wittier a man is, he is generally the more obnoxious. It succeeded as I wished; the jest went round, and he was laught at in his turn who began the frolic.'[54]

Marvell was extremely successful; unfortunately Parker ignored the lesson in decorum. Explaining that he could not refuse his friends' great urging, he answered the widely acclaimed ridicule with a final defence and summation of his position in *A Reproof to the Rehearsal Transpros'd, In a Discourse to its Authour*. Not quite as long as some of his previous tracts, this last effort covers essentially the same ground in a different tone. Parker cannot remain sufficiently detached to parry Marvell's irony, and indignation replaces the confidence of the earlier writings. This least successful of his refutations offers another example of the indecorum Marvell resists, and within the year the second part of *The Rehearsal Transpros'd* appeared.

The opening paragraphs of Marvell's second satire set a new tenor for the protracted controversy. Beginning once more with Parker's apology – this time the prefatory marks to *A Reproof* – Marvell in typical fashion seizes upon the remark, 'you might have been sooner informed, had I not immediately after I had undertaken your Correction been prevented by a dull and lazy distemper.' This ambiguous allusion to personal matters, like the earlier reference to 'comfortable importance,' is submitted to ironic scrutiny; the element of play, however, now seems less whimsical. With strained patience and delicacy Marvell asks whether the indefatigable author 'is grown so considerable, that the *Temper of his mind*, the *Juncture of his Affairs*, and the *State of his Body* should be transmitted to posterity? That after Ages must read in what Moon his invention was fluent, and in what *Epocha*, costive? That as in his late Preface he enter'd his *closer Importance* upon Record, so in this voluminous Pamphlet his close Stool too should be Register'd' (pp 149–50)? The exaggerated egotism prompts the first of several comparisons to Nero and initiates anew a conspicuous fabrication of a 'Fanatick kind of Spirit.'

The satiric reconstruction of character begins appropriately with a diagnosis of the disease symptomatic in the 'dull and lazy distemper.' Marvell abandons his first impression that 'Stupidity and Raving' reflect the feverish after-effects of an improperly cured lethargy and tentatively determines the disease to be an incurable form of *Abelteria*, a mental disorder that inevitably worsens whenever the afflicted thinks he is recovering from his silliness. But since this Greek affliction might be too farfetched, *The Rehearsal Transpros'd* entertains the suggestion of some who argue that Parker's disease 'derives its name from a Countrey much nearer.' Deliberately mimicking Parker's offence at his manner of satire, Marvell admits venereal disease seems rather doubtful for he 'question[s] much whether it could be *so Clownish and Licentious* (bold though it be) *to accost* a Personage of his Figure and Character. Yet who knows ...' (p 152). New stress on Parker's 'usual pompous explication of his own perfections,' a description of 'this blushing Gentleman, this very Picture of modesty,' and the intimation that his interests may be more than strictly theological are open mockeries. Marvell speculates whether the divine's 'Nature may have given his Divinity a slip,' but he coyly admits that he cannot prove his point and must respectfully refrain from pursuing the assertion. He concludes with the pun, 'there could not have been more conformity betwixt the Person and the Disease' (p 155). Later the satire returns to the suggestion of syphilis; now Marvell considers the possibility that Parker is sick of a new disease sweeping the nation, *The Rehearsal Transpros'd*. While in most cases the only effects are 'an innocent fit of uncessant laughter,' Parker's imbalanced humours may have caused a jaundice that changed him 'beyond all imagination.' Whatever the case, either the strong cathartic effects of *The Rehearsal Transpros'd* or the 'extraordinary foulness of his Stomack' produced a violent evacuation. Before proceeding with further treatment of Parker's distemper Marvell explains his former prescription of laughter.

The pernicious nature of Samuel Parker determines a defence of religious ridicule firmly premised on the necessity to repudiate 'opinions destructive to Humane Society and Christian Religion.' Marvell gives short shrift to the tracts that support Parker's complaints about 'such a clownish and licentious way of writing, as you know to be unsuitable both to the Civility of my Education, and the Gravity of my Profession'[55] and that concur with *Gregory, Father-Graybeard, With his Vizard off* in disapproval of 'right down [sic] rayling set off with a little Droll, the more takingly to calumniate and cast contempt on the Clergy.'[56] He invites those with leisure to construct their own character of Parker's pronouncements on ecclesiastical polity. His own impression of a dangerous writer who 'scarce ever opens his mouth, but that he may bite, nor bites, but that from the *Vesicles* of his Gums he may infuse a venom' (p 168) strengthens Marvell's determination to show truth, manners, and public tranquillity to be more important than misguided concern about implied disrespect for the clergy. Charges of profane ribaldry and unconscionable virulence repeat criticisms familiar from the first part of the satire, and

Parker's offensive arrogance again grates upon Marvell's sensitivity. Less circumspectly he explains that the civil disturbance provoked by the writings and the harmful disregard for the principles of Christianity 'appear'd so publick in the consequence and mischief, I could hold no longer, and I, though the most unfit of many, assumed upon him the Priviledge (if any such Priviledge there be) of an English *Zelote*' (p 169). Disclaiming any wish to harm the clergy, the second part of *The Rehearsal Transpros'd* once more assumes that Parker's manner warrants the satire's right to characterize his zealous fanaticism.

Commenting that his first effort 'intermixed things apparently fabulous, with others probably true' and that he would rather continue in a 'more manly way of argument' (pp 170–1), Marvell narrows the distance between truth and fiction. Rhetorically the gesture reconfirms a standard of moderation and reasonableness as it again shifts the onus for any departure from these ideals upon Parker. Then with its own version of events the satire suggests how the authorship of *A Reproof* makes this aim very difficult to achieve. Despite his private assurances that forthcoming answers would harm no reputations, Parker took up lodging in a 'Calumny Office' and encouraged all aspiring authors to aid a cause in which 'there was at last nothing so slight but it grew material, nothing so false but he resolved it should go for truth, and what wanted in matter he would make out with invention and artifice' (p 172). Lost among the outpouring of 'six *Scaramuccios*' that quickly entered upon the stage, his identity appears to undergo a transmigration analogous to that in Donne's 'Progress of the Soul.' Reluctant to pursue 'the same Ghost that hath haunted me in those differing dresses and Vehicles' any further than its reincarnation in the wife of Cain, Marvell abandons the parallel with 'that witty fable of Doctor *Donne's*' and demonstrates more directly 'how Syllogistical a life his hath been to the Stile and Principles that he has manag'd and prosecuted' (p 178).

In meeting Parker's complaint about the affront to the 'Gravity of his Profession' and the 'Civility of his Education' the second part of *The Rehearsal Transpros'd* develops a mock biography, similar in conclusion to that of the first part. The second biography, however, is on the whole less subtle than its predecessor. Marvell moves away from the droll manner of his 'diagnosis' and first invents an outrageous genealogy. With Parker's surname as his basis, he rejects as possible ancestors Henry Parker, a Carmelite who preached against the secular tendencies of the clergy, and Robert Parker, a 'Severe Non-conformist' whose writing led to his exile. Partial to a yeoman in Charles I's reign who was opposed to the Anglican communion table, the history finally settles on the balladeer Martin Parker, the subject of a petition condemning his efforts 'in disgrace of Religion, to the increase of all vice, and withdrawing of people from reading, studying, and hearing the Word of God and other good books' (p 179). The close kinship at least in style and effect accounts for Parker's desire to seek vengeance against all who dare criticize the author, but the obscurity of his ancestral origins makes any link with the balladeer admittedly conjectural. There is no question about his father, though, and Marvell is on more solid ground with an account that appears factual. Parker's father did publish a book on the principles of government, and the son did distinguish himself at Oxford for his devoted nonconformity. Noting the choice young Parker faced when the Restoration re-established Anglicanism, the biography describes with considerable satiric licence an indecisive man, now in London, 'where he spent a considerable time in creeping into all Corners and Companies, Horoscoping up and down concerning the duration of the Government: not considering any thing as best, but as most lasting and most profitable' (p 182). The ambitious man, who in Marvell's account would compromise any virtue for a living and is rumoured to have denounced his parents, then turned against his past with a series of books that reveal his true nature. The first publication on the non-controversial subject of atheism purportedly contains nothing of Parker's except 'the arrogance and the unparall'd censoriousness' written in a style that confuses 'the Skin and the Disease, the Faults and the Grammar' (p 183). A year later he further demonstrated his civility and education in a fulsome epistle to the man who influenced his conversion prefaced to a tangential attack on nonconformity: 'After this feat of activity he was ready to leap over the Moon: no scruple of Conscience could stand in his way, and no preferment seemed too high for him' (p 184). Successful as an archbishop's chaplain and with a vested interest in Lambeth, a palace he undoubtedly would desert at the first sign of trouble, Marvell's Parker undertook the series of writings on ecclesiastical polity that first define the law as he desires and then make certain this law is divinity. These are the 'pernicious' and 'foully managed' discourses that ultimately measure his gravity and civility, and the 'most noxious Creature' of this biographical anatomy demands representation suitable to his likeness. In an assurance to his readers that is a prelude to the rest of the satire Marvell declares: 'I have not used any harsh expressions but what were suitable to that Civility of Education which he practises, and that Gravity of Profession which he hath set up of: and even therein I have taken care, beside what my nature hath taken care for, to shoot below the mark, and not to retaliate to the same degree; being willing, as I must yield him the preference for many good qualities, so in his worst however to give him the precedence' (p 185).

Repeating several times a desire for something of substance, the second part of the satire reintroduces metaphors of pursuit and travel to describe its deliverance of Parker 'to Reason or Laughter, to Justice or Pity.' The quest also relies upon continued allusions to Bayes and *The Rehearsal* for a semblance of continuity and again lapses into bypaths as Marvell is forced to 'write too at adventure ... scumming off whatsoever comes uppermost, as it rises' (p 289), but a greater degree of earnestness reflects itself in more sustained and serious analysis. Instead of quickly dismissing the six major points or 'plays' of the controversy, Marvell answers Parker's clamour for dignified consideration with more straightforward discussions of the limits of public authority and private conscience, the relationship of morality and grace, and the wisdom of persecution and absolute conformity.[57] The new seriousness, however, also produces considerably more *ad hominem* attacks. Marvell, supplied with a number of Canterbury rumours, discloses intimate details and private statements to create a less fictitious and more unattractive figure, a morally reprehensible fool.

The essence of the man so indistinguishable from his beliefs is apparent in Marvell's contention that 'the sum of your Doctrine appears to be (if without offence I may name it) that your Priestly and Uncontroulable Power of the Civil Magistrate is Antecedent to *Christ*, Contemporary to the World, nay at least Co-eternal, if not Pre-eternal, to God himself' (p 213). The supreme embodiment of the political enthusiast, Parker is a mad zealot who indiscriminately violates divine and human law to achieve his self-serving ends. 'Having in his *Ecclesiastical Politie* created himself Perpetual Dictator, *Nequid Res-clerica detrimenti capiat*, and marching every where with four and twenty *Rods and Axes* before him, he deputes the *Consul* to be indeed both his *Magister Equitum* and his *Pontifex Maximus*: but all along speaks in the *Us* and the *We* of himself, and treats the good Civil Uncontrolable Magistrate with the *Must, Must*, to evidence his own rigorous Superiority' (p 194). Missing from this exaggerated image is the whimsy of the earlier scene in which the triumphant conqueror leads his captive Nonconformists off to prison. This figure is also ridiculous, but the aggressive laughter it provokes indicates a greater hostility towards his proud, menacing stature.

Familiar charges about giddy inspiration and insane railing also become more intensely serious and their consequences more urgent. The distempered divine, his 'profligate and loose rate' now figuratively exposed as syphilitic, loses himself in fits and raptures. Foaming at the mouth as though in the advanced stages of a falling sickness, he appears in the pages of his work to embroil himself in 'such *Froath* and *Growns* and *Taplash* of Wit, that it deserves compassion' (p 317). But Marvell is reluctant to dismiss Parker as a madman deserving of pity. Aware of the consequences of abusing a public, religious office and convinced of the great influence of the written word, he presses his main concern 'and all the matter depending betwixt your Book and me' that Parker 'cannot imagine what hurt a silly well-meaning book may do in the world far from its intention: but if it have on the contrary a felonious intention, and not having the fear of God before its Eyes, as I doubt yours has not, you know then that it may do more mischief than you can ever make amends for' (p 207). The images of disease and warfare in the satire make clear that such writing resembles bullets first chewed to increase their destructiveness and then envenomed with spittle. Any man who would poison wounds he has created, or would taunt, scoff, and jeer maliciously at afflictions he has aggravated, and then 'clap and crow at the Wit and Malice' has lost his most basic human sensitivity. Quite simply, *The Rehearsal Transpros'd* urgently insists that 'There is a certain Civility due to such as suffer, and to bruise a broken Reed is inhumane' (p 284).

The reaction to the dangerous implications of this zeal more often occurs in a discursive argumentation consonant with the increased seriousness, but the underlying attitude remains that of the satire's first part. Marvell recognizes that any form of absolutism is virtually impossible in a postlapsarian world, and he denies that Nonconformists offer a national threat. He counsels instead 'Christian Moderation and Patience.' Although he concedes the duty to obey a magistrate in all demands that do not contradict an obligation to God, pragmatic considerations reinforce a basic concern with the inviolability of conscience. *The Rehearsal Transpros'd* considers excess on the part of either the ruler or his subject counterproductive, and excessive concern for uniformity in religious matters described throughout the century as 'indifferent' is shortsighted. 'Had things been left in their own state of Indifferency,' Marvell argues, 'it is well known that the *English* Nation is generally neither so void of Understanding, Civility, Obedience, or Devotion, but that they would long ago have voluntarily closed and faln naturally into those reverent manners of Worship which would sufficiently have exprest and suited with their Religion' (p 242). Marvell refuses to define more exactly the limits that interrelate necessity, providence, ruler, and subjects; none the less he has no sympathy for those who meddle beyond their natural authority. Singling out the clergy in a passage reminiscent of Milton and Marprelate, he blames much of the religious controversy on ecclesiastics who have followed their appetites from multiple benefices to the courts of magistrates. Hypocrites who offer lip service to the gravity of their profession, they and their spokesman Samuel Parker have ignored the values Marvell links together as 'Nature, Law, and Discretion.' In abandoning 'all Modesty and Christianity' they have forgotten the bases of their religion – charity and 'that great and fundamental Law of Mercy' (p 249).

The witless violation of Christian proprieties overshadows questions of ecclesiastical polity; essentially the conflict becomes one of decorum. Particularly in the second part of the satire Marvell presses the accusation that 'thorow your whole *Reproof*, it seems that you do not trouble your self so much about the weight of the matter, as disquiet your mind with an Emulation of Wit'; he, on the other hand, modestly protests that 'Whether I have any at all I know not, neither, further then it is not fit for me to reject any good quality wherewith God may have indued me, do I much care: but would be glad to part with it very easily for any thing intellectual, that is solid and useful' (p 258). This willingness to disavow ridicule, itself an example of Marvell's humour, reflects his urbane wit and humane reasonableness. Like Milton and Marprelate, Marvell assumes that the right to decorous jest and earnest depends upon the dramatic opposition of personalities. His concern with Parker's rampant enthusiasm more extensively emphasizes the importance of 'personation,' but the integral presence of the satirist is not compromised. The consistent and deliberate inversion of Samuel Parker's ideals and image reveals a detachment and sophisticated playfulness that are paradoxically the appeal of his winning seriousness. Although Marvell may lapse from serious amusement into abusive criticism and may on occasion openly express an abhorrence of the 'noxious' divine, he never abandons his decision to deliver zeal bound in reason or laughter. Despite the protests of some contemporaries, Marvell shares Marprelate's and Milton's conviction that the humanistic values implicit in the satirist's manner and vision warrant the use of religious ridicule in necessary and important undertakings.

The approbation of most contemporaries and the silence of his opponent attest to the wisdom of this decision. Some years after Marvell's death Parker, now a bishop and attracted to the Catholicism of the new monarch, would add to one of his writings a lengthy and bitter digression against his former antagonist. When *Bp. Parker's History Of His Own Times* was posthumously published in 1728 with the editor's wish 'that this *Legendary History* of his *Life* and *Times*, had been buried with him,'[58] the controversy was already of little importance. The complexity of Marvell's calculated distortion of both Parker and his writings along with the ephemeral nature of polemics muted the initial success of *The Rehearsal Transpros'd*. By the beginning of the eighteenth century Marvell's reputation as a wit probably depended primarily on his verse satires, but at least one writer still considered *The Rehearsal Transpros'd* to be an example of the memorable satire produced 'when any great Genius thinks it worth his while to expose a foolish Piece; so we still read *Marvell's* Answer to *Parker* with Pleasure, tho' the Book it answers be sunk long ago.'[59] Swift's appreciation in his apology for *A Tale of a Tub* seems more than a gratuitous compliment, for, like Marvell, he too was deeply involved in issues that forced him to consider the propriety of religious ridicule and to place even greater emphasis than Marvell on the nature of his adversaries. The relentless disclosure of Parker's insane, messianic enthusiasm offers valuable precedent for Swift's counterparts, the Grubstreet Hack and the fanatical brothers Peter and Jack. Marvell's urbane, whimsical humour corresponds, moreover, to Swift's ideas of 'Men of Wit and Tast'; and his understanding of history anticipates Swift's involvement in the ancient-modern controversy.[60] But *The Rehearsal Transpros'd* is much more than an analogue for one of the greatest prose satires. Marvell memorably illustrates for later ages as well a sustained, imaginative exploration of the important role character plays in the delicate balance of jest and earnest. In the tradition of Marprelate and Milton he transforms conventional animadversion into a coherent vision of dramatic satire faithful both to its own and to traditional notions of decorum.

6

A Tale of a Tub

A Tale of a Tub continues the attack against abuses traditional in late sixteenth- and seventeenth-century polemic. Religious corruptions ridiculed in the satire are, as the author insists in his Apology, 'such as have been perpetually controverted since the Reformation';[1] and its digressive concern with errors in learning touches equally long-standing considerations. Despite a design which separates into sections a dual emphasis on 'the numerous and gross Corruptions in Religion and Learning,' Jonathan Swift's first significant prose satire unifies issues of polity and knowledge central to the controversy that earlier involved Marprelate, Milton, and Marvell. While the determination of a single form of religion no longer seems as urgent at the end of the seventeenth century and the preoccupation with learning is now more precisely delineated, Swift could still rely on an established polemical tradition. With even greater certainty than the earlier satirists he could also proclaim his resolution 'to proceed in a manner, that should be altogether new.'

Although the assertion of an early biography that the satire was written before he was nineteen and the persistent rumour that his 'little Parson-cousin' Thomas Swift wrote much of the religious allegory may be discounted,[2] the probable inception of the work does not entirely favour Swift's bid for originality. Several references in the Apology and one of the notes in the fifth edition support its assertion that the 'greatest Part' of the satire was written before 1696. Allusions to contemporary events indicate that Swift continued his work on the text until its 1704 publication;[3] however, modern editors agree that *A Tale of a Tub* developed in several stages. The religious allegory, which may have existed in some preliminary draft, seems likely to have been written largely during Swift's prebendary at Kilroot and prior to his return in 1696 to William Temple's estate. In fact the satire of learning introduced 'by way of Digressions' might well have been 'an afterthought.'[4]

But the involvement in a dispute originally between proponents of the ancients and of the moderns demanded more than secondary consideration. Temple had embroiled himself in the century-old controversy and left himself extremely vulnerable to attack with the ill-considered *An Essay upon the Ancient and Modern Learning* (1690). His sweeping dismissal particularly of modern scientific discoveries prompted in 1694 William Wotton's lengthy *Reflections upon Ancient and Modern Learning;* a second edition of Wotton's work three years later contained additional commentary by Richard Bentley which anticipated his extended criticism published in 1699. Wotton's moderate, thorough survey of modern contributions to learning and Bentley's forceful, scholarly scrutiny of certain questionably ancient authorships seriously damaged Temple's already weak case. 'Having no mind to Enter the List, with such a Mean, Dull, Unmannerly *Pedant*,'[5] Temple limited his engagement to an incomplete essay entitled *Some Thoughts upon Reviewing the Essay of Ancient and Modern Learning;* his defence was undertaken by the wits from Christ Church who responded to the combined 1697 edition of Wotton and Bentley with *Dr. Bentley's Dissertations on the Epistles of Phalaris, and the Fables of Aesop, Examin'd.* Their dismay that a man who 'had set the world a Pattern of mixing Wit with Reason, Sound Knowledge with Good Manners' had been mistreated 'by those that have writ against him, in a very rough way, and without that Respect which was due both to His Character, and their Own'[6] was shared by Swift. Explaining in the Apology to *A Tale of a Tub* that 'All the Men of Wit and Politeness were immediately up in Arms, through Indignation' at the affront given William Temple, Swift considers his satire in part a supplement to the refutation penned by Temple's supporters. Singling out William Wotton in a tale whose purported hero is Richard Bentley, Swift entered the entangled fray.

Once involved, he pursues a deliberately limited attack. While the Christ Church wits felt obliged to answer Bentley's devastating criticisms at least half-seriously, Swift avoids the complex issues related to the problem of the Aesop-Phalaris authorship and refuses to align himself with either the ancients or the moderns. The attitude of the *Tale* towards the Rosicrucians and the individual sections satirizing modern critics and the Royal Society indicate that Swift shares attitudes developed in Temple's essays, but he is not drawn into the contest on Bentley's and Wotton's terms. Abandoning any pretence to animadversion and acknowledging the writings of Temple's critics only through the satire's mimicry, *A Tale of a Tub* bypasses secondary issues. The important contention in Temple's essay, overshadowed by his mistaken notions about progress and ancient authorship, occurs near the end. 'But God be thanked,' Temple ironically begins his crucial paragraph, man 'is greater than his ignorance, and what he wants in knowledge, he supplies by sufficiency.'[7] Man's pride, his vain assumption that reason can absolutely measure truth, deludes him into the assurance that, 'though his opinions change every week or every day, yet he is sure, or at least confident, that his present thoughts and conclusions are just and true, and cannot be deceived: and among all the miseries to which mankind is born and subjected in the whole course of his life, he has this one felicity to comfort and support him, that in all ages, in all things, every man is always in the right.'[8] More specifically, in the final paragraphs of *Some Thoughts upon Reviewing the Essay of Ancient and Modern Learning* Temple contends that the absence of presumption and the willingness to admit 'a sense and acknowledgment of their own ignorance'[9] differentiate ancient writers from modern. The charity and humility forgotten by modern authors are manifested in the original essay's opposition of honour and avarice. The scornful dismissal of a virtue that inspired 'all the great and noble productions of wit' and the desire for gain have weakened modern learning; debilitated, the 'commonwealth of learning' has been further maimed by 'the scorn of pedantry, which the shallow, the superficial, and the sufficient among scholars first drew upon themselves.'[10] Earlier Andrew Marvell had levelled many of the same charges against Samuel Parker, and in general Martin Marprelate and John Milton agree with the substance of the criticism. Though individually the three satirists develop their own emphases, they share with Temple a tradition of humanism that abhors rigid absolutism consumed with pride and devoid of charity.[11] The ideal of manners to which they subscribe would support the denunciation in Swift's 'Ode To the Hon[ble] Sir William Temple' of those who

> purchase Knowledge at the Expence
> Of common Breeding, common Sense,
> And at once grow Scholars and Fools;
> Affect ill-manner'd Pedantry,
> Rudeness, Ill-nature, Incivility,
> And sick with Dregs of Knowledge grown,
> Which greedily they swallow down,
> Still cast it up and nauseate Company.[12]

A similar attitude shapes the work produced during a period Swift spent at Moor Park when, 'By the Assistance of some Thinking, and much Conversation, he had endeavour'd to Strip himself of as many real Prejudices as he could' (p 4).

Vanity and avarice unrelieved by charity, humility, or honour soon become the true subjects of a complex satire marked by polarized interpretations of vision and form. Those who find in Swift's intentions a defence of reason, common sense, and the established church are opposed by those who see a Swiftian scepticism indebted to Temple and those who see a Kafkaesque vision, dark and pessimistic.[13] The interpolation of allegorical narrative and aimless digression also poses seemingly irreconcilable differences. What appears carefully fitted together from one point of view seems intentionally formless from another. Still others see *A Tale of a Tub* most clearly as two distinct halves.[14]

The crux remains the relationship between the author of the satire and its speaker. Swift creates a fictional character more fully liberated from the confines of animadversion than Milton's Hall, Marprelate's Bridges, or even Marvell's Parker. In developing the dramatic element implicit in the other satirists' concern with character, he creates an ambiguously independent voice that functions in the manner of the Marprelate personae as both a vehicle and an object of the satire. Unlike the duncical speaker in the Elizabethan tracts, however, the narrator in *A Tale of a Tub* is not consciously distinguished from its creator. Without explicitly acknowledging a principle of decorum, the satire dramatizes the earlier satirists' manner: it establishes no firm limits separating the satirist and the satirized. Most readers 'always hear the voice of Swift,'[15] although its nature is by no means certain. Finding as many as six distinct voices in the work, they have differently labelled this persona an ingenue, a Grubstreet Hack, an epitome of the Moderns, or the embodiment of a specific individual.[16] Whether it is then assumed that the persona occasionally and unconsciously utters truths, that the author sometimes intrudes through his pretence to speak *in propria persona*, or that Swift is always the speaker who mimics a variety of writers,[17] the separation of voices remains inexact and subjective. The ambiguity, indeed, may be deliberately fostered as part of the tenuous boundary between the serious and the humorous which both encourages and frustrates division. The Apology, which purports to explain the satire's intention, illustrates the problems and the greatness in Swift's alliance of jest and earnest.

Of the four authors in this study Swift offers the most lengthy and the least straightforward defence of religious ridicule. 'Apology for the &c'

was originally conceived as one of the subjects for a miscellaneous volume and was written the year before it appeared as the Apology in the fifth edition of *A Tale of a Tub*, published in 1710.[18] Three printings since the *Tale* was anonymously published in 1704 and a separate edition in Ireland might not entirely justify the Apology's opening claim that 'the Book seems calculated to live at least as long as our Language, and our Tast admit no great Alterations' (p 3); still the satire had won considerable renown and some voluble criticism. Swift, whose advancement in the church was thwarted as a result of its publication, would later write to Esther Johnson: 'They may talk of the *you know what*; but, gad, if it had not been for that, I should never have been able to get the access I have had; and if that helps me to succeed, then the same thing will be serviceable to the Church.'[19] A year earlier in the Apology he openly and irritably expresses dissatisfaction with his satire's detractors and attempts to dismiss the leading criticisms. Though he adds little new to the conventional justifications for religious ridicule, the manner in which he develops his Apology is significant.

Biographical disclosures and the matter of the defence itself point somewhat uncertainly to the absence of fiction and the possibility of the author's candid presence. Much that Swift reveals about the satire's apparent composition and his reasons for undertaking it seems straightforward, though his memory is not entirely reliable. In the last paragraph of the Apology the author claims total ignorance about the set of explanatory notes appended to the fifth edition when in fact Swift saw them and perhaps had a hand in their composition. Earlier he is perhaps not truthful in denying that he ever read *A Letter Concerning Enthusiasm*, since his correspondence indicates that he was familiar with the work, which Shaftesbury published in 1708.[20] Similarly the satire's careful development of the number three does not correspond to the Apology's contention that the removal of a fourth wooden machine by 'those who had the Papers in their Power' altered the author's original manuscript and 'the Conceit was half spoiled by changing the Numbers' (p 8). The incidence of language resembling the conventional phraseology of apologies suggests that Swift may also be parodying himself.[21] Yet the evasiveness and the ironic play, if they are intentional, do not necessarily discredit the value of the Apology as a guide to the *Tale*'s satiric use of laughter. They may indeed contribute to its strategy.

Swift's task in the Apology is one of unusual defensiveness. An unconcealed disappointment that 'the Author's Intentions [had not] met with a more candid Interpretation from some whom out of Respect he forbears to name' (pp 5–6) and a hypersensitivity to 'the ill-placed Cavils of the Sour, the Envious, the Stupid, and the Tastless, which he mentions with disdain' (p 4), are apparent throughout the loose, uneven Apology. A defence intended in the author's view mainly to satisfy future readers does not need to bother with the carping of ephemeral criticism; but having made this contemptuous dismissal, Swift devotes half of the Apology to answering his most telling critic, William Wotton. Although he sarcastically rejects '*this* discreet, candid, pious, *and* ingenious *Answerer*,' Swift knows his ridicule may have transgressed traditional religious propriety; and when he cannot evade responsibility, he tries to qualify what seems objectionable.

Tacitly recognizing his indiscretion by making new changes in the original edition, Swift also openly admits at the outset of the Apology that 'there are several youthful Sallies, which from the Grave and the Wise may deserve a Rebuke' (p 4). Again at the end and twice more during the defence he acknowledges improprieties. By shifting responsibility Swift in each instance minimizes his lapses, which, he assures his audience, any reader with taste and candour will find few. His insistence on a precise dating of the composition corroborates 'The Bookseller to the Reader'[22] and reinforces the desired impression that such lapses were youthful errors. When he later emphasizes quite differently that several years and much revision produced his work, he adds, 'and if his Papers had not been a long time out of his Possession, they must have still undergone more severe Corrections' (p 10). The satire was not, in all probability, out of the author's hands and in the hands of the bookseller for the six years he claims, but the ruse allows Swift to again 'plead the Excuse offered already, of his Youth, and Franckness of Speech, and his Papers being out of his Power at the Time they were published' (p 12). By distancing himself from his text through time and the interference of his publisher Swift can recommend that his book 'with those Allowances above-required' be read.

The Apology argues directly that there can be no real offence for 'Why should any Clergyman of our Church be angry to see the Follies of Fanaticism and Superstition exposed, tho' in the most ridiculous Manner? since that is perhaps the most probable way to cure them, or at least to hinder them from farther spreading' (p 5). Without developing this rhetorical question Swift argues succinctly and conventionally on his own behalf that he supports the established church as 'the most perfect of all others,' attacks neither its clergy nor their calling, and proposes nothing critical of its doctrines. He further asserts that the abuses exposed are ones commonly recognized and 'perpetually ridiculed since the Reformation.' Wotton, who abhors 'making Sport with any way of worshipping God,'[23] contended that *A Tale of a Tub* blasphemes Christian tenets and is dangerously disruptive. Eighteenth-century England, he had written in *A Defense of the Reflections upon Ancient and Modern Learning*, must not be confused with the Reformation era; 'tho' the Rage and Spight with which Men treated one another was as keen and as picquant then as it is now, yet the Inclination of Mankind was not then irreligious, and so their Writings had little other effect but to encrease Mens Hatred against any one particular Sect, whilst Christianity, as such, was not hereby at all undermined. But now the Common Enemy appears barefaced, and strikes in with some one or other Sect of Christians, to wound the whole by that means.'[24] His appeal differs significantly from the arguments for compassion that Marvell, Rolle, and others had directed against Samuel Parker. Wotton displays the late seventeeth-century fear of atheism seen in Barrow's sermon, and he also shares the contemporary mistrust of ridicule's ability to undermine truth. Swift's textual modifications and his evasiveness in the Apology indicate that he may have heeded part of the criticism, but he does not compromise his insistence that the corruptions of religion should be ridiculed.

Ignoring Wotton's argument for a more tolerant attitude, the Apology instead almost scornfully concedes that 'the *weightiest* Men in the *weightiest* Stations are pleased to think it a more dangerous Point to laugh at those Corruptions in Religion, which they themselves must disapprove, than to endeavour pulling up those very Foundations, wherein all Christians have agreed' (p 6). In associating himself and his efforts with Christianity Swift presses a crucial difference between the enemies of religion and its friends. The real detractors, who endanger piety and good sense with their malicious falsehoods, are 'full of such Principles as are kindly received, because they are levell'd to remove those Terrors that Religion tells Men will be the Consequence of immoral Lives. Nothing like which is to be met with in this Discourse' (p 5). A later argument that some of his most objectionable passages are actually impersonations of the men he intends to expose singles out those like Dryden and L'Estrange 'who having spent their Lives in Faction, and Apostacies, and all manner of Vice, pretended to be Sufferers for Loyalty and Religion' (p 7). Both passages disclose a religious sensibility opposed to compromise and governed by a high moral seriousness. Compared to the disapproval of the Anglican hierarchy and the latitude of Wotton, Swift displays a commitment befitting the earnestness found in the earlier eras of Marprelate and Milton. A self-confessed 'high-churchman' and a supporter of the Test, he gives no quarter to the folly, superstition, and dissension that threatened religion.

This earnest, almost zealous disposition comprises, however, only part of the satirist's ethos. Anxious to qualify his intention, Swift insists that his work was never intended for an audience of Anglican clergymen. His first reference to the satire's youthful indiscretions explains that 'He was then a young Gentleman much in the World, and wrote to the Tast of those who were like himself' (p 4); later he allies himself with 'the Men of Wit and Politeness' who were incensed by the way in which Temple had been treated; and at the conclusion he states that 'He wrote only to the Men of Wit and Tast.' Throughout the Apology references to the 'Reader of Tast and Candor' sustain the assumption of a qualified, élite audience. Besides summarily dismissing his critics as injudicious, insensitive, and witless, the qualification allows him to dodge the possibility of impropriety with the contention that 'there generally runs an Irony through the Thread of the whole Book, which the Men of Tast will observe and distinguish, and which will render some Objections that have been made, very weak and insignificant' (p 8).

Swift appeals to values upheld in *The Rehearsal Transpros'd* and in the reaction of the Christ Church wits to Wotton and Bentley. Much of the defence published under Charles Boyle's name, and particularly the first sections of Bentley's 1699 answer, deal with countercharges of incivility, presumption, and indecorum. In a summation phrased much like that of both the Apology and *The Rehearsal Transpos'd* the wits who contributed to Boyle's effort conclude that a writer without sincerity, modesty, and humility should consider 'what the Men of Good Nature and Candor will think of his Fierce and Vindictive Temper; how the Men of Taste and Breeding will relish his Scurrilous Language, his Frigid Jests, his Low and Clownish Expressions; how the Men of Reason and Judgment will approve his Weak and Inconclusive Ways of Arguing.'[25] This focus on propriety is also important in *A Tale of a Tub*, and it in turn becomes an issue with the two critics Swift answers, William King and William Wotton. King in particular faults the satire for shaming conversation, manners, and education, as well as religion; and perhaps because of a desire to minimize these accusations Swift dismisses *Some Remarks on the Tale of a Tub* with the ironic admission that 'the manner how he has handled his *Subject*, I have now forgot, having just look'd it over when it first came out, as others did, meerly for the sake of the Title' (p 11). With Wotton Swift seizes the initiative by exaggerating the critic's ill-mannered conduct and fixing him unfavourably in an opposition between 'a paultry, imitating

Pedant' and 'a Person of Wit, Manners and Truth.' Advantageously making himself part of an audience alien to Wotton's insensitivity, Swift like Marvell presumes that readers with wit and taste will find his manner unobjectionable. But the same audience might not be equally receptive to a religious earnestness that could very well violate standards of urbane composure. Committed in the Apology to a taste that encompasses both sensibilities, Swift attempts to reconcile the divergence.

The final assertion of his apologia contends that 'the noblest and most useful Gift of humane Nature' is wit and 'the most agreeable' is humour; 'where these two enter far into the Composition of any Work, they will render it always acceptable to the World' (p 18). Several years later in 'The Author upon Himself' Swift would proclaim that 'Humour, and Mirth, had Place in all he writ: / He reconcil'd Divinity and Wit';[26] in the third number of The Intelligencer, written in 1728, he insists less playfully that, 'although some Things are too serious, solemn, or sacred to be turned into Ridicule, yet the Abuses of them are certainly not; since it is allowed, that Corruptions in Religion, Politicks, and Law, may be proper Topicks for this Kind of Satyr.'[27] None of these pronouncements adequately defines either wit or humour, although the Apology does recognize that those who 'have no Share or Tast of either, but by their Pride, Pedantry and Ill Manners, lay themselves bare to the Lashes of Both' will consider the blows 'weak, because they are insensible, and where Wit hath any mixture of Raillery; 'Tis but calling it Banter, and the work is done' (p 19). Swift's most specific definition of these protean terms in the verses written 'To Mr. Delany' recognizes that wit is

> as boundless as the Wind;
> Is well conceiv'd thô not defin'd;
> For, sure, by Wit is onely meant
> Applying what we first Invent;
> What Humor is, not all the Tribe
> Of Logick-mongers can describe;
> Here, onely Nature acts her Part,
> Unhelpt by Practice, Books, or Art.[28]

In his essay Of Poetry Temple similarly values wit as a process of composing the contrary forces of writing; humour he finds an elusive quality peculiar to the English.[29] Swift modifies Temple's claim that humour is uniquely native, but he follows Temple when he explains to Patrick Delany,

For Wit and Humor differ quite,
That gives Surprise, and this Delight:
Humor is odd, grotesque, and wild,
Onely by Affectation spoild,
'Tis never by Invention got,
Men have it when they know it not.[30]

Those who naturally possess a talent for humour have a gift too often derided as low comedy; 'It is certainly the best Ingredient towards that Kind of Satyr, which is most useful, and gives the least Offence; which, instead of lashing, laughs Men out of their Follies, and Vices; and is the Character that gives *Horace* the Preference to *Juvenal*.'[31] In combination with wit, 'we learn to Railly well,' a skill which passes now as repartee and mere ridicule, although the French and 'the politer Age of our Fathers' regarded it as the ability 'to say something that at first appeared a Reproach, or Reflection; but, by some Turn of Wit unexpected and surprising, ended always in a Compliment, and to the Advantage of the Person it was addressed to.'[32] Together all three, never more specifically defined by Swift,[33] hold in balance the mixture of humour and seriousness so resistant to definition. A strikingly original achievement, which Samuel Johnson found a 'wild work' and which modern critics describe as extravagant, robust, exuberant, and fanciful, *A Tale of a Tub* proves its author's claims to orthodoxy and originality, earnestness and urbanity. Subtly playful and grotesquely mirthful, yet neither Horatian nor Juvenalian, the polished yet uncompromising laughter both teases and lashes. Basic to this ridicule and its justification is the sophisticated presence of the author in a work which denies he is there.

The dimensions of this sophistication are more apparent when the claims of the Apology are seen in the perspective of the *Tale*'s Preface. From one point of view the contrast between the two prefatory pieces enhances the author of the Apology. As a self-professed and zealous 'Servant of all *Modern* Forms' the creator of the Preface ingenuously admits that he has exhausted his resources in the writing of the narrative and that he is not up to the kind of performance expected of a modern. The lengthy preface he then produces 'duly' to prepare the reader for 'the sublime Mysteries that ensue' ironically demonstrates a characteristically modern nothingness,[34] and his disclosures literally confirm his opening claim that his genius lies 'not unhappily' in the way of diversion. Since his own wit is governed by a modern decorum that rigidly fixes time, place, and person to the moment, he has no hope that his writing can appeal to any 'Taste of Wit' other than that exactly attuned to the literal circumstances of its creation. Resigned to the destructive effects produced by any shift in time or place, he can only relate the pressures of money, sickness, and hunger that prompted his writing in the hope that some sympathetic union will emerge between writer and reader. Should this not occur, he advises his audience to assume that any obscure or italicized passage is profoundly useful, witty, or sublime. By shamelessly avoiding the obligations of a defence while overtly paying lip service to the form, the *Tale*'s narrator blithely overturns conventional expectations and tacitly illuminates the serious nature of the counterpart Apology. The parallels between the two, however, create an opposite effect when the distinctions between them appear to collapse.

Apology and Preface tend towards a convergence in their discussions of authorial intent. Both initially emphasize an interest in diversion, and each concludes with a judgment of the manner chosen. According to the putative narrator the *Tale* was conceived as a temporary measure designed to divert those who 'find leisure to pick Holes in the weak sides of Religion and Government' (p 39) until a more substantial plan could be implemented; the explanation added to the 1710 edition states that the author 'thought the numerous and gross Corruptions in Religion and Learning might furnish Matter for a Satyr, that would be useful and diverting' (p 4). The Apology's subsequent disparagement of the 'illiterate Scriblers' who attack religion also suggests the similar antipathy of the Preface to Leviathan wits. Although the two prefatory pieces then reveal authors with extremely different motivations and sensibilities, the departures from the acceptable meant to characterize the speaker in the Preface tease the reader with suggestions of Swift's own self-mockery. When the speaker pompously proclaims he has written 'so elaborate and useful a Discourse without one grain of Satyr intermixt' and then launches into a discourse on satire before he catches himself with the admission that 'I forget that I am expatiating on a Subject, wherein I have no concern, having neither a Talent nor an Inclination for Satyr' (p 53), Swift seems to be poking fun at both the speaker and himself. The modern author, protesting that he is writing nothing satiric and has no gift for satire, cannot be confused with Swift and his actual performance in *A Tale of a Tub*; the self-laughter is less certain in the modern's claims to an elaborate and useful achievement. Here the speaker's boasting is meant to be undercut; however masked in his urbane play, Swift may indeed share a similar belief about his own success. The ambivalent relationship between author and speaker which fosters this self-parody becomes most complex in the narrator's lengthy disavowal of satire.

The Preface's dismissal of the satiric mode advances an argument that cannot be ignored. Writers inclined to satire 'might very well spare their Reproof and Correction: For there is not, through all Nature, another so callous and insensible a Member as the *World's Posteriors*, whether you apply to it the *Toe* or the *Birch*' (p 48). Despite his own preference for panegyric, which suits the modernist's smug content with the present, the speaker ingratiatingly adds that he will not degrade that which his audience of British writers values. Expansively recognizing that 'Nature her self has taken order, that Fame and Honour should be purchased at a better Pennyworth by Satyr, than by any other Productions of the Brain; the World being soonest provoked to *Praise* by *Lashes*, as Men are to *Love*' (p 49), the Preface initiates its own brief panegyric of satire. Consistent with the hack writers' craving for inexhaustible material and unlimited fame, the modern author finds the satiric vein richly rewarding. Whereas panegyric has a limited subject-matter and few possibilities for original expression, the speaker acknowledges that 'there is very little Satyr which has not something in it untouch'd before' (p 49). The ever-growing profusion of vices and follies retains, moreover, a quality distinct from mere abundance: for his pains the writer of panegyric will produce only envy and ill will; 'But Satyr being levelled at all, is never resented for an offence by any, since every individual Person makes bold to understand it of others, and very wisely removes his particular Part of the Burthen upon the shoulders of the World' (p 51). So long as he limits himself to generalities and abstractions the satirist may freely excoriate vices and will be applauded as 'a Deliverer of precious and useful Truths'; then all can consider his efforts 'but a *Ball* bandied to and fro, and every Man carries a *Racket* about Him to strike it from himself among the rest of the Company' (p 52). Should he foolishly mention a specific character or event, the panegyric abruptly ends, inevitable charges of defamation and slander will result in imprisonment, suit, or challenge.

A heavily pragmatic praise of satire couched in this manner becomes, of course, a mock encomium; its intention, however, remains perplexing. When the speaker draws back from his 'little Panegyrick' with the excuse that he is neither inclined towards satire nor discontented with the world, his explanation can be either taken at face value or viewed with suspicion. Whether he is indeed a naive writer insensitive to the implications of his panegyric or a guileful sycophant who is more a modern than he admits, his tribute raises unsettling doubts about Swift's attitude towards satire. Moderns may overlook satire's dubious usefulness in their desire for reputation, but even the speaker must hesitate before he turns the ineffectualness of satire into the inspiration for its praise. By deliberately transforming the world's insensitivity to satire into a virtue, the encomium appears to deny the satirist any laudable reasons for writing. Its limited options insist that, if he is not motivated by a desire for fame and honour, the writer of satire will be ignored or prosecuted for his troubles. The forcefulness of this assault against traditional assumptions about the constructive power of satire has a seriousness that cannot be ignored. The mock encomium retains its irony yet does not obscure the possibility of a self-mocking Swift. His voice becomes clearer in the fifth edition when the Apology parallels the Preface's statements with the comment that people who 'lay themselves bare to the Lashes' of wit and humour 'think the Blow is weak, because they are insensible' (p 19). Stated more directly in the *Battle of the Books*, the attitude assumes that 'Satyr is a sort of *Glass*, wherein Beholders do generally discover every body's Face but their Own; which is the chief Reason for that kind of Reception it meets in the World, and that so very few are offended with it.'[35] Those who ridicule the world's follies, it would appear to follow, can hope for only marginal success.

Nevertheless Swift does not forsake his own talents for ridicule. It may be that indignation prevented absolute cynicism, or it is possible that the self-doubts expressed in *A Tale of a Tub* should be carefully qualified.[36] The mock encomium is after all a rhetorical stratagem that deftly creates the illusion of a clear choice and insists upon a commitment without admitting any qualification – a satirist must be either an ambitious, unscrupulous hack or a hopelessly optimistic fool. Neither: Swift keeps the decidedly unmodern capacity to be both serious and playful. His deliberate self-questioning invites the audience to join him in the recognition of his own pretensions, and together they laugh at those who lack this largeness of vision. For the satirist's audience laughter signifies a sophisticated acceptance of complex, seemingly contradictory issues; while against the satire's victims it becomes a lash administered to their admittedly insensitive hides. The curative effects may be negligible; but Swift does not hope to achieve a radical transformation. Secure in his own religious beliefs and drawn reluctantly into the ancient-modern controversy, his efforts like Marprelate's, Milton's, and Marvell's are designed more for exposure than for correction. The Apology specifies that *A Tale of a Tub* will be 'useful and diverting' only for those with wit and taste. They may be amused by the antics of the modern enthusiasts and religious zealots even though the fanatics are beyond help. By isolating these incorrigibles and presenting them as ridiculous Swift draws more closely together his community of listeners and invites them to benefit from the spectacle. In doing so neither audience nor author is exempt from the satire's laughter. A confirmation of their wit and taste is their ability to avoid compartmentalizing the humour and the seriousness.

The moderns' lack of this requisite sensitivity becomes increasingly apparent in the speaker's own resolution of self-doubt. Quite openly his prefatory comments confess that 'it sometimes tenderly affects me to consider, that all the towardly Passages I shall deliver in the following Treatise, will grow quite out of date and relish with the first shifting of the present Scene' (pp 43–4). When a parallel passage in the Apology announces that the tale 'seems calculated to live at least as long as our Language, and our Tast admit no great Alterations' (p 3), the declaration may be both ironic and serious; but in the Preface there is no ambiguity. The speaker accepts the sentiments of 'the very newest, and consequently the most Orthodox Refiners' and finds a consoling justice in his fate 'because, I cannot imagine why we should be at Expence to furnish Wit for succeeding Ages, when the former have made no sort of Provision for ours' (p 44). Still he betrays some anxiety in his hope that any reader apprised of the prevailing taste for wit at the exact moment of composition will plumb the depths of his sublimity, and his absurd recreation of his state of mind in August 1697 additionally suggests that he is concerned with being understood. Continued stress on time and communication throughout the *Tale* reveals that the speaker in fact shares Swift's interest in the endurance of literature. But his embarrassingly candid and imperceptive comments combined with attitudes which sometimes betray guilefulness are not as easily confused with the author's. Noticeably Swift's antitype at these moments, the speaker does not quite come to terms with himself or his predicament.

He confronts the problem directly in his dedicatory epistle to Prince Posterity. The resemblance of the opening lines to Wotton's *Reflections upon Ancient and Modern Learning*, the admission that he himself has been 'laughed to scorn, for a *Clown* and a *Pedant*,' and an insistence that his praise of modern writers be accepted as 'a Specimen of our Learning, our Politeness and our Wit' characterize the speaker as a modern. On behalf of this body of writers and in a manner reminiscent of Marprelate's obtuse speaker, he proposes to defend their claims to posterity, although he actually shows their inevitable obscurity. Confessing outright that moderns worship the goddess immortality, the speaker protests that 'in vain we offer up to her our Devotions and our Sacrifices' (p 34). While the epistle recognizes time as the enemy of modernity, its short-sighted author remains impervious to the reasons why posterity's impartial governor should devour modern efforts. Allowing that particular instances of worthy writing are as difficult to fix as clouds on a windy day, he cites among his candidates for future fame a man 'of infinite Wit and Humour,' Richard Bentley, and that author with 'a most gentlemanly Style, adorned with utmost Politeness and Civility; replete with Discoveries equally valuable for their Novelty and Use: and embellish'd with *Traits* of Wit,' William Wotton (pp 37–8). More damaging to the cause of modern fame than this endorsement is the speaker's need to affirm his sincerity and to insist 'in the Integrity of my Heart, that what I am going to say is literally true this Minute I am writing' (p 36). Unconscious of the ironic tension between the quest for fame and the modern disposition to commit itself to the moment, the speaker also presumes to instruct posterity. With self-congratulation the penultimate paragraph concludes that the epistle is written to enlighten; 'Nor do I doubt in the least, but *Your Highness* will peruse it as carefully, and make as considerable Improvements, as *other* young *Princes* have already done by the many Volumes of late Years written for a Help to their Studies' (p 38). Undoubtedly Swift intends the parting irony, but the speaker in his character of modern apologist presumably has no doubts about the efficacy of his efforts.

As the narrative about the three brothers and the will finally begins to unfold, its narrator maintains an obtusely sanguine view. With only the tale's preliminary events behind him, his fretting about its reception in foreign translations is amusingly presumptuous. The speaker's confidence in his endeavours for the universal advancement of knowledge and his reflection about the great 'Emolument this whole Globe of Earth is like to reap by my Labours' (p 106) exaggerate modern pretensions to greatness while they question the value of any writing. In his next digression the narrator confides that usefulness is after all only relative. The 'Modern Authors' with whom he identifies himself could never accomplish 'our great Design of an everlasting Remembrance, and never-dying Fame, if our Endeavours had not been so highly serviceable to the general Good of Mankind' (p 123). The damning nature of this disclosure does not, however, occur to this modern; and at the conclusion of his description of Aeolism he declares that the removal of prejudice and the establishment of the truest perspective are highly desirable goals, 'which I therefore boldly undertake without any Regards of my own, beside the Conscience, the Honour, and the Thanks' (p 161). When he echoes the motto of the Royal Society as he prepares to launch into the last section of his narrative, there seems little credibility in his boast that, 'Since my *Vein* is once opened, I am content to exhaust it all at a Running, for the peculiar Advantage of my dear Country, and for the universal Benefit of Mankind' (p 184). The speaker, who can see no contradiction, remains consistently earnest, precisely because he is a modern. Moderns, the satire implies, have become so consumed with themselves that they are inured to absurd contradiction; without perspective, they can see nothing beyond themselves.

They are at the same time characteristically pragmatic. In his dedication the bookseller admits to 'a wise Piece of Presumption,' supplementing the inscription to posterity with a practical dedication to Lord Sommers that will guarantee the sale of the book. Awareness of the ploys available to the practical dedicator is only less obviously apparent in the narrator. Both the preposterous dedication to posterity and the Preface reveal considerable sensitivity to form. Their author knows enough, for example, to end his dedication with a trite, pointless tag or to include the rubric from modern prefaces; and his enthusiastic literal-mindedness does not completely exclude the possibility that he is consciously meeting demands of form. The last sentence of the Preface admits as much when it proposes to 'dismiss our impatient Reader from any farther Attendance at the *Porch*; and having duly prepared his Mind by a preliminary Discourse, shall gladly introduce him to the sublime Mysteries that ensue' (p 54). This deference to the reader reflects the narrator's own understanding of prefaces and dedications. He recognizes that they are often disbelieved and not even read, yet he cannot forsake a '*Modern* Inclination' to elaborate his achievement; therefore, 'I thought best to do it in the Body of the Work, where, as it now lies, it makes a very considerable Addition to the Bulk of the Volume, *a Circumstance by no means to be neglected by a skilful Writer*' (p 132). Now sufficiently disposed to 'resume my Subject, to the Infinite Satisfaction both of the Reader and the Author,' the narrator soon interrupts his tale with another digression, this time in praise of digressions. His straightforward admission that writers would have little to publish if they were held strictly to the purpose confirms the growing suspicion that he embodies the superficiality satirized in Marprelate's, Milton's, and Marvell's exposures of shallow dignity and empty gesture. Form and custom are convenient means to build the readers' anticipation and to promote the illusion of substance. Dedication, preface, introduction, and digression ensure that something will be literally created as they assure a significant production. The narrator never fully recognizes that content has lost its traditional supremacy over form.

His modern commitment to pretence assumes that true communication frustrates appreciation of substance. Before he finally begins his fable of the coats and the will, the narrator accordingly adds still another introductory section to explain his intentions. On the surface more digressive and unrelated than the previous sections, its elaborate 'Physico-logical Scheme of Oratorial Receptacles or Machines' and its defence of modern authors actually have a zany appropriateness. The pre-eminence given to the pulpit, the ladder, and the mountebank stage, which later figure in the tale proper, suggests a desire to be heard. The simplistic solution of finding a vantage-point from which the wisdom can literally sink in and the earnest, absurd calculations that demonstrate its feasibility minimize the need for substance. Since the correct altitude or the addition of more words will add to the impression, the system need not worry about troublesome issues of content. Besides, the Grubstreet writers included with the narrator under the sign of the mountebank stage already occupy weighty positions among the learned and witty. The narrator insists that their eminence would not even be an issue with their detractors if an impartial judge could find the means to measure the quantity of writing quickly lost in time. Blaming superficial readers as well for the neglect that sorely grieves those authors who share the emblem of the stage, the Introduction applauds the ignored writers who provide the models for its treatise. Like the pattern of panegyric in the dedication, this praise reverses conventional notions of worth, as indeed it does 'serve to give the Learned Reader an Idea as well as a Taste of what the whole Work is likely to produce' (p 69). Aware that the wisest Grubstreet writers have enclosed their wisdom within types or fables so superficially involved 'that the transitory Gazers have so dazzled their Eyes, and fill'd their Imaginations with the outward Lustre, as neither to regard or consider, the Person or the Parts of the Owner within,' he holds out the assurance that the more penetrating reader will find hidden within the best Grubstreet productions 'the most finished and refined Systems of all Sciences and Arts' (pp 66–7).

Throughout the mixture of tale and digression that follows the narrator persists in his confidence. His first interruption of the fable makes obeisance to all true critics; but having finished the rites 'Expostulatory, Supplicatory, or Deprecatory,' the next digressions increasingly confront the problems and triumphs of the modern author. Without pausing to consider the implications of an opening sentence that subordinates usefulness to fame, 'A Digression in the Modern Kind' pompously proclaims: "I have found a very strange, new, and important Discovery; That the Publick Good of Mankind is performed by two Ways, *Instruction*, and *Diversion*' (p 124). Superseding Horace, the narrator finds diversion well suited to a modern readership addicted to '*Fastidiosity, Amorphy*, and *Osci-*

tation,' particularly since he has little material left for instruction. Faithful to his own models, however, he promises to layer *utile* with *dulce* in the best modern manner. With the help of a recently discovered distillate that dilates within the brain into uncountable systems and of a liberal plagiarism from his inestimable master Wotton, the narrator is confident in his belief that he has 'included and exhausted all that Human Imagination can *Rise* or *Fall* to.' Those who might criticize his muddled concoction, the next 'Digression in Praise of Digressions' continues, should consider the alternative before they object. Writers limited to the purposeful and deprived of indexes, compendia, and all the other systems of modern abstraction would produce few if any books; the digression therefore proposes to overcome finite matter with a system that provides authors with the advantages of listing, 'for want of which, the Learned World would be deprived of infinite Delight, as well as Instruction, and we our selves buried beyond Redress in an inglorious and undistinguisht Oblivion' (pp 148–9). More exuberantly in the next two sections nostrums and lists find fanciful counterpart in the system of Aeolism and the 'Digression on Madness'; both represent the quintessential modern belief that substance resides in the substanceless. From here it is an easy and almost inevitable transition to the nothingness praised in the conclusion.

A narrator faithful to the emblem of the Grubstreet writers offers the mountebank's promise of something from nothing. With the illusion of form and the hope of universal gain, his literary confidence game solicitously guides its audience through an anticlimactic experience that proves to be in one sense as hollow as a tub. Displaying a charlatan's understanding of human vanity, the narrator in his Introduction distinguishes the learned from the superficial, appeals to their discerning taste, and repeatedly assures his increasingly impatient readers that they are on the threshold of the most sublime mysteries. When the digressions run out and the remainder of 'this miraculous Treatise' must be delivered, he then explains that the superficial reader may be prompted to laugh, 'But the Reader truly *Learned*, chiefly for whose Benefit I wake, when others sleep, and sleep when others wake, will here find sufficient Matter to employ his Speculations for the rest of his Life' (p 185). In the end the failure to retrieve the tale's conclusion from a faulty memory and the willingness to share his plans for writing upon nothing are very much in character. Amusingly, so is his final appeal to the reader not to expect too much 'but give some Allowance to the Author's Spleen, and short Fits or Intervals of Dullness, as well as his own' (p 209).

In the satire's penultimate paragraph the narrator unhesitatingly ex-

cuses the failure to make good all of the work's claims because he recognizes in the end that 'I am too much a Servant of the *Modern* Way.'
Invention has supplanted reason and method to such an extent that this
modern cannot resist the temptation to substitute wit whenever wisdom
proves elusive. This confession and a further disclosure that he will seize
any means to display his efforts are tantamount to an admission that he
has perpetrated a literary hoax, yet he is not daunted. He simply may not
comprehend what it means to be among the fraternity of mountebanks,
and in all likelihood he can see absolutely nothing wrong with his practices. For an author who earlier boasts a career spanning three monar-
chies and embracing thirty-six factions form and substance are, after all,
only means to public recognition. Outrageous in his pretensions, the
narrator dramatizes the ambition satirized in his counterparts, Samuel
Parker, Joseph Hall, and John Bridges. Unlike them, however, he lays
himself open to lashes of wit and humour he has no capacity to feel.[37]

In his double role as object and vehicle of satire the narrator unwittingly exposes the essential nature of modernism. By reducing Temple's
critics to this single embodiment, Swift avoids charges of hypocrisy or
duplicity that would grant the moderns at least a complexity denied them
in the transparent behaviour of their eager emulator. At the same time the
narrator's efforts to praise the qualities he admires methodically undermine the dignity of his particular heroes. Bentley and Wotton survive the
panegyrics suitably enhanced to the narrator's satisfaction, but this kind
of wit and perspicacity regularly appears satiric to the traditional sensibility possessed by 'any Reader of Tast and Candor.' Although the narrator
also indirectly compliments their writing by occasionally imitating stylistic
idiosyncracies, Swift is little interested in their actual writing. 'A Digression concerning Critics,' which supplements Boyle's attack on modern
critics, is among the satire's most specific links with the ancient-modern
controversy; and its satiric effect does not depend heavily upon the
marginal references to Wotton's and Bentley's books. Like the next digression, which specifies Wotton's and the Royal Society's claims to greatness, the most damaging satire remains the narrator's uncanny ability to
find the most objectionable characteristics of a critic or the most trivial
experiments of a scientist and to commend them with earnest enthusiasm.

Swift relegates questions of ancient authorship and modern advances
to the incidental satire and develops instead his own understanding of the
issue between Temple and his adversaries. Captured in a sentence, Temple's criticism of man's delusions about his ability to measure truth be-

comes the narrator's prerogative to 'think fit to lay hold on that great and honourable Privilege of being the *Last Writer*; I claim an absolute Authority in Right, as the *freshest Modern*, which gives me a Despotick Power over all Authors before me' (p 130). Aware that time will also take away this moment of importance, the prototypical modern nevertheless cannot accept the possibility that his commitment to the instantaneous has its limitations. Rather than recognize time as a determiner of worth, the narrator and his kind choose to exist in a memoryless void that stresses the uniqueness of the individual. They assume the right not to acknowledge an indebtedness outside of the self, and they refuse to yield this solipsistic privilege to the future. Absent in their vain claims to originality are the charity and humility Temple and the other satirists in this study value as essential attributes of learning; in their place the moderns have confused arrogance with honour and concealed superficiality with pedantry. For them indexes, compendia, and flagrant plagiarism become ballast. Perhaps this weightiness will survive into the future; at present the modern remains complacent in the elevation of his own worth. Within this narrow existence reality becomes a projection of the modern's limited view.

The ultimate manifestation of this autonomy is a mania for systems that provides the pedantic moderns with a wealth of material without 'an Expence of Time and Forms' and reinforces a false sense of control. This reductiveness, which Swift satirizes in the narrator's two digressions in praise of diversion, is complexly analysed in the final digressions. The sections on Aeolism and madness move away from ridicule of the modern penchant for empty form and endless catalogues to explore the tendency towards literal absoluteness. The quintessential element of air and the '*Phænomenon* of *Vapours*' are in the narrator's view the key to the most eloquent and profound human endeavours. But the theory of vapours in 'A Digression on Madness' is nothing short of madness. Perplexing in the extreme, this most intricate part of the satire demonstrates most memorably the wit and humour designated in the Apology as Swift's distinctive jest.

The proposal for 'the Use and Improvement of *Madness* in a Commonwealth' tenuously holds the ludicrous and serious together in a simple, insane prescription for greatness. Henry More had earlier outlined satirically the theory in *Enthusiasmus Triumphatus*, and Andrew Marvell ironically demonstrates it in *The Rehearsal Transpros'd*; it remains for Swift's narrator, however, fully to develop vaporous frenzy into an emptiness that resembles the 'Edifices in the Air' of the pulpit, the ladder, and the stage and that anticipates the conclusion's 'Ghost of Wit.' Closely allied in principle to Aeolism, the phenomenon of vapours traces greatness to a single source. All of history's most significant deeds – conquest of empire, advancement of new philosophies, and establishment of new religions – originate in hyperactive invention influenced by vapours 'ascending from the lower Faculties to over-shadow the Brain, and thence distilling into Conceptions, for which the Narrowness of our Mother-Tongue has not yet assigned any other Name, besides that of *Madness* or *Phrenzy*' (p 167). Grandiose schemes are thereby reduced to their fundamental inspiration and success is largely a matter of the moment. The timely release of choleric vapours stimulated by sexual frustration ended one world conquest, and in another circumstance war ceased when 'The same Spirits which in their superior Progress would conquer a Kingdom, descending upon the *Anus*, conclude in a *Fistula*' (p 166). Similarly the success of less violent schemers depends on the chance of the moment; observing that there is a harmony unique to individuals, the narrator stresses a proper tuning, 'for if you chance to jar the String among those who are either above or below your own Height, instead of subscribing to your Doctrine, they will tie you fast, call you Mad, and feed you with Bread and Water' (p 168). Circumstances of time, place, and person then literally assume great significance, and chance is an important factor. The unfortunate fate of William Wotton confirms the delicate line discriminating fool from philosopher, for the narrator is certain that Wotton's stature would not have diminished had he turned his talents away from philosophy 'into their proper Channels of *Dreams* and *Visions*, where *Distortion* of Mind and Countenance, are of such Sovereign Use' (p 169). Redundant humours in harmony with the 'Seasons' will, on the other hand, transform scoundrel to hero and madman to public benefactor. Seizing the opportunity 'long sought for,' the narrator demonstrates his theory with an appropriately mad scheme to transform the inhabitants of Bedlam into the servants of the state. Almost superfluously he adds in the last sentence of his digression that he too often allows his imagination to displace reason: 'upon which Account, my Friends will never trust me alone, without a solemn Promise, to vent my Speculations in this, or the like manner, for the universal Benefit of Human kind; which, perhaps, the gentle, courteous, and candid Reader, brimful of that *Modern* Charity and Tenderness, usually annexed to his *Office*, will be very hardly persuaded to believe' (p 180).

Yet this ironic conclusion to an increasingly bizarre proposal is not easily laughed away. While only an equally mad reader would accept the insane propositions, the narrator sometimes strikes a disquieting note. His wild notions about loosing the bedlamites into the government momentarily make sense when he describes the ways in which madmen could fill compatibly positions of public power. Discrediting the suggestion requires a belief in the essential sanity of statesmen, an affirmation which may not come easily. Once again unsettling disjunctive rigidity, Swift manipulates both the moderns and his own audience. 'Men of Wit and Tast' may smile at the narrator's efforts to capitalize on the appropriateness of the moment, and they may applaud his telling criticism of William Wotton, but their privileged detachment is not automatically secure.[38] At its most deliberately ambiguous moments the jest in 'A Digression on Madness' appears to be directed at everyone.

The laughter becomes most encompassing at the end of the narrator's contention that vapours underlie the greatest changes in empire, philosophy, and religion. Significantly the summation begins with a polarity between reason and imagination designed to support the justice of the theory. Content with the 'common Forms' and willing to form understanding by 'the Pattern of Human Learning,' man is reluctant 'to form Parties after his particular Notions; because that instructs him in his private Infirmities, as well as in the stubborn Ignorance of the People. But when a Man's Fancy gets *astride* on his Reason, when Imagination is at Cuffs with the Senses, and common Understanding, as well as common Sense, is Kickt out of Doors; the first Proselyte he makes, is Himself, and when that is once compass'd, the Difficulty is not so great in bringing over others' (p 171). The distinction sounds like the kind of discrimination Temple maintains in his essays, and a number of twentieth-century readers detect Swift *in propria persona* throughout this and the ensuing paragraph. Difficulties arise, however, as the subsequent statements appear to invert the traditional supremacy of reason in favour of a complete liberation of credulous imagination. By the end of the next paragraph the only choice appears to be a felicitous condition known as the '*Possession of being well deceived*'; there seems no alternative to this 'Serene Peaceful State of being a Fool among Knaves.' Even the narrator's insensitivity, more apparent in the paragraph's famous meiosis about the woman flayed and the beau stripped, does not offset a sense of compelling logic. A deliberate dialectical movement replete with subtle qualifications and striking aphorisms demands more than unusual attention. The development moves inexorably towards a resolution that prefers to sodder and patch imperfect nature rather than increase and uncover further fault.

The 'truly wise' man will follow Epicurus's example and 'content his Ideas with the *Films* and *Images* that fly off upon his Senses'; creaming off the top of nature, he will leave 'the Sower and the Dregs, for Philosophy and Reason to lap up' (p 174).

On the surface the dazzling motion of the two paragraphs appears to move logically away from the patterns and forms of learning that constitute traditional norms. Since what is left is a radical and troubling alternative, it is tempting to conclude that a cynical Swift has reached a bleakly negative dead-end.[39] But such a conclusion ignores the possibility that the essence of the paragraphs may be in reality the 'Sower' and 'Dregs.' An anatomy of the rhetoric reveals a tissue of words that covers limited alternatives and exclusive disjunctions with an appearance of sense. From the sound distinction between carefully formed understanding and transcendent fancy the paragraphs manipulate increasingly restrictive oppositions. Understanding-senses, fiction-truth, things past-things conceived, memory-imagination, womb-grave, credulity-curiosity, patch-expose, and wise-fool lead to the ultimate fool-knave. Lulling the reader with their precision and sweeping him along in their hypnotic ifs, buts, and so thats, the sentences disarm reason with the illusion of reason. Giving the reader the semblance of choice, they in turn dramatize the narrator's bias for a reductive superficiality.

Their success, moreover, cannot easily be denied. Readings contending that Swift actually implies an allegiance to common sense, forms, or a golden mean are not quite to the point. Although they are preferable to interpretations that find in Swift an unrelieved cynical strain, neither conclusion is necessary. These paragraphs primarily demonstrate the ease with which illusion becomes certainty and credulity replaces curiosity. Much of their humorous wit depends upon Swift's ability to develop a fallacious, mock-encomium of madness that threatens to become serious. 'Men of Wit and Tast' invited to admire the whimsy with which Swift ingeniously departs from the conventional find themselves uncomfortably caught with unexpected answers to profoundly important issues. The sign of the sophisticated man of taste is an ability to entertain ambiguity and to laugh at himself for being unable always to find satisfactory solutions to life's contradictions. Swift's distinctive laughter encourages his audience to repudiate the easy option and to admit the restrictions of any choice. Moderns do not have this capacity and insist on a solipsistic concreteness because they have cut themselves off from the past. The lessons of tradition instruct man in his own limitations; but they also temper despair with the comfort inherent in time's continuity. Lasting tradition teaches that man endures in spite of contradictions and paradoxes, and those who value time realize the virtue of the detachment it teaches. In contrast the moderns, faced with the prospect of emptiness and determined to assert themselves, do not have the ability to laugh. Blind to the foolishness which their earnestness creates and isolated from the repository of experience, they are hopelessly committed to the flux of time and the choices it appears to demand. In their insecurity they cannot comprehend a sensibility like Swift's that can both jest and be earnest, that can both laugh at the sometimes impractical yet desirable traditional ideals just as it entertains the possibility that persona and author are not always inseparably 'Outside' and 'In.' This refusal to accept the mutually exclusive is neither scepticism, elusiveness, nor coyness; for Swift and his select audience it originates in the wisdom that the earlier satirists too found in the tradition of humanism.[40]

In the *Tale* proper a clearer confidence determines a similar satiric laughter. Here the will and the coats, 'the Doctrine and Faith of *Christianity*, by the Wisdom of the Divine Founder fitted to all Times, Places and Circumstances' (p 73), provide Swift with a precise perspective from which to view the extremes of reductivism. Much of the jest remains within the purlieu of the narrator's emblematic pulpit, 'the Writings of our *Modern Saints* in *Great Britain*, as they have spiritualized and refined them from the Dross and Grossness of *Sense* and *Human Reason*' (pp 61–2), though Swift interprets the pulpit's province loosely. While he may have had specific treatises in mind, such as Bentley's on *critica sacra*,[41] and he certainly does acknowledge the conventional meaning of 'Saints,' the satire specifically involves Catholicism and Anglicanism in its survey of the coats' post-patristic alterations. When sense, reason, and biblical guidance are distorted for selfish purposes, the humour exempts none from ridicule consistent with the underlying attitude of the digressions.

The direction of the satire in the narrative emerges before the first digressive interruption. Despite its beginning 'Once upon a Time' in an era still inhabited by dragons and giants, the tale of the three brothers and their coats quickly assumes a distinctly modern cast. Appropriately, the time-bound narrator with no sense of the past allows Peter, Martin, and Jack to cultivate the manners of foppish eighteenth-century wits in a remote period indistinguishable from contemporary England. This confusion of time, person, and place particularly suits the narrative since fashionable appearance commanded respect then as it does now. The narrator, however, ignores the obvious parallel and instructs his readers in the mysterious attractiveness found in the Grand Monde. Unexpectedly the discourse on sartorism, which conveniently adds to the tale's bulk, contains 'Some Points of Weight' which have not been 'sufficiently illustrated.' Within a system that reverses the values essential to Marprelate, Milton, and Marvell clothing becomes the essential measure of rational beings and the outside takes precedence over the inside. Once mind and soul are recognized as more natural to the exterior, the real worth of sartorial splendour is obvious. Because Peter, Martin, and Jack worship fashion in the belief that clothes literally make the man, their mania for shoulder-knots, gold lace, and silver fringe appears less foolish than the ecclesiastical preoccupation with external signs of honour ridiculed by the three earlier satirists. Unfortunately, in order to remain consistent with the demands of sartorism, they must also disregard their father's will, a dilemma which the brothers solve with still another inconsistency. In their fidelity to the surface they distort the meaning apparent throughout the will; and when ingenious manipulation of single letters fails to yield the desired result, the brothers invoke a hidden, mythological, or allegorical dimension. As a last resort the will is locked away and interpretations are rendered by fiat. Peter and his two brothers have achieved the modern mentality. Like their later counterparts the brothers realize that religion also can profitably depend upon the individual whim of the beholder.

But the narrative is more than a religious satire that complements the digressions' concern with modern solipsism as it exposes the clergy's wilfull abandonment of its true office. While the three brothers are preoccupied with finding their own interpretations in the will, the narrator entangles his readers in a similar search below the surface of his tale. Already primed by the assertion in the Introduction that writers in his fraternity 'have darkly and deeply couched' in their works the 'most finished and refined Systems of all Sciences and Arts,' the 'courteous Reader' is advised after the initiation into sartorism 'to peruse with a world of Application, again and again, whatever I have written upon this Matter' (p 81). This transparent suggestion of great profundity, on another level a reflection of Swift's playful seriousness, invites the *adepti* to participate in the wisdom of Peter. It is no matter that the 'Learned Brother' has been schooled in Aristotle 'to find out a Meaning in every Thing but it self' or that the tale presents his '*Mythological*, and *Allegorical*' translation of broomsticks into fringes as more than a little absurd. Wills, coats, red satin linings, and embroidered Indian figures encourage secondary meanings, and the temptation to find them cannot be resisted. The narrative seems to support an allegorical dimension that Swift may have intended, yet it threatens to trap the reader into making a fool of himself. The humour within the seriousness could not have been more aptly demonstrated than in William Wotton's observations upon *A Tale of a Tub*. His eagerness to unravel the dark conceits, like that of Edmund Curll's *Complete Key*, demonstrates the natural tendency to seek deeper significance; and it is poetically just that Wotton is incorporated into the footnotes of the fifth and all later editions. The other footnotes whose authorship Swift must deny to sustain his ruse then increase the ambiguous joke. They may claim that 'It is likely the Author, in every one of these Changes in the Brother's Dresses, referrs to some particular Error in the *Church of Rome*' (p 86), but the one specific equation of 'flame Coloured Sattin' with Purgatory, re-gardless of how just it might be, has a strained congruity not dissimilar to that linking broomsticks and fringes. While the reader with 'Tast' can, of course, protest that his interpretations in no way resemble Peter's extreme distortions, the distance separating them is also less certain. The laughter remains; the objects simply must be more widely defined.

When the narrative resumes with an account of Peter's growing for-tunes, the jest is more pronounced. Again the section follows much the same rhythm as the eldest brother becomes more aggressive and in the end kicks Martin and Jack out. Wotton also contributes to the noticeably more intrusive footnotes, for Peter's increasingly bizarre creations of whispering-offices, universal pickling, and roaring bulls need extensive explanation. Since objects have now replaced the words found in the will, the brother's new, exaggerated distortions evoke a greater laughter. En-larged to the preposterous, 'the Ridiculous Inventions of Popery' are, Wotton recognizes, bantered and burlesqued as 'things to gull silly Superstitious People; and to rook them of their Money.'[42] The humorous renditions of confession, holy water, and other papal rites do not, how-ever, sit well with Wotton's fear that any sport at the expense of another religion may finally undermine the dignity of all religion. Swift's laughter assumes, on the contrary, that the ridicule of beliefs not founded in reason or sanctioned by Scripture amounts to the exposure of madness. He will not accept Wotton's more latitudinarian position, quite simply because, like Milton and Marprelate, and perhaps even Marvell, he believes that religion in its purest form cannot be compromised. By divorcing his satire from a doctrinal context and capturing the ludicrous in Peter's behaviour Swift moreover demonstrates that it is virtually impossible not to laugh at the absurd.[43]

The pontifical brother, in the narrative's estimation a 'Master of a high Reach, and profound Invention,' embodies the humour inherent in the modern mentality. Thus the narrator's opening intention of contributing to universal betterment and his later caution against overlooking 'certain dark points' of beneficial significance strike a tenor befitting the section's subject. Peter also promises easy panaceas for the most perplexing problems, and he too pretends that great meaning underlies all he propounds. Although his elaborate remedies go to ridiculous extremes that presumably succeed no better than the scheme for pardoning prisoners, which costs 'Wretches trusting to this ... their lives and Money too,' the most telling satire often singles out the believers. Those who hope to benefit from Peter's offices must duly rivet their eyes on one point 'and by no means break Wind at both Ends together, without manifest Occasion,' or perhaps place their mouths near a prescribed ass's head and 'by a fugitive Faculty, peculiar to the Ears of that Animal, receive immediate Benefit, either by Eructation, or Expiration, or Evomition' (p 108). With the inventor, the believers must accept the premise that windy force or mechanical operations will effect a metamorphosis. Their willingness to submit to these undignified postures reveals an absurdity more damaging than the rituals of penance, absolution, or confession which are ridiculed. Peter at least has an excuse: stretched to its limits, his brain finally *'shook* it self, and began to *turn round* for a little Ease. In short, what with Pride, Projects, and Knavery, poor *Peter* was grown distracted, and conceived the strangest Imaginations in the World' (pp 114–15). Inflated with new importance and inclined to blow the hats off disrespectful passers-by, the brother with a proven facility for finding hidden meanings in words now proposes to change bread into mutton and wine. What appears jest to his brothers remains totally serious to the increasingly intractable inventor. Deranged, arrogant, and 'no better than a Knave,' Peter succumbs to his own version of reality; self determines truth, *'and the D---l broil them eternally that will not believe'* (p 121).

When the history of the brothers continues after 'A Digression in the Modern Kind,' Jack develops an even more extreme madness. Unlike his temperate brother Martin, who sets about carefully restoring his coat in accordance with the will, Jack proceeds much too zealously. Martin wisely realizes that the alterations can never be entirely removed without damaging the original substance, and he restores a coat comparable to the view of the Anglican church presented in the Apology, 'the most perfect of all others.' An indignant Jack, smarting from Peter's imperious treatment, cares less about his father's exact commands; in his eagerness to rip out hateful remnants he ignores Martin's admonitions for cautious moderation. These arguments in fact so 'exalted *Jack's Levity'* that an opposite effect occurs: '*Martin's Patience* put *Jack* in a *Rage*; but that which most afflicted him was, to observe his Brother's Coat so well reduced into the

State of Innocence' (p 140). Maddened by excesses of spleen, spitefulness, and contradiction, Jack surpasses Peter's insantity with 'the oddest Whimsies that ever a sick Brain conceived.' In this state of mind he founds the sect of Aeolists.

Aeolism perfects the principle of wind that Peter had only begun to exploit. With an impossibly literal-minded logic fraught with puns the narrator proceeds after suitable digression to explain why eructation, or the 'Gift of BELCHING,' is for the Aeolist devotees 'the noblest Act of a Rational Creature' (p 153). Part of the inspiration for the description of dissenters may have been More's *Enthusiasmus Triumphatus* and Marvell's *The Rehearsal Transpros'd*, but the zany discourse remains characteristically Swiftian. In two short, allusive paragraphs of esoteric distinctions and cabalistic jargon '*Spiritus, Animus, Afflatus,* or *Anima*' are indiscriminately reduced to wind; in turn wind, the breath of life, is seen to be a fourth anima in man; and this observation leads with dazzling obscurity to the recognition that an extraction of all four forms in man the quintessential element. Seen from this point of view, the Aeolists gaping into the wind and united in a circle 'with every Man a Pair of Bellows applied to his Neighbour's Breech' make their own kind of sense. As the narrator points out with syllogistic finality, their efforts to achieve repletion end in public good, since '*Words are but Wind; and Learning is nothing but Words*; Ergo, *Learning is nothing but Wind.* For this Reason, the Philosophers among them, did in their Schools, deliver to their Pupils, all their Doctrines and Opinions by *Eructation*, wherein they had acquired a wonderful Eloquence, and of incredible Variety' (p 153). The understatement in the last passage becomes apparent in an ensuing description of Aeolist inventions that easily eclipse the preposterous creations of Peter's fantasy. Bladders filled at the sacred source, wind barrels efficiently equipped to funnel the northern blasts, and officers with the capacity to transform gusts introduced through lower regions into ecstatic emissions learnedly parody and literally supersede ancient and modern forms of inspiration. The laughter that ridicules Protestant dissenters captured ignominiously in postures more ludicrous than those of Peter and his followers is not subtle. Preachers, their facial features distorted, darkened, and transformed into a foam, deliver, often with prurient gusto, the most rarefied northern inspiration to 'panting' followers: 'some are greedily gaping after the sanctified Breath; others are all the while hymning out the Praises of the *Winds*; and gently wafted to and fro by their own Humming, do thus represent the soft Breezes of their Deities appeased' (p 156). For them the nothingness of wind represents everything.

The absurd delusion of Jack and his fellow dissenters culminates in the narrative's final, vigorous depiction of zealous madness. Before the tale about the coats and the will trails off into vague incompletion, its last section reveals the 'strange Variety of Conceptions' that succeeded Aeolism. Peter reappears with his brother in a crescendo of inanity and comes within a convenient lacuna of being confused with Jack, but the distance separating the two is still great. In his mania for increasingly remote levels of mystery the younger brother literally transforms his father's will into shapes of his own. Belittling the dissenters' penchant for self-justification based on a distortion of the Scriptures and caricaturing their excessive reliance upon predestination, the satire attacks with heavy hand fanatics who have reconstituted reality to fit their needs. Off in paroxysms of madness at the sound of music or the sign of colour, Jack adds to the image of the fervent reformer the groans and stripes of a religious enthusiast. These too, however, have little accord with reality, since secretly administered heat produces the groaning and public entreaties secure beatings 'sufficient to swell up his Fancy and his Sides' in emulation of martyrdom. This demented perversion accompanies a more repellent image. Because he can find no alternative at a crucial moment to the biblical directive, 'he which is filthy, let him be filthy still,' Jack chooses to live with his excrement. He also imparts a filthiness to others, attracted to his fits of prayer and rewarded when Jack would suddenly 'piss full in their Eyes' and 'all tobespatter them with Mud.' Dirtiness, disease, and noxious odour further complement the mad quirks that dehumanize the zealot; and in the dark, illuminated only by the glow emanating from his orifices, Jack is seen to possess 'the Scull of an Ass.' The metamorphosis into bestiality completes a series of jokes in *A Tale of a Tub* probably based on Bentley's references to an ass with the last jest on ears. Outside and inside receive still another turn and the history draws to its end with the suggestion that 'as in the *Ears* and *Nose*, there must be a Parity also in the *Inferior*' (p 201). The *double entendre* uses verbal confusion to praise the leaders and their 'devouter Sisters, who lookt upon all extraordinary Dilations of that Member, as Protrusions of Zeal, or spiritual Excrescencies, were sure to honor every head they sat upon, as if they had been *Marks of Grace*' (p 202). England's recent history of cropped ears then provides the parting joke in 'a brief Survey of the falling State of *Ears*' and the efforts to 'advance their antient Growth in the present.'

Further particulars of the dissenters' subsequent adventures lost in the narrator's faulty memory hint at their rise in popularity; Jack's personality, however, undergoes no further alteration. Reduced to the level of a raving madman controlled by vaporous influences and inflated with

Aeolist inspiration, Jack is hopelessly beyond change. The unrelenting satiric metamorphosis shows the dissenting brother impervious to either reason or laughter. The serious implications of the transformation, even with the rather short shrift given Martin, offer no quarter to any outside the Anglican Church. While the Church of England may not possess the original doctrinal purity, which, as the tale of the coats indicates, can now be only approximated, its authority in tradition and in reason offers for Swift the most acceptable means to the ideal. Sixteenth- and seventeenth-century controversies about necessary and incidental belief are then, quite simply, indifferent matters; and all who undermine the established church are freely ridiculed in an anatomy of madness that surpasses earlier depictions of dissenters in its extremeness and its sexual humour.

From the beginning of the tale ambiguous puns on the tailor idol as a 'God of Seamen' and explicit references to the brothers' venereal diseases establish a tenor that culminates in the final jokes on ears.[44] Along with the numerous references to excremental functions and physical peculiarities, coarse jests and prurient allusions found in seventeenth-century satire are transformed through robust imagination into an effective ridicule that never loses sight of the satirist's deliberate self-consciousness.[45] At the expense of his victims' dignity Swift encourages his audience to applaud the means as well as the end when, for example, common assumptions about the salaciousness of female fanatics support the satire's suggestion that these women accept oracular inspiration 'entring and passing up thro' a Receptacle of greater Capacity' or when Jack's penchant for excrement is carefully set up in a potentially bathetic joke compounded by the added footnote, 'I cannot guess the Author's meaning here, which I would be very glad to know, because it seems of Importance' (p 191). The satire in turn gains force from a vision that mechanically traces all extraordinary behaviour beyond perversions of the mind and body to common origins. Even though the phenomena of vapours and Aeolism cannot be seriously entertained, they contain a peculiarly satisfying logic. Combining the exterior with the interior and greatness with madness, their pseudoscientific air gives the illusion of credibility to a satire that finds humour in the most ignominious expressions of mind and body. At the same time it cannot be forgotten that this insistent ridicule of a reductive insanity remains itself unmistakably and unrelentingly reductive.

The ironic and artistic control that sustains this duality encourages still further complexity in the satire's unity. As the narrative and the digressions continue to unfold, the differences between the religious enthusiasts and the moderns seem to disappear in a commonly shared pride that extends finally to the complete denial of reality, madness. Tale and digressions alike lose the rigid distinctions established by the section headings, and the two parts tend to come together in a crescendo of nothingness. The obvious likeness between sections VIII and IX, Aeolism and the 'Digression on Madness,' and the reversal of the normal order of narrative and interruption in sections X and XI tempt the reader to find additional relationships and even an organic unity in a work that does not conceal its flagrantly pragmatic intention. Its putative author may be a literary confidence-man who promises profundity but delivers only cryptic and open-ended narration; and his digressions often postpone the deception with a pastiche of gestures common to the modern writers, as chance or an unreliable memory appears to govern their position; still the satire entices its audience into limited commitments. The tale of the brothers promises to make more sense when dragons and whispering offices yield ecclesiastical meanings; tone becomes more exact if Swift can be distinguished from his persona or personae; and attitudes towards moderns and Nonconformists will emerge as soon as suspect passages are traced to their origins. Like the choice between fool and knave offered in 'A Digression on Madness,' *A Tale of a Tub* deliberately poses a dilemma. Once the reader tries to impose an interpretation on its elusive material, he runs the risk of compromising in part his right to laugh at the satire's victims; detachment, however, remains very difficult. The satire makes its basic point when the reader recognizes that he himself possibly must acknowledge a kinship with the moderns.

Wotton and Bentley, Swift, and the readers are caught in an artistry that defies comfortable stasis. Erudite scholars and churchmen find their writings incorporated into a work that renders them fools, and then allows one of the main subjects of ridicule to comment on the folly. Their inclination to oversimplify is exposed in a maddeningly simplistic vision in which the authorial viewpoint shifts uncertainly among various voices, and the reader who thinks he can define the author and pinpoint his position may find himself betrayed by his own presumption. But 'Men of Wit and Tast' who have the necessary circumspection will accept the all-encompassing laughter, knowing that jest and earnest do not necessarily exclude each other. Profound dilemmas of human existence are humorously examined with a dazzling rhetorical virtuosity and the opponents of Anglicanism are ridiculed in an apparently uncompromising attack that recognizes that any claim to seriousness runs the danger of oversimplification. As a sign of certainty and/or an admission of limitation the laughter in *A Tale of a Tub* paradoxically strengthens credibility. Although the union of jest and earnest admits a diversity of interpretations, appropriately it eludes definition.

The achievement is impressive, particularly when seen in terms of the tradition of Marprelate, Milton, and Marvell. Like the earlier satirists Swift recognizes within the specific issues of church polity much larger questions of human conduct central to the tradition of humanism. By extending the literal decorum that governs the earlier satirists' preoccupation with manner he gives further dimension to the principle of *decorum personæ* and the emphasis on characterization. In the process the dramatic element crucial to the other satires becomes intrinsic not only to the narrator and his tale but to the themes themselves. The reader who attempts to unfold tale within tale finds himself involved in an experience that dramatizes much that the satire attacks. And the author who apologizes for his elaborate satiric joke must himself subordinate this justification to the experience of the *Tale* itself. Here, more completely than his predecessors in their satires, Swift dramatizes the precept that the satirist's manner does indeed determine the decorous use of religious ridicule.

The immediate success and the numerous subsequent editions of *A Tale of a Tub* suggest considerable receptivity in a decade when divines purportedly rivalled jesting deists and scoffing atheists 'with an attempt of raillery and humour, as a more successful method of dealing with heresy and infidelity.'[46] But the period which applauded Swift's 'most audacious Example' of a 'pernicious Abuse of Wit' seemed to Richard Blackmore in 1716 an era dominated by influential arbiters of taste who valued wit at the expense of religion.[47] And Anthony Ashley Cooper, the Earl of Shaftesbury, also singles out 'that detestable writing of that most detestable author of the *Tale of a Tub*, whose manners, life, and prostitute pen and tongue are indeed exactly answerable to the irregularity, obscenity, profaneness, and fulsomeness of his false wit and scurrilous style and humour.'[48] While these comments reveal the biased exaggeration common among contemporary reactions to Swift's satire, Shaftesbury's judgment in particular reflects a growing opposition to the religious satire not only of Swift but also of the other writers considered in this study.

Shaftesbury has no sympathy for one of the greatest satires on religious zeal even though he himself is the foremost eighteenth-century advocate of the freedom to ridicule fanatical beliefs or enthusiasm. "Tis only in a free nation, such as ours,' the opening argument of *A Letter Concerning Enthusiasm* (1708) contends, 'that imposture has no privilege; and that neither the credit of a court, the power of a nobility, nor the awfulness of a Church can give her protection, or hinder her from being arraigned in every shape and appearance.'[49] No religion, much less the superstitious and the enthusiastic, should then be exempt from the province of laughter: free exchange determines when 'unnatural' humour will not survive and 'ill-placed' ridicule must fail. An important proviso, however, limits the actual freedom of wit and humour. Brushing aside any harm that might occur to religion, Shaftesbury defends his proposal in a later essay with the reminder that 'I am writing to you in defence only of the liberty of *the club*, and of that sort of freedom which is taken amongst gentlemen and friends who know one another perfectly well.'[50] Swift was in fact not indifferent to 'the Tast of those who were like himself'; and for that matter, all of the satirists in this tradition recognize a specific audience, and all are aware of the arguments that lead Bacon among others to prohibit public criticism. Nevertheless they do not accept Bacon's corollary that 'we contend about ceremonies and things indifferent,' for the issues seem to them to involve profound personal and national considerations. They might agree in principle with Shaftesbury that the larger public must not 'be laughed at to its face,' condescended to in disdain, or threatened with disturbance; however, in practice they overcome misgivings and even risk repression to seek the wider audience offered by printing.

The manner in which the satirists pursue their ideals, furthermore, does not readily conform to Shaftesbury's understanding of temperate evenness and 'amicable collision.' His good humour insists upon the naturally appropriate and the moderation he sees in the biblical example of Christ. Unlike Milton and the proponents of zeal, who believe that divine behaviour sanctions a harsh, aggressive, and even scornful laughter, Shaftesbury applauds the sharp, witty, and felicitous language he finds throughout Christ's humourous pleasantry. He disapproves, moreover, of Restoration and contemporary eighteenth-century church controversialists who have ignored the New Testament lesson and have created a 'burlesque divinity' in their eagerness to employ raillery and humour on behalf of orthodoxy. Authors prone to extremes of harshness or clownishness appear to him peevish, wanton, and childish, caught always 'between anger and pleasure, zeal and drollery.' Given a freedom of exchange conducted with 'decent language' and pursued without any 'offense to the arguer,' the essays argue that acceptable limits for wit and humour would soon emerge and no need would exist for the extremes of ridicule which, Shaftesbury believes, flourish in periods of suppression.

In short, the religious satires of Marprelate, Milton, Marvell, and Swift assume an engagement too radical for a view of religious ridicule more suited to the theories of an essayist than the practice of a satirist. None would disagree with the values to be found in freely conducted exchange – indeed all share to some degree Marprelate's desire for open confrontation – but they also recognize the realities of the times. Whether primarily motivated by the urgency of their religious convictions or by their reactions to intemperance the four satirists respond to a sense of public necessity that often transcends very real threats to their personal welfare. Their development of distinct forms of religious ridicule confirms a tendency that Shaftesbury finds typical in periods of limited freedom, and their desire for a general forum reflects an intense seriousness at odds with the essayist's manner and with the eighteenth century's changing temperament.[51]

Yet none of the satires compromises its sense of decorum. Despite an expediency that prompts them, however reluctantly, to develop new modes of ridicule, none of the satirists in this study is content merely to accept the obvious advantages ridicule offers the public disputant. Like other contemporary prose controversialists they all insist upon a literal-minded sense of decorum that allows them to excuse their methods with the need to answer ridicule in kind. However, they do not base their manners solely upon this proverbial tenet. Although necessity prompts them to write religious satire, they undertake their obligations to jest with thought and imagination.

Their responsibility is most apparent in the apologies each satirist develops. Generally the arguments in support of ridicule add little to the rhetorical and religious traditions summarized in Barrow's sermon, but the presence of the apologies themselves reveals a characteristic sensitivity. Though somewhat defensive, the justifications indicate the satirists' fundamental belief that generic definitions of animadversion are less important than considerations of proper method. All of the satirists recognize that classical and religious precedents sanction only the possibility of ridicule: the decision to mix jest and earnest ultimately depends on the circumstances; and each of the satirists realizes that these judgments must be determined individually and largely in terms of character.

As the strategy of Marprelate's *decorum personæ* suggests, the essential approach balances the ethos of the satirist against that of his adversary.

Thus Marprelate's satires against Bridges and the Anglican establishment vindicate themselves with the justification, 'I jested because I dealt against a worshipful jester'; but this claim to a method based on the example of the opponent gives way to a greater insistence upon the satirist's own integrity. In the course of his writing Marprelate like Milton realizes that the success of his radical position depends primarily upon his own moral integrity. All of the authors in fact recognize the central importance of the satirist's character, and even the elusive Swift finally appeals to 'Men of Wit and Tast' who can appreciate the ethos obscured by the satire's complexity. By seizing opportunities and manipulating carefully drawn impressions of character they make the defence and the fulfilment of the satire integral to each other.

This sense of character, which represents an emerging and markedly modern consciousness,[52] sets the satires apart from the welter of contemporary prose tracts and warrants the attention given to their forms. While other writers such as Richard Overton and John Eachard assume personae or interject witty jibes, their efforts do not rise above the *ad hoc* attack of animadversion. Marprelate, Milton, Marvell, and Swift transform tractarian controversy into literature at least partly through the organic unity of their works. In each instance their innovative fictions depend upon a dramatic opposition of characters. Where the apologies can only state justifications, the satires elaborately translate into concrete form and action abstract ideas and specific individuals: a duncical Bridges, an incompetent Hall, Bayes the Second, the enthusiastic moderns, and Peter, Martin, and Jack. Always the satirists' presence, unmistakable in Milton's self-dramatization as well as in Swift's self-effacement, is apparent in the dramatic manipulation of personalities and issues for artistic ends. Whatever liberties are taken with the circumstances, the result is a seriousness that expresses the satirists' intense personal engagement. Because they sustain a remarkable degree of artistry in often very trying situations, they give additional support to the demeanours they claim for themselves, and they ensure a wide and enduring audience.

The achievement of the four satirists discussed here depends upon a common, and crucial, conviction absent in the essays of Shaftesbury and in the modern temperament. As in other apologies for religious ridicule, the decorum which Shaftesbury's essays invoke accepts the importance of one's manner, though it is soon evident that such careful attention to behaviour reflects a revealing hypersensitivity to laughter's abuse. While the offers of the essays 'to stand the test of ridicule' idealistically proclaim that 'One may defy the world to turn real bravery or generosity into ridicule,' their larger contexts and the subsequent eighteenth-century reactions to them discourage vigorous ridicule.[53] Some reservations about the inviolability of truth are also apparent earlier, particularly in the momentary bitterness of Marprelate and in the scepticism of Marvell, but all four satirists finally refuse to compromise. The fundamental obligation of their satires, as well as the ultimate justification for their manner, therefore, remains charity, the essence of Christianity. Although they may disagree about doctrine, each of the satirists in his own way is willing to run the risks of public confrontation in order to teach Christian civility. The love may take different forms, and it may be envisioned with varying degrees of passion, eloquence, or urbanity, but each satirist insists upon its paramount importance both as an end and a means. Within a circularity that inextricably links charity with truth and manners, relationships and distinctions tend to blend. The satirists are earnest when they assure their audiences of decorous modes of jest which, in the words of Barrow, are 'innocent and reasonable, conformable to good manners, (regulated by common sense, and consistent with the tenour of Christian Duty, that is, not transgressing the bounds of Piety, Charity and Sobriety).'

They do so with the convictions still possible in the era which their satires reflect. Although in a simplified sense the four satirists follow a historical pattern of the growing demand for revolution and its reactionary aftermath, they are primarily interested in the responses to the underlying conflicts. Their attention to tradition, their concern for individualism, and their preoccupation with the tension between the superficial and the essential indicate a common refusal to disavow the pressing issues of the historical moment. Without succumbing to the opposite temptations of either absolutism or compromise, they recognize the greatness of human potential. At the same time they also acknowledge the wisdom of the past and the importance of social order. Because they believe in the attainability of truth, they strive for a liberality and harmony absent in narrow, simplistic visions. Thus it is not surprising that in pursuit of their ideal they reconcile the additional opposition of jest and earnest.

The four are, in conclusion, Christian humanists sensitive to the traditions and the pressures of a tumultuous era. When this historical moment passes and the unfinished tale of the third brother Martin ends happily for him in Georgian stability, the religious ridicule these writers developed becomes less significant. Marprelate enjoys only a semblance of the notoriety accorded him in the Restoration, Milton and Marvell are diminished in stature, and the initial controversy surrounding *A Tale of a*

Tub becomes less urgent.[54] But the satirists' common respect for the power of language and truth seems now once again remarkable even though the religious issues that inspired them are more remote than ever. In their commitments to pursue error and deliver it 'bound either to Reason or Laughter' the satirists undauntingly assume that in the search for truth both human faculties harmoniously though paradoxically coexist. In their very different ways each demonstrates that earnestness is a condition of jest; as an expression of truth and a means to their ends religious ridicule becomes then its own justification. Overcoming in practice what they lack in their often conventional arguments, Marprelate, Milton, Marvell, and Swift demonstrate that the uniqueness of man is indeed '*animal rationale, mortale, risus capax.*'

Notes

1 Anthony Collins, *A Discourse Concerning Ridicule and Irony in Writing* (London 1729), p 5.

2 The importance of fiction in satire was first significantly discussed by Northrop Frye, and the concept has been used by Edward W. Rosenheim Jr in *Swift and the Satirist's Art* (Chicago 1963) to distinguish satire from polemic. Rosenheim argues that some form of 'manifest fiction' is central to all satire: 'For all satire involves, to some extent, *a departure from literal truth* and, in place of literal truth, a reliance upon what may be called a *satiric fiction*' (p 17). 'And if the rhetorician departs at any point from literal truth into a deliberate fiction which he intends the audience to recognize for what it is, if this fiction is a means for conveying or augmenting his literal argument, and if that argument involves an "attack" as we have been using the term, then the rhetoric assumes, however transiently and transparently, the character of satire' (p 18). Melville Clarke explores the range of emotion in 'The Art of Satire and the Satiric Spectrum,' in *Studies in Literary Modes* (London 1958), pp 31–49.

3 Blaise Pascal provides a convenient seventeenth-century summary of patristic precedents in letter xi of *The Provincial Letters* (1656). Early illustrations of religious satire are presented in G.R. Owst's *Literature and Pulpit in Medieval England* (Cambridge 1933) and in John Peter's *Complaint and Satire in Early English Literature* (Oxford 1956). Although Peter's study focuses primarily on sixteenth-century verse and dramatic satire, he emphasizes the tension between the nature of satire and 'the Christian principle of sufferance and restraint.' The analysis of the major prose satirists presented here is at odds with the solution to the dilemma Peter finds; he feels that a temporary dependence upon the classical norms of satire displaces Christian ethics.

4 William Vaughan, *The Golden Fleece* (London 1626), pp 9–10.

5 Aristotle makes this observation in *De partibus animalium*: 'That man alone is affected by tickling is due firstly to the delicacy of his skin, and secondly to his being the only animal that laughs' (trans William Ogle in *The Works of Aristotle*, ed J.A. Smith and W.D. Ross [Oxford 1912], v, 673a). Socrates' dual role is described by Thomas Sprat in *The History of the Royal-Society* (London 1667), p 417.

6 Thomas Jackson, *A Treatise of the Holy Catholike Faith and Chvrch* (London 1627), p 176.

7 William Prynne, *The Falsities and Forgeries of the Anonymous Author of a late Pamphlet ... Intitled The Fallacies of Mr. William Prynne* (London 1644), p 1.

8 Thomas Edwards's complaints in the first parts of *Gangraena* (London 1646) about Goodwin's manner are answered by John Goodwin in *Anapologesiates antapologias* (London 1646).

NOTES TO CHAPTER TWO

1 For a sense of the general traditions which the satirists relied upon and the directions of future movements see Lane Cooper, *An Aristotelian Theory of Comedy* (Oxford 1924); Mary A. Grant, *The Ancient Rhetorical Theories of the Laughable*, University of Wisconsin Studies in Language and Literature 21 (Madison 1924); V.A. Kolve, 'Religious Laughter,' in *The Play Called Corpus Christi* (London 1966), pp 124–44; Ernst R. Curtius, *European Literature and the Latin Middle Ages*, trans Willard R. Trask (London 1953), pp 417–35; Alan H. Gilbert, *Literary Criticism: Plato to Dryden* (New York 1940); Marvin T. Herrick, *Comic Theory in the Sixteenth Century* (Urbana, Ill. 1950); Norman Knox, *The Word Irony and Its Context, 1500–1755* (Durham, NC 1961); David Farley-Hills, *The Benevolence of Laughter* (London 1974); P.K. Elkin, *The Augustan Defence of Satire* (Oxford 1973); and Stuart M. Tave, *The Amiable Humorist* (Chicago 1960).

2 Richard Greenham, 'Of Ioy and Sorrow,' in *Godly Instrvctions for the Dve Examination and Direction of All Men*, in *The Workes*, ed H. Holland (London 1612), p 726.

3 Corbyn Morris, *An Essay Towards Fixing the True Standards of Wit, Humour, Raillery, Satire, and Ridicule* (London 1744). Morris considers Barrow, Cowley, Dryden, Locke, Congreve, and Addison to have made important statements on wit.

4 Barrow was a master of Trinity College who distinguished himself as one of his country's foremost scholars. Before he voluntarily yielded the Cambridge chair of mathematics to his protégé Isaac Newton, Barrow held successively the professorships in Greek at Trinity and mathematics at Gresham and Cam-

bridge. His designation as doctor of divinity in 1670 then allowed him to devote his remaining years more exclusively to the study of divinity. See Irène Simon, *Three Restoration Divines, Barrow, South, Tillotson* (Paris 1967), pp 213–28.

5 Erasmus, *The Seconde tome or volume of the Paraphrase of Erasmus upon the new testament* (London 1552), fol cxxxvii[v].

6 John Chrysostom, *An Exposition Vpon the Epistle of S. Paule the Apostle to the Ephesians* (London 1581), p 222.

7 John Trapp, *Annotations Upon the Old and New Testament* (London 1662), v, 766.

8 John Mayer, *A Commentary Vpon The New Testament ... Vpon all the Epistles of the Apostle Pavl* (London 1631), p 373. Mayer lists 156 classical and religious authors whose opinions he claims to represent.

9 Henry Hammond, *A Paraphrase, and Annotations Upon all the Books of the New Testament* (London 1659), p 626. Chrysostom recognizes the danger of 'filthie talke' (p 222); and Calvin's sermon on this passage, which in Arthur Golding's translation attacks 'foolishe talke that is full of vayne bibblebabble,' focuses almost entirely on covetousness and lewdness (*The Sermons of M. Iohn Caluin, vpon the Epistle of S. Paule too the Ephesians*, trans Arthur Golding [London, 1577], fols 240[v] ff). See also Nicholas Hemming [Niels Hemmingsen], *The Epistle of the Blessed Apostle Saint Paule ... to the Ephesians*, trans Abraham Fleming (London 1581), p 168; and Obadiah Walker, *A Paraphrase and Annotations Upon the Epistles of St. Paul – Ephesians* (Oxford 1675), p 225.

10 Edward Leigh, *Annotations Upon all the New Testament Philologicall and Theologicall* (London 1650), p 287. Gouge, Gataker, Downame, Ley, et al., in their *Annotations Upon all the Books of the Old and New Testament* (London 1657), note that 'The word in the Original Ευτραπελία, signifieth facetiousnesse of speech, and by the Philosophers is taken in a good sense, who make it a virtue' (II, HHH4[v]). In *Ethica nicomachea* Aristotle had written: 'The kind of people one is speaking or listening to will also make a difference. Evidently here also there is both an excess and a deficiency as compared with the mean. Those who carry humour to excess are thought to be vulgar buffoons, striving after humour at all costs, and aiming rather at raising a laugh than at saying what is becoming and at avoiding pain to the object of their fun; while those who can neither make a joke themselves nor put up with those who do are thought to be boorish and unpolished. But those who joke in a tasteful way are called ready-witted, which implies a sort of readiness to turn this way and that; for such sallies are thought to be movements of the character, and as bodies are discriminated by their movements, so too are characters' (IX, 1128a), in *The Works of Aristotle*, trans W.D. Ross (Oxford 1940).

11 James Fergusson, *A Brief Exposition of the Epistles of Paul to the Galatians and Ephesians* (London 1659), II, 330–1.

12 'Gr. *Eutrapelia*, which word is sometimes taken in good part for honest pleasant discourses, which in times and opportunities are lawful and edifying, as there are examples thereof in Gods Word, 1 *Kings*. 18.27' in *The Dutch Annotations Upon the whole Bible*, trans Theodore Haak (London 1657), sig Rra[v]; also John Diodati, *Pious and Learned Annotations Upon the Holy Bible* (London 1651), sig Ddd4[v].

13 Isaac Barrow, *Several Sermons Against Evil-Speaking* (London 1678), p 41; hereafter cited in the text.

14 Trapp, *Annotations Upon the Old and New Testament*, v, 766.

15 Quintilian observes: 'the effect of a jest depends not on the reason, but on an emotion which it is difficult, if not impossible, to describe. For I do not think that anybody can give an adequate explanation, though many have attempted to do so, of the cause of laughter' (*The Institutio Oratoria of Quintilian*, trans H.E. Butler [Cambridge, Mass. 1966], II, 441).

16 Walter Charleton, *Two Discourses* I. *Concerning the Different Wits of Men* (London 1675), pp 140, 141. Although the work was written in 1664, the first edition was published in 1669.

17 Morris, p x.

18 The central passage is Cicero's statement: 'For Nature has not brought us into the world to act as if we were created for play or jest, but rather for earnestness and for some more serious and important pursuits. We may, of course, indulge in sport and jest, but in the same way as we enjoy sleep or other relaxations, and only when we have satisfied the claims of our earnest, serious tasks. Further than that, the manner of jesting itself ought not to be extravagant or immoderate, but refined and witty ... In our jesting let the light of a pure character shine forth' (*De Officiis*, trans Walter Miller [Cambridge, Mass. 1958], pp 105, 107). Cf *Marcvs Tullius Ciceroes thre bokes of duties* (1556), fol 41[r]; *The First Book of Tullies Offices* (London 1616), pp 211–12; Robert Whittington, *The thre bookes of Tullyes Offices* (1534), fol F7[v]; Roger L'Estrange, *Tully's Offices* (London 1680), p 55.

19 Paul Bayne[s], *An Entire Commentary Vpon the Whole Epistle of the Apostle Pavl to the Ephesians* (London 1647), pp 587–8.

20 William Chillingworth, *The First Sermon. 2 Tim. III 1–5*, in *The Works of William Chillingworth* (London 1704), p 330.

21 Thomas Granger, *A Familiar Exposition or Commentarie on Ecclesiastes* (London 1621), p 50.

22 The phrase is Notker Labeo's version of the Aristotelian notion; it is quoted by Kolve, p 127.

23 William Perkins, *A Direction for the Government of the Tongve according to Gods word*, in *The Works* (London 1631), I, 448.

24 Perkins follows closely Chrysostom's *Homily VI. Matt. 11. 1,2*: 'Yea, for He also wept, both over Lazarus, and over the city; and touching Judas He was greatly troubled. And this indeed one may often see Him do, but no where laugh, nay, nor smile but a little; no one at least of the Evangelists hath mentioned this' (*The Homelies of S. John Chrysostom on the Gospel of Matthew*, trans George Prevost, in *A Library of Fathers* [Oxford 1843], XI, 88).

25 Perkins, I, 447. The Bible also offers other passages for writers such as George Ridpath intent upon denouncing mirth and pleasure. In *The Stage Condemned* (London 1698) Ridpath condemns 'those foolish Jests, filthy Discourses, and immoderate Laughters that are occasioned by Comedies' with the biblical prohibitions: 'John 2.16; Ro. 13.14; Col. 3.2,5; Gal 5.24; 2 Tim. 3.4.; Tit. 3.3; Jam. 4.3; Luk. 8.14; Col 3.5; Mat 5.28; 1 Tim 2.9; 1 Pet 3.3; Pro 23.1; Ro 13.13; Col. 3.8; Col. 4.6; Eph 5.4; 1 Tim. 5.6' (p 179).

26 Jeremy Taylor, *Sermon xxiii*, in *The Whole Works of the Right Rev. Jeremy Taylor*, ed Reginald Heber, rev Charles Page Eden (London 1868), IV, 288.

27 Taylor, IV, 292. Taylor believes: 'The whole state of this question is briefly this; 1. If Jesting be unseasonable, it is also intolerable ... 2. If it be immoderate, it is criminal, and a little thing here makes the excess; it is so in the confines of folly, that as soon as it is out of doors it is in the regions of sin. 3. If it be in an ordinary person, it is dangerous; but if in an eminent, a consecrated, a wise, and extraordinary person, it is scandalous ... 4. If the matter be not of an indifferent nature, it becomes sinful by giving countenance to a vice, or making virtue to become ridiculous. 5. If it be not watched that it complies with all that hear, it becomes offensive and injurious. 6. If it be not intended for fair and lawful purposes, it is sour in the using. 7. If it be frequent, it combines and clusters into a formal sin. 8. If it mingles with any sin it puts on the nature of that new unworthiness, beside the proper ugliness of the thing itself' (IV, 290–1).

28 Taylor, IV, 292.

29 Among others: [Thomas Twyne], *The Schoolemaster, or Teacher of Table Philosophie* (London 1576), 'The fourth Booke: of mery Iestes, and delectable deuises'; Richard Rogers, *Seven Treatises* (London 1603), p 370; William Vaughan, *The Golden Fleece* (London 1626), p 11.

30 Edward Reyner, *Rules for the Government of the Tongue* (London 1656), pp 225–6. See also John Northbrooke, *A Treatise wherein Dicing, Dauncing, Vaine plaies or Enterludes ... are reprooued* (London 1579), fol 26ᵛ; Henry Crosse, *Vertues Common-wealth: Or The Highway to Honovr* (London 1603), sig. O4ʳ; Robert Barclay, *An Apology For the True Christian Divinity* (1678), pp 366–70. William Prynne's 'Actvs 5. Scena Vndecima,' in *Histrio-Mastix* (London 1633), pp 290–301, a valuable seventeenth-century source for patristic, classical, and biblical comments on laughter, further reveals that criticism of laughter is most

often associated with an attack on something else; even then the reaction is against 'profuse immoderate laughter' (p 296).

31 Erasmus, *On Copia of Words and Ideas (De Utraque Verborum ac Rerum Copia)*, trans Donald King and H. David Rix (Milwaukee 1963), pp 102–3. Aristotle, Cicero, and Quintilian still remain the authorities on ridicule for Henry Kames in *Elements of Criticism* (London 1769), I, 377.

32 Aristotle, *Rhetorica*, trans W. Rhys Roberts, in *The Works of Aristotle*, (Oxford 1924), XI, 1419b.

33 In his 'abridgement containing the most useful part of Aristotle's Rhetoric' Hobbes translates '*Iests* are dissolved by serious and grave discourse: and grave discourse is deluded by *Iests*' (*A Briefe of the Art of Rhetorique* [London 1637], p 200). The same translation occurs in the 1681 edition, *The Art of Rhetoric*.

34 Cicero, *De Oratore*, trans E.W. Sutton and H. Rackham (Cambridge, Mass. 1942), I, 373.

35 Representative examples are: John Jewel, *Defence* (1570), in *The Works of John Jewel*, ed John Ayre (Cambridge 1850), IV, 916; John Frith, *The Workes of the excellent Martyr of Christ, Iohn Frith*, in *The Whole workes of W. Tyndall, Iohn Frith, and Doct. Barnes* (London 1573), p 68; Northbrooke, *A Treatise wherein Dicing, Dauncing, Vaine plaies or Enterludes ... are reprooued*, fol 26ᵛ; [Dudley Fenner], *The Artes of Logike and Rhetorike, plainelie set foorth in the English tongue* (1584), sig D2ᵛ; Henry Peacham, *The Garden of Eloquence*, intro William G. Crane, Scholars' Facsimiles and Reprints (Gainesville, Fla 1954), p 36; Thomas Granger, *Syntagma Logicvm. Or, The Divine Logike* (London 1620), pp 381–2; Richard Bernard, *Thesaurus Biblicus* (London 1661), pp 140–1; John Boys, *The Workes of Iohn Boys Doctor in Diuinitie and Deane of Canterburie* (London 1622), p 57; John Smith, *The Mysterie of Rhetorique Unvailed* (London 1657), pp 47–8; Thomas Hall, *Rhetorica sacra* (London 1654), p 168, in *Vindiciae literarum* (London 1655); Gouge, et al., *Annotations Upon all the Books of the Old and New Testament*, I, B2ʳ; Fergusson, *A Brief Exposition of the Epistles of Paul to the Galatians and Ephesians* II, 329; Trapp, *Annotations Upon the Old and New Testament*, I, 369; Simon Patrick, *A Commentary Upon the Two Books of Kings* (London 1705), p 267.

36 Thomas Sprat, *The History of the Royal-Society* (London 1667), p 419.

37 John Fell, *The Character of the last Daies. A Sermon Preached before the King* (Oxford 1675), p 20.

38 Mary Claire Randolph, 'The Medical Concept in English Renaissance Satiric Theory,' *Studies in Philology*, 38 (1941), 125–57; also Alvin P. Kernan, *The Cankered Muse* (New Haven 1959).

39 Almost a century earlier Puttenham had defined *Asteismus*, or the 'ciuill iest,' as the mirthful civility with which a gentleman can indirectly mock without intending grief or offence. Reyner, whose justification of delight anticipates

Barrow's, also expresses a similar likeness in his declaration that 'There is a dexterity in speaking truth in an Irony; or in a pleasant sentence, which may be taken sometimes with lesse offence, then a plain downright speech.' Although Reyner includes his discussion under the heading 'Rules of Urbanity' and Puttenham is highly conscious of 'decency,' they do not stress the Restoration nexus between playful jest and behaviour. See George Puttenham, *The Arte of English Poesie*, ed Gladys Willcock and Alice Walker (Cambridge 1936), p 190; Reyner, *Rules for the Government of the Tongue*, p 227.

40 Tom Brown, *Twenty Select Colloquies out of Erasmus Roterodamus. To which are added, Seven New Colloquies, as also The Life of Erasmus* (London 1699), sig C2ʳ. Brown's comments and colloquies are added to the twenty selected by Roger L'Estrange.

41 'Neither is it true, that this fineness of raillery is offensive. A witty man is tickled while he is hurt in this manner, and a fool feels it not. The occasion of an offence may possibly be given, but he cannot take it. If it be granted, that in effect this way does more mischief; that a man is secretly wounded, and though he be not sensible himself, yet the malicious world will find it out for him; yet there is still a vast difference betwixt the slovenly butchering of a man, and the fineness of a stroke that separates the head from the body, and leaves it standing in its place' (*A Discourse concerning the Original and Progress of Satire*, in *Essays of John Dryden*, ed W.P. Ker [New York 1961], II, 93).

42 Richard Flecknoe, 'Of Raillerie,' in *Enigmaticall Characters* (London 1658), p 30.

43 Flecknoe, p 31.

44 'You might have considered,' Samuel Rolle writes in *A Sober Answer To the Friendly Debate, Betwixt a Conformist and a Nonconformist* (London 1669), 'the temper of the age you live in, which is almost all *froth, Air, humor, Droll, Hudibras feathers*, yea *alamode of France* ... which is already almost *mad with mirth*' (sig B2ʳ). *Remarques on the Humours and Conversations of the Town* (London 1673), similarly notes: 'I do believe, that never in any Age, was there such a violent and universal thirst after the Fame of being wits, and yet no Age has possibly discharg'd it self, with less real applause' (p 93). 'This Age of ours,' Fell concurs in *The Character of the last Daies*, 'has somwhat of mockery for its particular Genius' (p 19).

45 Peacham, *The Garden of Eloquence*, p 35. Robert South more pointedly asks in his *Sermon on Matt. XIII. 52* (1660): 'For is it possible, that a man in his senses should be merry and jocose with eternal life and eternal death, if he really designed to strike the awful impression of either into the consciences of men?' (*Sermons Preached Upon Several Occasions* [Oxford, 1842], II, 359). Thomas Sprat also sees a secular dimension: 'For the ordinary ill breeding is only an indecence and offence against some particular Custom, or Gesture, or Behaviour in use. But

this prophaneness is a violation of the very support of humane Society, and a rudeness against the best Manners that all mankind can practise, which is a just reverence of the Supreme Power of all the World' (*An Account of the Life and Writings of Mr. Abraham Cowley* [1668], in *Critical Essays of the Seventeenth Century*, ed J.E. Spingarn [Oxford 1957], II, 134). The attempt to justify, though not publish, certain dialogues of Lucian, that 'most impious blasphemer of our Saviour Christ, and of his sacred doctrine,' reflects the dominant attitude – see Francis Hickes, *Certaine Select Dialogves of Lvcian* (Oxford 1634), and Jasper Mayne, *Part of Lucian made English from the Original in the Yeare 1638* (Oxford 1663).

46 Joseph Glanvill, *The Sin and Danger of Scoffing at Religion*, in *Seasonable Reflections and Discourses In Order to the Conviction, & Cure Of the Scoffing, & Infidelity Of a Degenerate Age* (London 1676), p 6.

47 *A Dialogue between Tom and Dick over a Dish of Coffee Concerning Matters of Religion and Government* (London 1680), p 12. Further support for this characterization can be found in Clement Ellis, *The Vanity of Scoffing* (London 1674); *Remarques on the Humours and Conversations of the Town*, p 69; and Richard Blackmore, *A Satyr Against Wit* (London 1700), p 6. But this charge must be as cautiously qualified as the mistaken notion that the Puritan was 'the archenemy of laughter' who 'hated and denounced it in daily life no less than in the theater' (Louis Cazamian, *The Development of English Humor. Parts I and II* [Durham, NC 1952], p 114). The accusation of atheism arises often in reaction to Hobbes or in the heat of pamphlet warfare; it is hurled at people who are often neither extremely irreligious nor very witty.

48 Glanvill also objects in *The Sin and Danger of Scoffing at Religion* that 'the Scoffer is not *sure* that he is wiser than *all mankind*, that hath reverence for it. He hath *no demonstration* to prove Religion *false* and *ridiculous*: Nor is he *absolutely certain*, that there is no *Immortality* or *future judgement*' (p 37).

49 Stephen Ford offers an extended statement of the prevailing attitudes in *The Evil Tongue Tryed, And found Guilty: Or, The Hainousness, and exceeding Sinfulness of Defaming and Back-biting, open and declared* (London 1672).

50 Ben Jonson, *Timber: or, Discoveries*, in *Works*, ed C.H. Herford and Percy and Evelyn Simpson (Oxford 1947), VIII, 633–4. William Congreve quotes this passage in *Amendments of Mr. Colliers False and Imperfect Citations, &c.* (London 1698), p 64. The distinction is very commonly made: Trapp, for example, cites Elijah to contend that 'All mocking therefore is not unlawful: not that which tendeth to the discountenancing of sin; but that which is to the unjust disgrace, and just grief of another' (*Annotations Upon the Old and New Testament*, I, 369). In the many editions of *The Isle of Man* (London 1668) Richard Bernard argues: 'In discovery, attaching, arraigning and condemning of Sin, I tax the Vice, and not any Mans person' ('Epistle to the Reader,' sig A5^r).

51 John Dryden, *A Discourse concerning the Original and Progress of Satire*, II, 79 ff. Jonathan Swift, 'Verses on the Death of Dr. Swift,' in *The Poems of Jonathan Swift*, ed Harold Williams (Oxford 1958), II, 571. Elkin, who observes that 'It is tempting to conclude that more personal satire was written in the late seventeenth and early eighteenth centuries than in any other period in English history,' emphasizes the Augustans' inconsistent attitudes towards personal references; see *The Augustan Defence of Satire*, pp 118–45.

52 Thomas Wilson, *A Complete Christian Dictionary* (London 1655), p 358. Quintilian, II, 443.

53 Greenham, *Of a Good Name*, in *The Workes*, p 261.

54 Richard Baxter, *A Christian Directory* (London 1673), pp 438–46.

55 John Goodwin, *Cretensis* (London 1646), pp 4–5. The standard argument often cites the prohibition implicit in the fifth commandment and the inviolability of the divinely annointed; in *Amendments of Mr. Colliers False and Imperfect Citations, &c.* Congreve interestingly uses Article 26 of the 39 Articles to contend that 'If he is found to play the Knave, he is subject to the Penalties of the Law, equally with a Lay-man; if he plays the Fool, he is equally with a Lay-fool, the subject of Laughter and Contempt' (p 63).

56 William Vaughan, *The Spirit of Detraction* (London 1611), p 318.

57 Vaughan, *The Spirit of Detraction*, p 319. In another appeal for moderation Joseph Hall reminds the readers of *Christian Moderation* (London 1640) that 'wee refraine from all rayling termes, and spightful provocations of each other in the differences of Religion. A charge too requisite for these times; wherein it is rare to finde any writer, whose inke is not tempered with gall, and veneger, any speaker, whose mouth is not a quiver of sharpe, and bitter words' (pp 151–2). Among the most interesting of the moderate statements is Jacobus Acontius [Giacomo Aconcio], *Satans Stratagems* (London 1648). This reissue of the sixteenth-century tract has testimonies by John Goodwin, Ramus, and Samuel Hartlib.

58 See particularly Thomas Edwards's numerous examples in his preface to the first part of *Gangraena* (London 1646).

59 Boys, *The Workes of Iohn Boys*, p 276.

60 Boys, p 57.

61 Robert Abbot, *A Triall of Ovr Chvrch-forsakers* (London 1639), sig A4ᵛ. Thus Joseph Hall explains in *Christian Moderation*: 'The Chirugian stroakes the arme, before hee opens the Veine: But where lenitie prevailes not, wee are cruell to the Church, if we strike not home; when singing will not still the Childe, the Rod must: If they bee such as are without the reach of our Authoritie, wee must first doe our best, to make them sensible of the wounds they give to our common Mother, and those Rubs which they lay in the way of the Gospel; since it cannot be otherwise now, then the Historian noteth in those first Ages of the

Church, that the difference of Opinions, whereof one arose out of another, was a great hinderance to many, in pitching upon our holy Profession' (pp 172–3).

62 Edwards, *Gangraena*, p 178. Edwards conveniently summarizes the standard biblical references to Christ and the apostles when in *The Second Part of Gangraena* (London 1646) he asserts: 'Whosoever doth but well read the Scriptures, and observe what quick sharp passages are there recorded to have come from the mouth of Christ and his Apostles against Errors, Heresies, and false Teachers, yea sharper and more spoken against false Doctrines and false Teachers, then against bad manners (as for instance, *Mat.* 7.15. *Gal.* 1. 8,9. *Gal.* 5. 10. 12. 2 *Pet.* 2. 1, 2,3. 2 *John* 9. 10, 11. *whole Ep.* of *Jude Revel.* 2. 14, 15. 20. 22, 23. with a hundred other such) will never blame me for bitternesse, bloudinesse, inveteratenesse, &c.' (p 65).

63 John Edwards, *A Defence of Sharp Reflections on Authors and their Opinions*, in *Some New Discoveries of the Uncertainty, Deficiency, and Corruptions of Human Knowledge and Learning* (London 1714), p 187.

64 William Falkner, *Two Treatises. The First, Concerning Reproaching & Censure* (London 1684), p 121.

65 Falkner, pp 127–8.

66 Edward Stillingfleet, *Sermon XXXVI*, in *The Works* (London 1710), I, 567.

67 Stillingfleet, I, 567.

68 René Rapin, *Reflections upon the Eloquence of These Times; Particularly of the Barr and Pulpit* (London 1672), sigs A8^{r-v}.

69 Jonson, *Timber: or, Discoveries*, VIII, 634.

70 R. Selden, 'Roughness in Satire from Horace to Dryden,' *Modern Language Review*, 66 (1971), 264–72; Elkin, *The Augustan Defence of Satire*, pp 146–66.

71 Quintilian, II, 453. Later he repeats: 'above all *doubles entendres* and obscenity, such as is dear to the Atellan farce, are to be avoided, as also are those coarse jibes so common on the lips of the rabble, where the ambiguity of words is turned to the service of abuse' (II, 463).

72 As Clement of Alexandria tells the reader in *Christ the Educator*, trans Simon P. Wood (Washington 1954), Plato's *Republic* (x, 606c) does not condone men given to laughter or ridicule (p 134). Plato's comments on laughter are conveniently found in Cooper, *An Aristotelian Theory of Comedy*; and also in Grant, *The Ancient Rhetorical Theories of the Laughable*, who concludes that 'Plato [*Republic* 452d] makes the tacit admission that deserved ridicule is legitimate' (p 22).

73 Quintilian, II, 441.

74 Clement of Alexandria, *Christ the Educator*, p 135. Acknowledging Aristotle, he contends: 'It is true that man is an animal who can laugh; but it is not true that he therefore should laugh at everything' (p 135).

75 Peacham, *The Garden of Eloquence*, p 40. But they were assured that laughter's inherent element of distortion cannot be considered a lie. Roger Hutchinson

argues in *The Image of God* (1550): 'Jests and merry conceits be no lies, forasmuch as they be uttered not to harm, nay, or hinder any man, but for mirth sake. A man may affirm that which is false, and yet make no lie: for to lie is to affirm an untruth with a mind to hurt, endamage, and deceive, some man thereby' (*The Works of Roger Hutchinson*, ed John Bruce, Parker Society [Cambridge 1842], p 52).

76 Baxter, *A Christian Directory*, p 355.

77 George Williamson, 'The Restoration Revolt against Enthusiasm,' *Studies in Philology*, 30 (1933), 571–603.

78 Joseph Glanvill, *A Letter to the Reverend and Learned Dr. Henry More ... Reflections on Drollery and Atheism* in *Palpable Evidence of Spirits and Witchcraft ... with two letters* (London 1668), pp 144–5. In *A Discourse of Wit* (London 1685) David Abercromby similarly states that pretenders to wit 'are not clear enough sighted to discern what is true Sence, or down right Nonsense in a Discourse: They are only capable to judge of a polite Expression, of a Word *A-la-mode*, and other such like Childish niceties. They have, I confess, some confused Notions of every thing, which emboldens them to debate things that are beyond the reach of their Capacity. They are the professed Censurers of Mankind, and can speak good of none, themselves only excepted' (pp 42–3).

79 Glanvill, *A Letter To the Reverend and Learned Dr. Henry More ... Reflections on Drollery and Atheism*, p 152. Fell, *The Character of the last Daies*, also warns: 'The brightest evidence and vertue disguis'd and render'd monstrous by burlesque, like the Primitive Christians in the skins of wild beasts, will easily be worried and destroied. Nay so it fares, that the most venerable persons, things, and actions, are most liable to be thus expos'd and made ridiculous: for whatever this beloved acquisition proves, be it the gift of Nature, meant certainly for better purposes, or the product of drunkenness or frenzy, or what is yet a shorter method, of spight or malice, it has a peculiar faculty to pervert the best and most useful things' (pp 20–1).

80 Richard Allestree, *The Government of the Tongue* (Oxford 1674), pp 114–15.

81 Most prominent in the post-Shaftesburian controversy, the image is used as early as 1664 by Walter Charleton to deplore Aristophanes' unjust ridicule of Socrates.

82 Sprat, *The History of the Royal-Society*, p 417.

83 In *Contexts of Dryden's Thought* (Chicago 1968) Phillip Harth makes this important distinction about much Restoration thought mistakenly labelled as scepticism.

84 Glanvill, *The Sin and Danger of Scoffing at Religion*, p 31.

85 Sprat, *The History of the Royal-Society*, p 419.

86 Richard Blackmore, *An Essay Upon Wit*, in *Essays Upon Several Subjects* (London 1716), pp 206–7.

87 Edward Filmer, *A Defence of Plays* (London 1707), p 92.
88 In *Two Essays of Love and Marriage* (1657), pp 77–83, as quoted by Benjamin Boyce, *The Polemic Character 1640–1661* (Lincoln, Neb. 1955), p 14.
89 Edward Stillingfleet, *The New Way of Answering Examined in a Reply To Two late Pamphlets* (London 1672), p 7. Stillingfleet has no misgivings: 'we think the separating of *Fanaticism* from true inspiration to be one of the best Services that can be done to the *Christian Religion*' (p 11).
90 Tillotson, whom Blackmore values as 'a good Judge of Wit, and as great a Master of it as perhaps any Nation ever bred,' states: 'For though every man have a right to dispute against a false religion, and to urge it with all its absurd and ridiculous consequences, as the ancient fathers did in their disputes with the heathen; yet it is a barbarous incivility for any man scurrilously to make sport with that which others account religion not with any design to convince their reason but only to provoke their rage' (*The Folly of Scoffing at Religion* [London 1911], pp 11–12).
91 Quintilian, II, 445.

NOTES TO CHAPTER THREE

1 Martin Marprelate, *Hay any Worke for Cooper*, in *The Marprelate Tracts, 1588, 1589*, ed William Pierce (London 1911), p 239; hereafter cited in the text. Among the suspected authors of the Marprelate tracts, John Penry and Job Throkmorton were singled out by contemporary writers: the anonymous *An Almond for a Parrat* (1590) contends Penry wrote the tracts (*The Works of Thomas Nashe*, ed R.B. McKerrow [Oxford 1958], III, 365 ff); Matthew Sutcliffe accuses Throkmorton of the authorship in *An Answere vnto a Certaine Calumnious letter published by M. Iob Throkmorton* (London 1595). Despite their denials Penry and Throkmorton were generally recognized as the most probable authors until the late nineteenth century. More modern scholarship has suggested a number of different identities for Marprelate; they are conveniently summarized by Leland H. Carlson in 'Martin Marprelate: His Identity and His Satire,' in *English Satire, Papers Read at a Clark Library Seminar, January 15, 1972* (Los Angeles 1972), pp 3–53. Carlson, who justly criticizes Donald J. McGinn's arguments in favour of Penry (*John Penry and the Marprelate Controversy* [New Brunswick, NJ 1966]), believes Throkmorton is the sole author.
2 William Pierce, *An Historical Introduction to the Marprelate Tracts* (New York 1909), p 139.
3 John Bridges, *A Defence of the Government Established in the Chvrch of Englande for Ecclesiasticall Matters* (London 1587), sig q3ᵛ.
4 [Dudley Fenner], *A Defence Of the godlie Ministers, against the slaunders of D. Bridges, contayned in his answere to the Preface* (London 1587), sig A2ᵛ.

5 Thomas Wilson, *The Arte of Rhetorique* (London 1562), fol 2^{r-v}. In *The Garden of Eloquence*, intro William G. Crane, Scholars' Facsimiles and Reprints (Gainesville, Fla 1954), pp 144, 145, Henry Peacham, however, demands a 'discreet obseruation of necessarie circumstances': 'for in diuine Orations, and Sermons, to moue laughter doth much diminish and oppose the modestie of so graue an action, and so serious a cause.'

6 Wilson, fol 69^{v}.

7 Andreas Hyperius [Gerardus], *The Practice of Preaching, Otherwise Called the Pathway to the Pulpet*, trans John Ludham (London 1577), fol 42^{v}. Hyperius claims for the preacher a liberty not given the orator: 'For the Preacher chargeth, commaundeth, sharply rebuketh, threateneth, pronounceth, as one in place of authoritie, and as a Judge, the sentence of excommunication: But the Rhetoritian supposeth none of these thinges to bee lawfull unto him, but rather he is compelled nowe and then sowly to flatter and fawne upon the Judges.'

8 Fenner, sig E2^{v}.

9 Henry Sharpe's deposition as quoted by Edward Arber, *An Introductory Sketch to the Martin Marprelate Controversy. 1588–1590*, The English Scholar's Library of Old and Modern Works 8 (London 1879), p 97.

10 Matthew Sutcliffe, *The Examination of M. Thomas Cartwrights late apologie* (London 1596), fol 48^{v}.

11 John Jewel, *Defence* (1570), in *The Works of John Jewel*, ed John Ayre, Parker Society (Cambridge 1850), IV, 915.

12 John Frith, *The Workes of the excellent Martyr of Christ, Iohn Frith*, in *The Whole workes of W. Tyndall, Iohn Frith, and Doct. Barnes* (London 1573), p 68.

13 Celio Secondo Curione, *Pasquine in a Traunce* (London 1584), sig Aiij^{r}. Thomas More, in *The Apologye of Syr Thomas More Knyght* (1533), ed Arthur Irving Taft, Early English Text Society 180 (London 1930), answers those that 'reproue that I brynge in amonge the moste ernest maters, fansyes and sportes, and mery tales' with typical irony: 'For as Horace sayeth, a man maye somtyme saye full soth in game. And one that is but a lay man as I am, it maye better happely become hym meryly to tell hys minde, than seryously and solempnely to preache. And ouer thys I can scant beleue that the brethern fynde any myrth in my bokes. For I haue not myche herde that they very merely rede them' (p 194).

14 Listing a number of classical precedents in his prefatory letter to More, Erasmus contends: 'St. Jerome amused himself in this way with far more freedom and sarcasm, sometimes even mentioning names. I have not only refrained from naming anyone but have also moderated my style so that the sensible reader will easily understand that my intention was to give pleasure, not pain' (Erasmus, *Praise of Folly and Letter to Martin Dorp 1515*, trans Betty Radice [Harmondsworth/Baltimore 1971], p 60). The letter to Dorp adds Christ and

Socrates to the authorities sanctioning laughter; and Erasmus further argues: 'the two greatest orators, Cicero and Quintilian, had every reason for laying down rules for raising a laugh. Speech which has wit and charm has such power to please that we can enjoy a well-turned phrase even if it is aimed at ourselves' (p 221). Citing others who have vigorously ridiculed the clergy, he again claims that he has mentioned no individuals by name. 'If anything I've said seems rather impudent or garrulous,' he adds, 'you must remember it's Folly and a woman who's been speaking' (p 236).

15 John Coolidge, 'Martin Marprelate, Marvell and *Decorum Personæ* as a Satirical Theme,' PMLA, 74 (1959), 526.

16 Coolidge also cites Folly's precedent. The passage from Proverbs in the 1535 Coverdale Bible is 'make ye foole an answere to his foolishnesse, least he be wyse in his owne cõceate'; the Geneva Bible has 'Answere a foole according to his foolishnes, lest he be wise in his owne conceite.'

17 Quoted by Simon Patrick in a letter defending his own use of religious laughter, appended to *A Defence and Continuation of the Ecclesiastical Politie* (London 1671), p 738. Beza's argument from Proverbs was published in 1585.

18 *An Address to Demetrianus*, in *The Treatises of S. Caecilius Cyprian*, trans Charles Thornton, in *A Library of Fathers of the Holy Catholic Church* (Oxford 1839), III, 200.

19 Robert Allen, *An Alphabet of the holy Proverbs of King Salomon* (London 1596), p 13. Simply stated in *The Bookes of Salomon* (1551): 'Geue not the fole an aunswere after his folishnes, leste thou become lyke vnto him, but make the fole an aunswere to hys folyshnesse, lest he be wyse in his owne conceyte' (sig Giiii^v). Although they might agree with Cyprian that it is usually pointless to answer a fool, commentators believe that when 'The glory of God may be obscured,' when scandal or offence may be given, or when the fool becomes more insolent, 'then it is fit he should reprove the fool' (Arthur Jackson, *Annotations Upon ... Iob, the Psalms, the Proverbs, Ecclesiastes, and the Song of Solomon* [London 1658], p 892; also Robert Bolton, *The Workes* [London 1641], II, 121–2).

20 'Some make the sense of both verses to be this; that a fool ought not to be answered with words, but with a rod & correction' (Jackson, p 892). Michael Cope [Michel Cop], in *A Godly and learned Exposition vppon the Prouerbes of Solomon*, trans M.O. [Marcelline Outred] (London 1580), believes the verses allow answers to a fool that 'rebuke him, and tel him sharply and seuerly, that there is nothing but follie in him, and that he is voide of all wisdome' (fol 520^v); Joseph Hall prescribes a 'discreet and sober manner' in *A Plaine And Familiar Explication (by way of Paraphrase) of all the Hard Texts of the whole Divine Scripture* (London 1633), p 238. But a fool should not be met 'by conforming himself to his vain jangling, & weak manner of reasoning' (Jackson, p 892; Robert

Cleaver, *A Briefe Explanation of the Whole Booke of the Prouerbs of Salomon* [London 1615], p 436; Simon Patrick, *The Proverbs of Solomon Paraphrased* [London 1683], pp 443, 450).

21 [William Prynne], *A Revindication of the Anoynting and Priviledges of Faithfull Subjects* (1643), p 1.

22 *A Briefe and plaine declaration, concerning the desires of all those faithfull Ministers, that haue and do seeke for the Discipline and reformation of the Church of Englande* [usually referred to as *The Learned Discourse*], (London 1584), sig A3ʳ.

23 *The Learned Discourse*, sig A3ʳ.

24 Bridges, p 45.

25 Richard Hooker, *Of The Lawes of Ecclesiasticall Politie* (London 1594), pp 24 ff.

26 Bridges, p 46.

27 Fenner, sigs D1ᵛ–D2ʳ.

28 Fenner, p 150.

29 Walter Travers, *A Defence Of The Ecclesiastical Discipline* (1588), p 138.

30 Travers, p 38.

31 George Puttenham, *The Arte of English Poesie*, ed Gladys Willcock and Alice Walker (Cambridge 1936), pp 267 ff.

32 Aristotle, *Rhetorica*, trans W. Rhys Roberts, in *The Works of Aristotle* (Oxford 1924), XI, 1356a.

33 Bridges, pp 82–3.

34 Pierce, *An Historical Introduction to the Marprelate Tracts*, p 283.

35 Cicero, *De Oratore*, trans E. W. Sutton and H. Rackham (Cambridge, Mass. 1967), I, 375; also Cicero, *Orator*, trans H.M. Hubbell (Cambridge, Mass. 1939), p 371.

36 Wilson, fols 69ᵛ–70ʳ; Cicero, *De Oratore*, I, 379.

37 Wilson, fol 84ᵛ; Puttenham, pp 144–5.

38 *The Beehive*, cited by Penry as a precedent for the jest, illustrates a similar form of satiric praise.

39 Cf Travis L. Summersgill, 'The Influence of the Marprelate Controversy upon the Style of Thomas Nashe,' *Studies in Philology*, 48 (1951), 156–8.

40 Thomas Cooper, *An Admonition to the People of England*, ed Edward Arber, The English Scholar's Library 15 (Birmingham 1882), frontispiece, p 1.

41 Cooper, p 31.

42 Ronald B. McKerrow, 'The Martin Marprelate Controversy,' in *The Works of Thomas Nashe* (Oxford 1958), V, 44. The suggestion is based on a letter written by Whitgift and quoted in Strype's *Whitgift* (1718).

43 *The Learned Discourse*, sig A3ᵛ.

44 *On Christian Doctrine*, trans J.F. Shaw, in *The Works of Aurelius Augustine* (Edinburgh 1873), IX, 167–8.

45 Augustine, ix, 168.

46 In *The Plea of the Innocent: Wherein is auerred; That the Ministers & people falslie termed Puritanes, are iniuriouslie slaundered for enemies or troublers of the State* (1602) Josias Nichols writes: 'So great hurt is it, when an honest and lawfull course is begon, for foolish and hayrbraine men to trust in them selues, and to hazard such meanes as God neuer sanctified' (p 33). According to Samuel Clarke, Richard Greenham 'spake freely against that Book, manifesting his dislike of the same: For (Said he) the tendency of this Book is to make sinne ridiculous, whereas it ought to be made odious' (*A Martyrologie ... Together With the Lives of ten of our English Divines* [London 1652], ii, 85). Thomas Fuller, speaking 'on certain knowledge from the mouths of such whom I must believe,' also reports that many repudiated the writings as 'unbeseeming a pious spirit' (*The Church-History of Britain* [London 1655], book ix, p 193).

47 Thomas Cartwright, *A brief Apologie of Thomas Cartwright* (1596), sig C2^v.

48 Richard Bancroft, *Daungerovs Positions and Proceedings, published and practised within this Iland of Brytaine, under pretence of Reformation, and for the Presbiteriall Discipline* (London 1593), p 170; Matthew Sutcliffe, *An Answere vnto a Certaine Calumnious letter published by M. Iob Throkmorton* (London 1595), fol 48^r, and *The Examination Of M. Thomas Cartwrights late apologie* (London 1596), fol 48^r.

49 *Doctor Reignolds His Letter to Sir Fravnces Knollis, Concerning Doctor Bancrofts Sermon at Paules crosse.9. Feb: 1588. In the Parliament time,* in *Informations* (1608), p 75.

50 Richard Harvey, *A Theologicall Discovrse of the Lamb of God and His Enemies: Contayning a brief Commentarie of Christian faith and felicitie, together with a detection of old and new Barbarisme, now commonly called Martinisme* (London 1590), sig a1^v.

51 Sutcliffe, *An Answere vnto a Certaine Calumnious letter*, fol 75^r. In *Pappe with an hatchet* Lyly complains about '*Martins* dogged humour, who without reuerence, regard, or exception vseth such vnfitting tearmes, as were hee the greatest subiect in England hee could not iustifie them' (*The Complete Works of John Lyly*, ed R. Warwick Bond [Oxford 1902], iii, 405).

52 In his preface Harvey also criticizes Nashe. T.T. in *A Myrror for Martinists* (London 1590) writes: 'I cannot but on the one side condemne the late Martine libellers, and their fauorites, who hauing a bad cause, do as lewdly handle the same: and on the other mislike some repliers, who notwithstanding they haue chosen the better part, yet handle it not so charitably and modestly as it requireth' (p 1).

53 Sutcliffe, *An Answere vnto a Certaine Calumnious letter*, fol 80^r. Also Lyly's *Pappe with an hatchet*, iii, 396.

54 Leonard Wright, *A Friendly Admonition to Martine Marprelate, and his Mates* (London 1590), p 2.

55 Cooper, p 12.

56 Richard Bancroft, *A Sermon Preached at Paules Crosse the 9. of Februarie ... 1588* [1589], p 88.

57 Cooper, pp 11 ff. Bancroft, *Daungerovs Positions and Proceedings*, sigs A4^{r-v}.

58 Luke 10:16, as quoted by Harvey, p 186.

59 This fear is commonly voiced: Sutcliffe, *An Answere unto a Certaine Calumnious letter*, fol 48^r; Bancroft, *A Sermon*, p 68; Cooper, p 31; Wright, p 1.

60 Cooper, p 11. And in any case criticism should not be publicly made by private individuals: see Harvey, p 148; Wright, p 5; Bancroft, *Daungerovs Positions*, p 63.

61 Francis Bacon, *A Wise and Moderate Discourse, Concerning Church-Affaires. As it was written, long since, by the famous Author of those Considerations, which seem to have some reference to this. Now published for the common good.* The pamphlet is dated 1641; Spedding in his edition says it 'was first printed ... in 1640.' With a new title but the same errors in pagination it reappears in 1663 as *True Peace: Or a Moderate Discourse to Compose the unsettled Consciences, and Greatest Differences In Ecclesiastical Affaires.* William Rawley also includes it in *Resuscitatio* (London 1657) as *An Advertisement touching the Controversies of the Church of England.* James Spedding's edition in volume VIII of *The Works of Francis Bacon* (London 1861) will be cited.

62 Bacon, VIII, 76.

63 Bacon, VIII, 75.

64 Bacon, VIII, 88.

65 Bacon, VIII, 76–7.

66 Bacon, VIII, 77.

67 Bacon, VIII, 101.

68 *Hay any Worke* with the new title *Reformation no Enemy* appeared in 1641; the same year Margery Mar-Prelat wrote *Vox Borealis, or the Northerne Discovery* and *A Sermon Preached in London by a Faithfull Minister of Christ.* Marprelate's name was also added to *The Character of a Puritan* (1643), and Richard Overton used the pseudonym Martin Mar-Priest for five tracts printed in 1645–46.

NOTES TO CHAPTER FOUR

1 John Milton, *Of Reformation*, ed Don Wolfe and William Alfred, in *Complete Prose Works of John Milton*, ed Don Wolfe, et al (New Haven 1953), I, 540; hereafter cited in the text.

2 *A Second Defence of the English People*, ed Donald A. Roberts and trans Helen North, in *Complete Prose Works*, IV, i, 622.

3 *Animadversions*, ed Rudolf Kirk and William P. Baker, in *Complete Prose Works*, I, 653; Wolfe, ed, I, 79–80.

4 This is William Haller's description of Milton's style in *Liberty and Reformation in the Puritan Revolution* (New York 1955), p 50; Joan Webber characterizes the 'I' in this way in 'John Milton: The Prose Style of God's English Poet,' in *The Eloquent 'I'* (Madison 1968), pp 184–218. Both offer particularly valuable insights into Milton's antiprelatical tracts; some of their implications are developed in the following analysis.

5 In fact, only the year before the publication of *Animadversions* Edward Reynolds's *A Treatise of the Passions and Facvlties of the Soule of Man* (London 1640) describes anger as the most dominant and uncontrollable passion which 'of all other, hath the least recourse to Reason' sig Xx4ʳ. Coeffeteau observes in *A Table of Humane Passions*, trans Edward Grimstone (London 1621), that 'profound cogitations and meditations hinder laughter: wherefore wise men doe not laugh so easily as others' (p 303).

6 John Bastwick, *The Answer of Iohn Bastwick ... This is to follow the Letany as A second part thereof* (London 1637), p 1.

7 Bastwick, p 2.

8 *A Modest Confutation of A Slanderous and Scurrilous Libell* (1642), p 2.

9 When later in the Salmasian controversy Milton refutes the charge that his book 'abounds with the pleasantries of dissolute prodigals' he again cites the precedent of Cicero – this time quoting from *De oratore* – and adds: 'Even to Plato and the Socratics nothing appeared more seemly or decorous than pleasantries intermixed and interspersed sometimes in the gravest matters' (*Pro Se Defensio*, in *Complete Prose Works*, iv, ii, 771).

10 Milton claims that Bacon 'leaves an aspersion upon *Job*, which by any else I never heard laid to his charge. For having affirm'd that *there is no greater confusion then the confounding of jest and earnest*, presently he brings the example of Job *glancing at conceits of mirth, when he sate among the people with the gravity of a Judge upon him*. If jest and earnest be such a confusion, then were the people much wiser then *Job*, for *he smil'd, and they believ'd him not*' (1, 907). As the editor points out, Milton has combined two sentences actually separated by two paragraphs; in doing so, he distorts Bacon's contention that Job proves that serious issues demand reverence rather than mirth. Milton apparently does this, at least in part, to avoid entertaining any biblical alternative to Elijah and the authorities he mentions.

11 Richard Greenham, 'Of Conference and Godly wisdome in the gouernment of the tongue,' in *Godly Instrvctions*, in *The Workes* (London 1612), p 647; see also Thomas Kranidas's discussion in *The Fierce Equation: A Study in Milton's Decorum* (The Hague 1965), pp 49–71.

12 Oratorical traditions have also been suggested as models for Milton's prose. Cf Joseph Anthony Wittreich Jr, '"The Crown of Eloquence": The Figure of the

Orator in Milton's Prose Works,' in *Achievements of the Left Hand*, ed Michael Lieb and John T. Shawcross (Amherst 1974), pp 3–54; Annabel Patterson, 'The Civic Hero in Milton's Prose,' *Milton Studies*, 8 (1975), 71–101. Milton's general indebtedness to the prophetic tradition has been discussed in Michael Fixler's *Milton and the Kingdoms of God* (Evanston 1964) and William Kerrigan's *The Prophetic Milton* (Charlottesville 1974).

13 John Smyth, *Paralleles, Censvres, Observations* (1609): 'That Mr. Barrow eironically vpbraydeth the preaching and Worship of the assemblies, following therein Elias his example, I dare not censure that as an vngodly act of his' (p 134).

14 Richard Sibbes, *Violence Victorious*, in *The Complete Works*, ed Alexander B. Grosart (Edinburgh 1863), VI, 304–5.

15 Joseph Hall, *Contemplations vpon the Principall Passages of the holy Storie*, in *The Works* (London 1628), III, 1262.

16 Daniel Featley, *Clavis Mystica* (London 1636), pp 779, 792; see also pp 794 ff.

17 Oliver Bowles, *Zeale for Gods House Quickned* (London 1643), p 25.

18 George Gifford, *Sermons vpon the Whole Booke of the Revelation* (London 1596), p 207.

19 Gouge, Gataker, Downame, Ley, et al, *Annotations Upon all the Books of the Old and New Testament* (London 1657), I, 1113ᵛ. Milford C. Jochums also notes that Milton may have been influenced by the Helios myth as well as by the fiery chariots of the Bible (Isaiah 66:15; 2 Kings 2:11, 6:17) in *An Apology*, Illinois Studies in Language and Literature 35, nos. 1–2 (Urbana 1950), p 142.

20 Arthur Jackson, *Annotations upon the remaining Historicall Part of the Old Testament* (Cambridge 1646), p 552.

21 Bowles, pp 36–7.

22 George Hutcheson, *A Brief Exposition of the XII. Small Prophets* (London 1657), p 426.

23 In *Animadversions* Milton contends: ' 'Tis not Ordination nor Jurisdiction that is Angelicall, but the heavenly message of the Gospell, which is the office of all Ministers alike; in which sense *John* the *Baptist* is call'd an *Angel*, [Math. 11.], which in Greek signifies a Messenger, as oft as it is meant by a man' (pp 713–14).

24 Here Reynolds, who stresses the opposition between anger and reason in *A Treatise of the Passions and Facvlties of the Soule of Man*, is particularly interesting. To 'mannage this Passion as to be *Angry but not sinne*, it will be requisite,' he adds, 'To let it have an Eye *upward*, as *Moses* did, whonever [sic] expressed any other Anger that wee read of but zealous, and Religious, when the injury directly aimed at God and his honour' (sig Xx4ᵛ).

25 Webber also makes this point, p 203.

26 *A Modest Confutation*, sig A3ʳ.

27 In the sixth of the *Prolusions* Milton apologizes: 'If in the course of this I outgo by a finger's breadth, as they say, my usual custom and the strict rules of modesty, I beg you, gentlemen, to accept this explanation: it is to give you pleasure that I have put off and for the moment laid aside my usual habit, and if anything I may say is loose or licentious, put it down to the suggestion, not of my real mind and character, but of the needs of the moment and the genius of the place' (I, 276–7). More seriously he argues in *A Second Defence of the English People*: 'if anyone should find our rebuttal at any point somewhat frivolous, let him consider that we are engaged, not with a serious foe, but with a troupe of actors. So long as the nature of my *Defence* had to be suited to them, I thought that I ought to aim, not always at what would have been more decorous, but at what they deserved' (IV, i, 574). Milton also makes a number of statements supporting his jesting earnest in *Pro Se Defensio*; some of them may be found in Irene Samuel's 'Milton on Comedy and Satire,' *Huntington Library Quarterly*, 35 (1971/2), 107–30.

28 Thomas Kranidas, who examines 'Milton and the Rhetoric of Zeal,' *Texas Studies in Literature and Language*, 6 (1964/5), 423–32, relies mainly upon Thomas Brightman and the commentary on Revelation 'to examine Puritan fervor and its "rhetoric of zeal" as it relates to its antithesis, the Anglican *via media* and its claims for moderation' (p 423). In *Ecclesiastes, Or, A Discourse concerning the Gift of Preaching as it fals under the rules of Art* (London 1647), p 79, John Wilkins suggests important pronouncements on zeal can be found in Cornelius Burges's *The Fire of the Sanctuary*, Oliver Bowles's sermon on John 2:17, Sibbes's sermon on Matthew 11:12, and Greenham's on Revelation 3:19. These among other contemporary observations indicate that Anglican decency was often seen as undesirably lukewarm; but they also reveal that zeal was very complexly understood and not readily sanctioned. As an alternative to Joel Morkan, who argues in 'Wrath and Laughter: Milton's Ideas on Satire,' *Studies in Philology*, 69 (1972), 475–95, that 'It was Milton's unique achievement to bring together both the medieval *vir bonus* and the raging Renaissance satiric personality' (p 486), the following suggests Milton consciously fulfils seventeenth-century notions of religious zeal and satire.

29 Greenham, 'Of Zeal,' in *Godly Instrvctions*, p 829. Greenham's comments are also found in John Winston's *A Briefe Tract Concerning Zeale*, the 'principall of such as were scattered heere and there in Master R. Greenham's Workes,' which is added to *Fovre Godlie and Frvitfvll Sermons ... by I. Dod and R. Cleauer* (London 1610).

30 Greenham, 'Of Zeal,' p 829.

31 Edward Boughen, *A Sermon Concerning Decencie and Order in the Church* (London 1638), p 12.

32 Thomas Brightman, *The Revelation of St. Iohn* (London 1644), p 49; Cornelius Burges, *The Fire of the Sanctvarie newly uncouered, Or, A Compleat Tract of Zeale* (London 1625), pp 82–3.

33 Winston, *A Briefe Tract Concerning Zeale*, p 72.

34 Winston, p 81; Richard Barnerd [Bernard], *The Faithfvll Shepheard* (London 1609), sig Bl^r; Samuel Ward, *A Coal From the Altar, To Kindle the Holy fire of Zeale* (London 1615), p 24; Burges, p 490.

35 Burges, p 491. The great attention given to a self-searching awareness is particularly apparent in the nine conditions for zeal found in Winston's *A Briefe Tract Concerning Zeale*, pp 75 ff.

36 Sibbes, *Violence Victorious*, p 305.

37 Cf pp 108–13 in James Egan's 'Milton and the Marprelate Tradition,' an essay which has since applied some of the observations made about Marprelate to Milton (*Milton Studies*, 8 [1975], 103–21).

38 Joseph Hall, *A Defence of the Humble Remonstrance* (London 1641), pp 1–2.

39 William Haller, *The Rise of Puritanism* (New York 1957), pp 142 ff. Milton's use of military imagery has been noted by James H. Hanford, 'Milton and the Art of War,' *Studies in Philology*, 18 (1921), 232–66; Webber, pp 204 ff; D.M. Rosenberg, 'Satirical Techniques in Milton's Polemical Prose,' *Satire Newsletter*, 8 (1971), 96–7.

40 *Of Reformation*, 1, 583, 547–8.

41 John Chrysostom, *An Exposition Vpon the Epistle of S. Paule the Apostle to the Ephesians* (London 1581), p 222.

42 John Bastwick, *The Letany of John Bastwick* (1637), p 14.

43 Milton's justification for this passage is in *An Apology*, 1, 930.

44 Joseph Mede, *The Key of the Revelation*, trans Richard More (London 1643), p 24.

45 In this context the contemporary associations between the Song of Songs and Revelation are particularly relevant. Stanley N. Stewart discusses the relationship in *The Enclosed Garden: The Tradition and the Image in Seventeenth-Century Poetry* (Madison 1966).

46 Kranidas surveys the tradition in *The Fierce Equation*.

47 In *Reason of Church-Government* Milton asserts: 'if Christ be the Churches husband expecting her to be presented before him a pure unspotted virgin; in what could he shew his tender love to her more, then in prescribing his owne wayes which he best knew would be to the improvement of her health and beauty with much greater care doubtlesse then the Persian King could appoint for his Queene *Esther*' (1, 755).

48 Ward, *A Coal From the Altar*, p 6.

49 In addition to an increasing number of scholarly articles, two book-length

studies of Milton's prose have recognized the significance of the antiprelatical tracts. See *Achievements of the Left Hand*, ed Lieb and Shawcross; and Keith W. Stavely, *The Politics of Milton's Prose Style* (New Haven 1975).

50 William Riley Parker, who also quotes Milton's statement, argues that the absence of printed reactions to the tracts is not an indication of their true influence; see *Milton A Biography* (Oxford 1968), I, 201. Haller, on the other hand, believes that 'They made little impression on parliament or public in 1641–1642' (*Liberty and Reformation in the Puritan Revolution*, p 57).

51 Richard Leigh in *The Transproser Rehears'd* (Oxford 1673) writes about Marvell's manner: 'here he has all the terms of that Art which *Smectimnuus, Marchmont Needham, J. Milton*, or any other of the Professors ever thought of' (p 32). 'So black a Poyson has he suckt from the most virulent Pamphlets, as were impossible for any Mountebank but the Author of *Iconoclastes* to swallow, without the Cure of Antidotes. And certainly if that Libeller has not clubb'd with our Writer (as is with some reason suspected) we may safely say, there are many *Miltons* in this one Man' (p 147). *S'too him Bayes* (Oxford 1673) also asserts: 'You had all this out of the Answerer of *Salmasius*: and your way had been to have transcrib'd the whole side again just as it lay' (p 130). No biographical information yet supports any possible association between Milton and the writing of *The Rehearsal Transpros'd*. The accusations may be nothing more than Restoration animus towards both Milton and Marvell; possibly the allusions have in mind Marvell's use of a theatrical decorum and Milton's statement in *A Second Defence*: 'let him consider that we are engaged, not with a serious foe, but with a troupe of actors. So long as the nature of my *Defence* had to be suited to them, I thought that I ought to aim, not always at what would have been more decorous, but at what they deserved' (IV, i, 574).

NOTES TO CHAPTER FIVE

1 Andrew Marvell, *The Rehearsal Transpros'd* and *The Rehearsal Transpros'd The Second Part*, ed D.I.B. Smith (Oxford 1971), p 135; hereafter cited in the text.

2 Richard Leigh in *The Transproser Rehears'd* (Oxford 1673) observes: 'Once, perhaps in a Century of years, there may arise a *Martin-Mar-Prelate*, a *Milton*, or such a *Brave* as our present Author' (p 55). Despite some objection and a threat 'By the Eternal God I will cut thy Throat,' *The Rehearsal Transpros'd* enjoyed wide contemporary popularity; indeed, according to the often cited statement of Gilbert Burnet, 'from the king down to the tradesman, his books were read with great pleasure' (*Bishop Burnet's History of His Own Time*, ed. M.J. Routh [Oxford 1833], I, 478).

3 Samuel Parker, *A Discourse of Ecclesiastical Politie* (London 1670), p 10.

4 At the time he wrote his tracts on ecclesiastical polity Parker, although Marvell's junior by twenty years, had already begun to rise in the clerical ranks towards an eventual bishopric. As early as 1669 the anonymous author of *Insolence and Impudence triumphant* questions Parker's motives; and Marvell, who knew Parker personally, often accuses him of ambition in *The Rehearsal Transpros'd*. Subsequent contemporaries – aware of his Presbyterian origins, his conversion to Anglicanism, and his later willingness to aid the Catholic monarch James – further emphasize Parker's ambition. 'Being of an eager Spirit,' he was, in the opinion of Richard Baxter, 'turned with the Times' (*Reliquiæ Baxterianæ* [London 1696], III, 41).

5 Henry Stubbes, *Rosemary & Bayes: Or, Animadversions Upon A Treatise Called, The Rehearsall Trans-prosed. In a Letter to a Friend in the Countrey* (London 1672), p 18.

6 Samuel Parker, *A Free and Impartial Censvre of the Platonick Philosophie* (Oxford 1666), p 27.

7 Parker, *A Discourse of Ecclesiastical Politie*, p iv.

8 Samuel Parker, *Bishop Bramhall's Vindication of himself ... Together with a Preface Shewing What Grounds there are of Fears and Jealousies of Popery* (London 1672), sigs. b8ᵛ–c1ʳ; c2ᵛ.

9 Simon Patrick, *A Friendly Debate Betwixt two Neighbors, The one a Conformist, The other A Non-Conformist* (London 1669), p 25.

10 *Bishop Bramhall's Vindication of himself*, sig c3ᵛ.

11 Samuel Rolle, *A Sober Answer To the Friendly Debate, Betwixt a Conformist and a Nonconformist* (London 1669), p 147.

12 John Owen, *Truth and Innocence Vindicated: In a Survey of a Discourse Concerning Ecclesiastical Polity* (London 1669), p 294.

13 Annabel Patterson also has since considered Marvell's qualified acceptance of jest (*Marvell and the Civic Crown* [Princeton 1978], pp 193 ff). She suggests that by the conclusion of the second part of *The Rehearsal Transpros'd* Marvell realizes that 'There is, perhaps, no viable poise "betwixt Jest and Earnest"' (p 210).

14 See Cicero, *De Oratore*, trans E.W. Sutton and H. Rackham (Cambridge, Mass. 1942), I, 359.

15 Patrick argues: 'the best Masters of Rhetorick have given precepts about ways of facetious speaking and moving laughter, in the making of Orations' (p 730). He cites Cicero's second book of *De oratore* and *Orator ad Brutum, ad Herennium*, and Quintilian. Much of his defence is devoted to a justification of the dialogue; he does, however, contend that 'a scurrilous Companion jests after one fashion, an honest man after another' (p 738); desirable models offered are Socrates, Erasmus, Beza, and Minucius Felix.

16 Samuel Parker, *A Defence and Continuation of the Ecclesiastical Politie* (London 1671), p 176.

17 Samuel Parker, *A Reproof to the Rehearsal Transprosed, In A Discourse to its Author* (London 1673), p 105.

18 John Humfrey, *The Authority of the Magestrate, About Religion, Discussed, In a Rebuke to the Prefacer of a late Book of Bishop BRAMHALLS* (London 1672), p 7.

19 *Raillerie a la Mode Consider'd: or the Supercilious Detractor. A Joco-serious Discourse* (London 1673), p 7. For Edmund Hickeringill, in *Gregory, Father-Greybeard, With his Vizard off* (London 1673), the gentleman à la mode 'shall catch at a phrase, chew to a Crumb some chymical term of Art, or a new-coin'd word pick'd up at a club; and away he struts, repeats to himself, admires his own Improvements, laughs at the Clergy, dictates policy; ... then nothing less contents him than to sublimate his silver into a vapour and smoak, to be a *Virtuoso*; and with new experiments confound all Order, Government and Policy, and thereby commence new *Politicoso*' (p 119). Hickeringill judges Marvell a fanatic, crazed lunatic.

20 Parker, *A Reproof to the Rehearsal Transprosed*, p 234.

21 James R. Sutherland, 'A Note on the Satirical Poetry of Andrew Marvell,' *Philological Quarterly*, 45 (1966), 47.

22 Parker, *A Discourse of Ecclesiastical Politie*, p i.

23 Parker, *A Free and Impartial Censure*, pp 73, 15.

24 *Bishop Burnet's History of His Own Time*, III, 145. In assessing his later career as an Anglican polemicist and minister Burnet dismisses Parker as 'a man of no judgment, and of as little virtue, and as to religion rather impious' (I, 477). A fuller account of Parker's youthful nature is found in Anthony à Wood, *Athenae Oxonienses* (London 1691), II, 616.

25 Parker, *A Discourse of Ecclesiastical Politie*, p xvii.

26 Parker, *A Defence and Continuation of the Ecclesiastical Politie*, sig A8ʳ.

27 Later in *A Reproof to the Rehearsal Transprosed* Parker replies: 'You have (I thank you) bestowed upon me a Prebend, a Sine-cure and a Rectorship, now why might I not at the time of writing that Preface be busied in attending the Seals for my Sine-cure, and in taking order for the repairs of my Parsonage Barns, and in providing Goods and Furniture for my Prebend-house. These I take to be close and comfortable things as well as a female Importance. And what if beside all this I had newly sold my little inheritance and engaged in a purchase elsewhere that lay better for my own convenience; and what if at that very nick of Affairs a stop were put to the payments of the Exchequer, and my Money in the Bankers hands, do you think it did not closely concern me to disengage it from their keeping, and whether it would not have been some comfort to have effected it. But it seems there is nothing so far from the thoughts of you

Gamesters as purchasing of Lands' (pp 242–3). Actually Marvell may have been closer to the truth than Parker will admit: as D.I.B. Smith points out, Parker was married to Rebecca Pheasant soon after *A Reproof* appeared in print. Ruth Nevo indicates in *The Dial of Virtue* (Princeton 1963) that the phrase 'comfortable importance' is also used by Rochester and Butler (p 200).

28 John Coolidge develops this point in 'Martin Marprelate, Marvell and *Decorum Personæ* as a Satirical Theme,' PMLA, 74 (1959), 529–30.

29 George Villiers, Second Duke of Buckingham, *The Rehearsal*, in English Reprints, ed Edward Arber (London 1869), III, 89.

30 Ibid, p 51.

31 Ibid, p 97.

32 Parker, *A Discourse of Ecclesiastical Politie*, pp xx–xxi.

33 Ibid, p xxiii.

34 Parker, *Bishop Bramhall's Vindication of himself*, sig e3ʳ.

35 Parker, *A Defence and Continuation of the Ecclesiastical Politie*, p 125.

36 Phillip Harth, *Swift and Anglican Rationalism* (Chicago 1961), particularly chapter 3.

37 Parker, *A Defence and Continuation of the Ecclesiastical Politie*, p 342.

38 Ibid, p 587.

39 More's *Enthusiasmus Triumphatus*, which first appeared in 1656, was reissued in revised and completed form in 1662. All quotations are from the 1662 edition, edited by Michael V. DePorte in The Augustan Reprint Society Publications 118 (Los Angeles 1966), p 12.

40 Ibid, p 6.

41 Ibid, p 16.

42 John Owen also stresses several times military imagery; see especially his image of Parker following the triumphant chariot of Patrick and dragging the Nonconformists behind in *Truth and Innocence Vindicated*, p 65.

43 Parker, *A Defence and Continuation of the Ecclesiastical Politie*, p 714.

44 Parker, *A Free and Impartial Censvre*, p 50.

45 More, p 14.

46 Parker, *A Defence and Continuation of the Ecclesiastical Politie*, p 340.

47 Parker, *A Discourse of Ecclesiastical Politie*, p 75.

48 Parker, *A Free and Impartial Censvre*, p 76.

49 See, for example, *A Free and Impartial Censvre*, p 78.

50 Parker, *A Defence and Continuation of the Ecclesiastical Politie*, pp 97–8.

51 Parker, *Bishop Bramhall's Vindication of himself*, sig e8ʳ.

52 Ibid, sig d4ʳ.

53 Robert Ferguson, *A Sober Inquiry Into The Nature, Measure, and Principle of Moral Vertue, Its distinction from Gospel-Holiness* (London 1673), sigs A6ʳ, A6ᵛ.

54 John Dryden, *A Discourse concerning the Original and Progress of Satire*, in *Essays of John Dryden*, ed W.P. Ker (New York 1961), II, 93–4.

55 Parker, *A Reproof to the Rehearsal Transprosed*, p 1.

56 Hickeringill, *Gregory, Father-Greybeard, With his Vizard off*, p 37.

57 John Wallace analyses Marvell's serious objections in *Destiny His Choice: The Loyalism of Andrew Marvell* (Cambridge 1968), pp 184–206; see also Patterson, pp 200 ff.

58 *Bp. Parker's History Of His Own Times, In Four Books* (London 1728), p 7. Another edition without the prefatory comments appeared in 1727.

59 Jonathan Swift, *A Tale of a Tub*, ed A.C. Guthkelch and D. Nichol Smith (Oxford 1968), pp 9–10.

60 Swift's evaluation and the similarities between the two satires are discussed by Raymond A. Anselment in '*A Tale of a Tub*: Swift and the "Men of Tast," ' *Huntington Library Quarterly*, 37 (1974), 265–82.

NOTES TO CHAPTER SIX

1 Jonathan Swift, *A Tale of a Tub*, ed. A.C. Guthkelch and D. Nichol Smith (Oxford 1968), p 8; hereafter cited in the text.

2 W.H. Dilworth in *The Life of Dr. Jonathan Swift* (1758) mentions 'a person of undoubted veracity' who saw the *Tale* in Swift's possession at this early age (in *Swift: The Critical Heritage*, ed Kathleen Williams [London 1970], p 157). Robert Martin Adams's suggestion in 'Jonathan Swift, Thomas Swift, and the Authorship of *A Tale of a Tub*,' *Modern Philology*, 64 (1967), 198–232, that Thomas Swift wrote the religious allegory has provoked considerable scholarly resistance.

3 Guthkelch and Smith, eds, 'Date of Composition,' pp xliii–xlvii; and Ronald Paulson's review of Phillip Harth's *Swift and Anglican Rationalism*, in *Journal of English and Germanic Philology*, 61 (1962), 406–8.

4 Guthkelch and Smith, eds, p xlvi; and particularly Phillip Harth, *Swift and Anglican Rationalism* (Chicago 1961), pp 6 ff.

5 Quoted by Guthkelch and Smith, eds, p xlviii.

6 Charles Boyle, *Dr Bentley's Dissertations on the Epistles of Phalaris, and the Fables of Aesop, Examin'd*, (London 1699), Preface, no pagination.

7 William Temple, *An Essay upon the Ancient and Modern Learning*, in *Five Miscellaneous Essays by Sir William Temple*, ed Samuel Holt Monk (Ann Arbor 1963), p 62.

8 Ibid, p 62.

9 William Temple, *Some Thoughts upon Reviewing the Essay of Ancient and Modern Learning*, in *Five Miscellaneous Essays*, p 96.

10 Temple, *An Essay upon the Ancient and Modern Learning*, p 69.

11 Irvin Ehrenpreis discusses Swift's indebtedness to the tradition of humanism in his biography *Swift: The Man, His Works, and the Age* (Cambridge, Mass. 1962), I, 188 ff.

12 Swift, 'Ode To the Honble Sir William Temple,' in *The Poems of Jonathan Swift*, ed Harold Williams (Oxford 1958), I, 27.

13 Ricardo Quintana surveys the range of readings in 'Emile Pons and the Modern Study of Swift's *Tale of a Tub*,' *Études Anglaises*, 18 (1965), 5–17.

14 Representative of the many readings are Miriam Starkman, *Swift's Satire on Learning in A Tale of a Tub* (Princeton 1950); Robert C. Elliott, 'Swift's *Tale of a Tub*: An Essay in Problems of Structure,' PMLA, 66 (1951), 441–55; Harth, *Swift and Anglican Rationalism*; Edward Rosenheim Jr, *Swift and the Satirist's Art* (Chicago 1963); Jay Arnold Levine, 'The Design of *A Tale of a Tub* (With a Digression on a Mad Modern Critic),' ELH, 33 (1966), 198–227; Frank Kinahan, 'The Melancholy of Anatomy: Voice and Theme in *A Tale of a Tub*,' *Journal of English and Germanic Philology*, 69 (1970), 278–91; Philip Pinkus, *Swift's Vision of Evil* (Victoria, BC 1975).

15 Herbert Davis, 'Swift's Use of Irony,' in *The World of Jonathan Swift*, ed Brian Vickers (Harvard 1968), p 157.

16 Ricardo Quintana, in *Swift: An Introduction* (Oxford 1955), identifies the voices as 'the one who is writing the *Apology*, "the author" referred to therein, "the bookseller," the modern author, and the latter's *alter ego*, the historian. But there is still another, a sixth character, who appears on the stage only briefly but without whom the others would lose their meaning in the satiric comedy being enacted. This sixth character is not Swift, but he is a satirist – perhaps we should say, he is *the* satirist' (p 55).

17 Michael V. DePorte, 'Digressions and Madness in *A Tale of a Tub* and *Tristram Shandy*,' *Huntington Library Quarterly*, 34 (1970/1), 43–57; Elliott, "Swift's *Tale of a Tub*: An Essay in Problems of Structure'; Gardner D. Stout Jr, 'Speaker and Satiric Vision in Swift's *Tale of a Tub*,' *Eighteenth-Century Studies*, 3 (1969/70), 175–99. Robert C. Elliott, who concedes that 'one can never be sure' Swift 'is truly speaking – or speaking truly – for himself' (p 386), lucidly analyses a tendency among modern critics to question the value of the persona; see his defence of the persona in 'Swift's "I",' *Yale Review*, 62 (1972/3), 372–91.

18 Irvin Ehrenpreis, *Swift: The Man, His Works, and the Age* (Cambridge, Mass. 1967), II, appendix B, 768–9.

19 In a letter dated 7 October 1710, as quoted by John Middleton Murry, *Jonathan Swift: A Critical Biography* (London 1954), p 83.

20 Robert M. Adams notes that, 'in a letter to Ambrose Philips, written two years earlier (14 September 1708), Swift described the *Letter Concerning Enthusiasm* as "very well writ" and asked if Philips did not write it himself. On 12 January

1708–9 he wrote to Colonel Robert Hunter, then a prisoner of war in Paris, to assure him that he (Swift) had not written the *Letter* and to ask whether Hunter is perhaps the author' ('The Mood of the Church and *A Tale of a Tub*,' in *England in the Restoration and Early Eighteenth Century*, ed H.T. Swedenberg Jr [Berkeley 1972], p 90).

21 Ronald Paulson, for example, suggests that the passage excusing youthful indiscretions 'is merely a parody of similar disclaimers in writers like Dryden' (*Theme and Structure in Swift's Tale of a Tub* [New Haven 1960], p 163).

22 The bookseller says: 'It is now Six Years since these Papers came first to my Hands, which seems to have been about a Twelvemonth after they were writ; For, the Author tells us in his Preface to the first Treatise, that he hath calculated it for the Year 1697' (p 28).

23 William Wotton, *A Defense of the Reflections upon Ancient and Modern Learning, In Answer to the Objections of Sir W. Temple, and Others. With Observations upon The Tale of a Tub* (London 1705), reprinted in Guthkelch and Smith, eds, p 318.

24 Ibid, p 324.

25 Boyle, p 222.

26 Jonathan Swift, 'The Author upon Himself,' in *Poems*, ed Williams, i, 194.

27 Jonathan Swift, *The Intelligencer Number III*, in *The Prose Works*, vol xii, ed Herbert Davis (Oxford 1955), p 33.

28 Jonathan Swift, 'To Mr. Delany,' in *Poems*, ed Williams, i, 215.

29 William Temple, *Of Poetry*, in *Five Miscellaneous Essays*, pp 180, 198.

30 Swift, 'To Mr. Delany,' i, 215–16.

31 Swift, *The Intelligencer Number III*, xii, 33.

32 Jonathan Swift, *Hints towards an Essay on Conversation*, in *The Prose Works*, vol iv, ed Herbert Davis and Louis Landa (Oxford 1957), p 91.

33 See also John M. Bullitt, 'Swift's "Rules of Raillery",' in *Veins of Humor*, ed Harry Levin, Harvard English Studies 3 (Cambridge, Mass. 1972), pp 93–108.

34 For alternative approaches to the nature of modernism and the preoccupation with nothingness consider, for example, John R. Clark, *Form and Frenzy in Swift's Tale of a Tub* (Ithaca 1970); W.B. Carnochan, 'Swift's *Tale*: On Satire, Negation, and the Uses of Irony,' *Eighteenth-Century Studies*, 5 (1971), 122–44; Frederick N. Smith, 'The Epistemology of Fictional Failure: Swift's *Tale of a Tub* and Beckett's *Watt*,' *Texas Studies in Literature and Language*, 15 (1973/4), 649–72; Marjorie Beam, 'The Reach of Wit of the Inventor: Swift's *Tale of a Tub* and *Hamlet*,' *University of Toronto Quarterly*, 46 (1976/7), 1–13.

35 Jonathan Swift, *The Battle of the Books*, ed Guthkelch and Smith, p 215.

36 Gardner D. Stout Jr, who has interestingly considered Swift's doubts about satire's usefulness, finds a 'radically disaffected satiric vision' that leads him to conclude that 'Swift is torn between amused laughter, contemptuous scorn,

and a suppressed rage intensified by its own impotence. Unable to decide
whether to laugh or weep at the spectacle of his own and other men's folly, he is
stretched on the tough rack of his own satiric vision' ('Speaker and Satiric
Vision in Swift's *Tale of a Tub*,' p 196).

37 Cf Pat Rogers, 'Form in *A Tale of a Tub*,' *Essays in Criticism*, 22 (1972), 142–60.

38 Cf Neil Schaeffer, ' "Them That Speak, and Them That Hear": The Audience
as Target in Swift's *Tale of a Tub*,' *Enlightenment Essays*, 4 (1973), 25–35. Schaeffer, who emphasizes 'Swift's gloomy view of life,' suggests that ultimately 'The
best, or the ideal reader, seems an impossibility' (p 28).

39 The more negative view F.R. Leavis finds in 'The Irony of Swift' in *Determina-
tions*, ed F.R. Leavis (London 1934), pp 79–108, has stimulated much modern
criticism. More recently Robert Martin Adams's reading, 'Swift and Kafka' in
Strains of Discord (Ithaca 1958), pp 146–79, has also had considerable influence.

40 Several studies which appeared after this chapter was written differently emphasize Swift's sensibility. In 'Divinity and Wit: Swift's Attempted Reconciliation,' *University of Toronto Quarterly*, 46 (1976/7), 14–30, George Falle concludes: 'Swift uses his wit as a means of intensifying the complexity of the
perennial problems that confront the Christian world, and this practice serves
in turn to enhance the order of divine providence, to make us more fully aware
of God's benevolence and grace ... The wisdom of this world is indeed foolishness with God. One of the ultimate services of wit judiciously employed is to
illustrate that paradox and to suggest that the ultimate resolution of all seeming
antinomies rests in the divine will' (p 29). Alan S. Fisher, on the other hand,
finds a greater urgency in 'a sense of *having* fun.' He contends in 'An End to the
Renaissance: Erasmus, Hobbes, and *A Tale of a Tub*,' *Huntington Library Quarterly*, 38 (1974/5), 1–20, that 'Erasmus believed that paradox embodied full
truth, and Swift, to be sure, did not. Yet Swift is fond of paradox in his way. I
sense here a Swift who longs for the sure footed perceptions of an Erasmus but
knows, helplessly, that he lives in another era, an era where truth is required to
conform to method and to purely "objective" sources of what is known' (p 10)
Without Erasmus's assurance that wise men and fools 'dissolve ... in the ultima
reality of heaven,' and aware that a desirable 'integrity and right reason'
are now anachronisms, Swift only tentatively implies his values. 'His despair
about proceeding this way is real, but not total, for the jokes and amusing
touches are the essence of the *Tale*, and one presumably does not make jokes in
a vacuum. Swift expects his readers – enough of his readers – to understand
him' (p 20).

41 Levine, 'The Design of *A Tale of a Tub* (With a Digression on a Mad Modern
Critic),' pp 200 ff.

42 Wotton, p 321.

43 For a more critical view, see William John Roscelli, '*A Tale of a Tub* and the "Cavils of the Sour",' *Journal of English and Germanic Philology*, 64 (1965), who argues: 'But when he ventures to assail specific doctrines, no matter by whom they may be held, as a satirist he can do so only by implicitly denying that there exists any real distinction between faith and reason. And it is this implicit denial of any reality to faith apart from reason which alienates those readers who perceive the terrible consequences such an attitude portends for religion as such. No matter how much they admire Swift's genius or how sympathetic they are to his purposes, such readers must at last come to look upon his satire as an instrument for subverting faith' (p 56).

44 Paulson emphasizes the possible sexual humor on pp 199 ff. Martin Kallich supplements this discussion in 'Swift and the Archetypes of Hate: *A Tale of a Tub*,' in *Studies in Eighteenth-Century Culture*, ed Harold Pagliaro (Madison 1975), particularly pp 53–4.

45 In a series of essays on the background of *A Tale of a Tub* Clarence M. Webster contends: 'Those critics who believe that Swift was coarse are invited to read many of the satires' he lists in 'The Satiric Background of the Attack on Puritans in Swift's *A Tale of a Tub*,' PMLA, 50 (1935), 210–23. See also his 'Swift's *Tale of a Tub* Compared with Earlier Satires of the Puritans,' PMLA, 47 (1932), 171–8; and 'Swift and Some Earlier Satirists of Puritan Enthusiasm,' PMLA, 48 (1933), 1141–53. Selections from the long bibliographies he provides reveal a generally crude, not sustained attack characterized by little wit and quite unlike Swift's satire.

46 Shaftesbury, *Miscellaneous Reflections*, in *Characteristics of Men, Manners, Opinions, Times*, ed John M. Robertson (New York 1964), II, 337.

47 Richard Blackmore, *An Essay Upon Wit*, in *Essays Upon Several Subjects* (London 1716), p 217.

48 Shaftesbury, *The Life, Unpublished Letters, and Philosophical Regimen of Anthony, Earl of Shaftesbury*, ed Benjamin Rand (New York 1900), p 504.

49 Shaftesbury, *A Letter Concerning Enthusiasm*, in *Characteristics*, I, 9.

50 Shaftesbury, *Sensus Communis; An Essay on the Freedom of Wit and Humour*, in *Characteristics*, I, 53.

51 Among discussions of the changing temperament, Stuart Tave's *The Amiable Humorist* (Chicago 1960) is most comprehensive. Other studies include R.S. Crane, 'Suggestions Toward a Genealogy of the "Man of Feeling",' ELH, 1 (1934), 205–30; Andrew M. Wilkinson, 'The Decline of English Verse Satire in the Middle Years of the Eighteenth Century,' *The Review of English Studies*, 3 (1952), 222–33; Edward N. Hooker, 'Humour in the Age of Pope,' *Huntington Library Quarterly*, 11 (1947/8), 361–85; Thomas B. Gilmore Jr, *The Eighteenth-Century Controversy over Ridicule as a Test of Truth: A Recon-*

sideration, Georgia State University School of Arts and Sciences Research Papers, 25 (1970).

52 See Hugh M. Richmond's discussion of 'Historical Psychology,' in 'Personal Identity and Literary Personae: A Study in Historical Psychology,' PMLA, 90 (1975), 209–21.

53 Gilmore is the most recent scholar to suggest that the controversy over Shaftesbury's views of ridicule contributed to the decline of satire in the eighteenth century. In any case Shaftesbury's endorsement of ridicule is both elusive and qualified throughout his essays.

54 Kathleen Williams summarizes the position of others who agree that 'The *Tale*, an old-fashioned work when it was published, emerged into a world not altogether suited to it' (*Swift: The Critical Heritage*, p 4). An interesting exception, however, is Robert M. Adams's 'The Mood of the Church and *A Tale of a Tub*.' Adams suggests that the satire be seen 'as if it were a book composed by a man who had some reason to doubt that there was going to be an eighteenth-century establishment in which he would be a distinguished dean, who did not know and could not guess that the English church was going to drone and drowse peacefully (undisturbed save by a few errant Methodists) through a long Hanoverian summertime' (p 73). John Edwards finds Marprelate 'a dull Ass in respect of this more impudent one' [the author of some dialogues between Timothy and Philatheus] (*A Defence of Sharp Reflections on Authors and their Opinions*, in *Some New Discoveries of the Uncertainty, Deficiency, and Corruptions of Human Knowledge and Learning* [London 1714], p 212). In *A Letter To the Reverend Subscribers To a late voluminous Libel, Entitled, The History of England, during the Royal House of Stuart* (London 1731) Milton and Marvell are compared to Sir Anthony Welden, 'three Men for libelling and defaming infamous' (p 4). Kathleen Williams surveys Swift's critical fortunes.

Index

This book
was designed by
WILLIAM RUETER
and was printed by
University of
Toronto
Press